Studies in Musical Genesis and Structure

General Editor: Malcolm Gillies

Studies in Musical Genesis and Structure

Mahler's Fourth Symphony

JAMES L. ZYCHOWICZ

OXFORD
UNIVERSITY PRESS

OXFORD
UNIVERSITY PRESS

Great Clarendon Street, Oxford OX2 6DP

Oxford University Press is a department of the University of Oxford.
It furthers the University's objective of excellence in research, scholarship,
and education by publishing worldwide in

Oxford New York

Athens Auckland Bangkok Bogotá Buenos Aires Calcutta
Cape Town Chennai Dar es Salaam Delhi Florence Hong Kong Istanbul
Karachi Kuala Lumpur Madrid Melbourne Mexico City Mumbai
Nairobi Paris São Paulo Singapore Taipei Tokyo Toronto Warsaw
with associated companies in Berlin Ibadan

Oxford is a registered trade mark of Oxford University Press
in the UK and in certain other countries

Published in the United States
by Oxford University Press Inc., New York

British Library Cataloguing in Publication Data
Data available

Library of Congress Cataloging in Publication Data

Library of Congress Cataloging-in-Publication Data
Zychowicz, James L.
Mahler's Fourth Symphony/James L. Zychowicz.
p. cm.—(Studies in musical genesis and structure)
Includes bibliographical references and index.
1. Mahler, Gustav, 1860–1911. Symphonies, no. 4, G. major.   I. Title.   II. Series.
MT130.M25 Z93   2000   784.2'184 21—dc21   99-046013
ISBN 0 19 816206 5

1 3 5 7 9 10 8 6 4 2

Typeset in MGaramond
by Kolam Information Services Pvt Ltd, Pondicherry, India
Printed in Great Britain
on acid-free paper by
Biddles Ltd, www.biddles.co.uk

Editor's Preface

Since Philip Gossett's inaugural monograph on Donizetti's *Anna Bolena* in 1985, the series *Studies in Musical Genesis and Structure* has sought to chart the currents of musical creation through studies of single works by eminent composers. Under the editorship of Lewis Lockwood those currents have mainly been of the nineteenth or early twentieth centuries, with a particular emphasis on Beethoven. The series' volumes have both pioneered new approaches to sketch study and provided penetrating insights into the detail of the compositional routine of half a dozen leading composers.

James L. Zychowicz's meticulous examination of Mahler's Fourth Symphony continues that series tradition. This symphony stands at the stylistic cross-roads, culminating the 'Wunderhorn' period yet laying the foundations for Mahler's next band of symphonies initiated by the Fifth. Originally planned as a six-movement 'symphony humoresque', the Fourth was born as Mahler's shortest symphony, with four movements lasting for around three-quarters of an hour: 'a symphony of normal dimensions', Mahler modestly commented. Zychowicz's study of the sketch materials is exciting because of its information by a rich (although not complete) chain of sources, leading from rough preliminary ideas to fair copy. After an opening survey of the symphony's overall structure, Zychowicz adopts a chronological approach and progressively documents the emergence of Mahler's renowned precision of musical thought, sometimes early suggested in the sketches by his characteristic attention to issues of timbre and tone colour.

One particularly important aspect of this study is its pursuit of Mahler's symphonic vision beyond the work's first edition of 1902. He thought of his symphonies as evolving phenomena needing periodic revision. As Zychowicz reveals, Mahler engaged in at least three revisions of the Fourth Symphony, which in their changed detail accorded with his search in more recent works for purer colours and greater differentiation of texture. In Chapter 9 the consequences of these painstaking revisions for any attempt at a definitive reading of Mahler's symphony are outlined, with Zychowicz rejecting the notion that Mahler's final revisions necessarily lead to an edition of the greatest authority since even they can be 'transitional and untested'. Rather, he asserts that each source of revision has its own particular historical context.

In early 1999 Oxford University Press reconceived this series as *Studies in Musical Genesis, Structure and Interpretation*. Its intention is to retain the central focus on genesis, but to encourage inclusion of the wider gamut of Western repertory through an extension of possible perspectives to include, as appropriate, issues of performing interpretation and performance practice. In pushing the end-point of his study beyond the first edition to take in revisions informed by Mahler's own performing interpretation of this work and indeed later symphonies, Zychowicz provides a convenient bridge between the original and the reconceived purposes of this series.

Malcolm Gillies

University of Queensland

Preface

The study of Gustav Mahler's music, especially his manuscripts, often involves working with materials in a variety of locations and with a number of individuals. The Fourth Symphony, like other music of Mahler, requires as much patience on the part of the researcher to find the sketches as it does the good will of those who own or have charge of the manuscripts to make them available for study. With regard to the latter, I am grateful for the kindness extended to me by a number of institutions, and especially the following individuals, who gave me access to manuscript materials: Dr Günther Brosche and the staff of the Österreichische Nationalbibliothek, Vienna; Dr Otto Biba and the staff of the Gesellschaft der Musikfreunde, Vienna; Dr Herta Blaukopf, Frau Emmy Hauswirth, Frau Gerda Hanf, and the Internationale Gustav Mahler Gesellschaft, Vienna; M. Henry-Louis de La Grange of the Bibliothèque Musicale Gustav Mahler, Paris; Dr Hans Braun of the Bibliotheca Bodmeriana, Cologny-Genève, Switzerland; Mr J. Rigbie Turner of the Pierpont Morgan Library, New York; the Newberry Library, Chicago; the Stanford University Library, Stanford; the Music Library of the University of Western Ontario, London, Ontario; and the Public Library of Cincinnati and Hamilton County (Ohio).

I was first able to work on Mahler manuscripts in 1985, with the assistance of a summer research fellowship from the University of Cincinnati for study in Vienna. It was possible to continue work through a Fulbright scholarship for study in Vienna, 1986–7. The generosity of M. Henry-Louis de La Grange allowed me to continue my work in Europe between 1987 and 1988. Subsequent visits to archives and libraries have been on my own, but not without the help and support of family and friends.

In addition, my research on Mahler benefits from the friendships of colleagues, particularly Robert Bailey, Susan M. Filler, and Steven D. Coburn. I am also grateful to Professor Lewis Lockwood, the former series editor, for his interest in my work. I appreciate the previous assistance of Bruce Phillips and the current support of Maribeth Payne and Helen Peres da Costa at Oxford University Press. Bonnie Blackburn contributed much in her thoughtful and insightful editing. I am indebted to my family, particularly my mother Jean Zychowicz, for her understanding and support. I should also like to thank Salvatore Calomino, whose meticulous eye proved invaluable in countless ways during the latter stages of this project.

J.L.Z.

Acknowledgements

I should like to acknowledge the following for permission to use the facsimiles found in this publication:

J. Rigbie Turner, Pierpont Morgan Library, Lehman Deposit
Department of Special Collections, Stanford University Libraries
Henry-Louis de La Grange, Bibliothèque Musicale Gustav Mahler
Dr Günther Brosche, Österreichische Nationalbibliothek, Musiksammlung

Contents

List of Illustrations

List of Tables

List of Musical Examples

List of Sigla and Abbreviations

A-Wgm	Vienna, Gesellschaft der Musikfreunde
A-Wigmg	Vienna, Internationale Gustav Mahler Gesellschaft
A-Wn	Vienna, Österreichische Nationalbibliothek, Musiksammlung
C-Lu	London, University of Western Ontario
CH-CObodmeriana	Cologny, Bibliotheca Bodmeriana
D-B	Berlin, Staatsbibliothek der Stiftung Preußischer Kulturbesitz
F-Pbmgm	Paris, Bibliothèque Musicale Gustav Mahler
US-CIpl	Cincinnati, Public Library of Cincinnati and Hamilton County [Ohio]
US-Cn	Chicago, Newberry Library
US-NYpm	New York, Pierpont Morgan Library
US-STu	Stanford, Stanford University Library
New Grove	*The New Grove Dictionary of Music and Musicians*, ed. Stanley Sadie, 20 vols. (London: Macmillan, 1980)

1. Introduction: Sketches and Drafts

Gustar Mahler's Fourth Symphony (1899–1900)[1] is one of the composer's most accessible compositions, and while it is difficult to find a single work that unequivocally embodies his style, this Symphony contains elements that may be seen to emerge throughout his oeuvre. For some the Fourth Symphony is Mahler's response to Beethoven's Ninth Symphony,[2] while others assign other meanings to it. To probe the Fourth Symphony thoroughly, however, it is important to understand Mahler's approach to its composition, and this is possible through analysis that includes an exploration of the sketches documenting the process that Mahler used to create it.

The Fourth Symphony is also an excellent subject for the study of Mahler's sketches because of the number of different manuscripts that survive. More kinds of sketches and drafts survive for the Fourth than are known to exist for any of his other works. They include sketches from almost every stage of work on the symphony, from the earliest plans to the fair copy, as well as several sets of autograph revisions that extend throughout the last decade of the composer's life.

To date relatively more attention has been drawn to Mahler's sketches for his later works, especially the Ninth and Tenth Symphonies; earlier compositions, like the Fourth, have received less attention. Recent studies deal with specific aspects of various manuscripts,[3] including several for the

---

[1] For the current critical edition of the work see Gustav Mahler, *Symphonie No. 4—G-Dur*, edited by Erwin Ratz (Sämtliche Werke, Kritische Gesamtausgabe, 4; Vienna: Universal, 1963). This edition represents the 'Ausgabe letzter Hand' and essentially includes Mahler's final revisions. The ramifications of this edition are explained by James L. Zychowicz, 'Toward an *Ausgabe letzter Hand*: The Publication and Revision of Mahler's Fourth Symphony', *Journal of Musicology*, 12 (1995), 260–72. See also id., 'Sketches and Drafts of Gustav Mahler 1892–1901: The Sources of the Fourth Symphony' (Ph.D. diss., University of Cincinnati, 1988), 391–405. See also Stephen E. Hefling, '"Variations *in nuce*": A Study of Mahler Sketches and a Comment on Sketch Studies', in *Gustav Mahler Kolloquium 1979*, ed. Rudolf Klein (Österreichische Gesellschaft für Musik, 7; Kassel: Bärenreiter, 1981), 102–26.

For the purpose of this discussion, Mahler's Fourth Symphony in G Major is a four-movement work: (1) Bedächtig. Nicht eilen (G major); (2) In gemächlicher Bewegung. Ohne Hast (C minor); (3) Ruhevoll (G major); and (4) Sehr behaglich (G major–E major). For a conventional analysis of the work, see Rudolph Stephan, *Gustav Mahler: IV. Symphonie G-Dur* (Meisterwerke der Musik, 5; Munich: Wilhelm Fink, 1966).

[2] Mark Evan Bonds, 'Ambivalent Elysium: Mahler's Fourth Symphony', in *After Beethoven: Imperatives of Originality in the Symphony* (Cambridge, Mass.: Harvard University Press, 1996), 176.

[3] Two concise surveys of sketch studies have been published to date: Stephen Hefling, 'Perspectives on Sketch Study in Mahler Research', in *Das Gustav-Mahler-Fest: Hamburg 1989*. Bericht über den Internationelen Gustav-Mahler-Kongreß, ed. Matthias Theodor Vogt (Kassel: Bärenreiter, 1991), 445–58 at 456–8 (bibliography of sketch and manuscript studies); and Edward R. Reilly, 'Mahler's Manuscripts and What They Can Tell Us', *Muziek & Wetenschap*, 5 (1995/96), 363–83.

Second,[4] Third,[5] and Fourth Symphonies, but few investigations approach the sketches from a broader perspective. This may be the result of the paucity of materials, since many of the surviving manuscripts are fragmentary at best. Portions of different movements at various stages of composition are extant, but it is almost impossible to locate a complete set of all the materials that preceded the fair copy. The situation is further complicated by the fact that Mahler's manuscripts are scattered around the world, with a number of them still in private collections. In his study of another symphony of Mahler, Peter Andraschke aptly describes the situation with many of the composer's manuscripts: 'For the most part, Mahler destroyed the preparatory work for his compositions. The few sketches, mostly in private hands, cannot yet be centrally registered. The material known hitherto represents only a selection surviving by chance.'[6]

Andraschke's comments point up the difficulties that exist with obtaining manuscript materials, and the shortcomings that occur when entire sets have been dispersed. When he made that remark, however, Andraschke was referring to the Ninth Symphony and may not have known of the extent of sketches for the Fourth that have turned up in various places. In fact, enough different kinds of materials for the Fourth survive to allow for an examination of the compositional process from its perceived beginnings to the final revisions.

Mahler's Sketches

With regard to the kinds of sketches that Mahler used in creating his symphonies, it is useful to differentiate between the stages of compositions. While some would call everything before the fair copy a 'sketch', Mahler's systematic approach to composition is apparent in the style of the manuscripts that he used to proceed from one phase of work to the next. The framework devised by Edward R. Reilly for his proposed catalogue of the composer's manuscripts is useful in separating each compositional stage:

[4] As to the sketches for the Second Symphony see Edward R. Reilly, 'Die Skizze zu Mahlers zweiter Symphonie', *Österreichische Musikzeitschrift*, 34 (1979), 266–84. The early version of the first movement, the tone poem 'Todtenfeier', is the subject of 'The Making of Mahler's "Todtenfeier": A Documentary and Analytical Study' by Stephen E. Hefling (Ph.D. diss., Yale University, 1985) and Stephen E. Hefling, 'Mahler's "Todtenfeier" and the Problem of Program Music', *19th Century Music*, 13 (1988), 27–53.

[5] Several studies exist for the sketches and drafts for the Third Symphony: Susan M. Filler, 'Editorial Problems in Symphonies of Gustav Mahler: A Study of the Sources of the Third and Tenth' (Ph.D. diss., Northwestern University, 1976), esp. 20–369; Edward R. Reilly, 'A Re-examination of the Manuscripts of Mahler's Third Symphony', in *Colloque International Gustav Mahler* (Paris: Association Gustav Mahler, 1986), 62–72; Peter Franklin, 'The Gestation of Mahler's Third Symphony', *Music and Letters*, 58 (1977), 439–46; and John Williamson, 'Mahler's Compositional Process: Reflections on an Early Sketch for the Third Symphony's First Movement', *Music and Letters*, 61 (1980), 338–45.

[6] Quoted by Williamson, 'Mahler's Compositional Process', 338. The passage is found in Peter Andraschke, *Gustav Mahlers IX. Symphonie: Kompositionsprozeß und Analyse* (Beihefte zum Archiv für Musikwissenschaft, 14; Wiesbaden: Franz Steiner, 1976), 1.

1. First ideas for a work, sometimes jotted down in pocket notebooks.

2. Preliminary sketches, exploring the possibilities of developing and combining different themes or motifs, and, in some cases, pointing to the sequence in which they will ultimately appear. These were usually written in a reduced score of from two to four staves, and sometimes contain limited indications of plans for scoring.

3. Preliminary drafts, in which the basic sequence of musical thought for a full movement, or a substantial portion of the movement, is laid out, most often in a short or condensed score of four staves, and with fuller indications of scoring. Additional sketches connected with specific passages in the draft may also be found associated with this phase and the two that follow.

4. Draft full scores, in which the instrumentation of one or more movements is worked out in some detail, but not necessarily filled in completely. Modifications of melody, harmony, and other elements are also found.

5. 'Final' autograph full score, in a relatively fair copy, with scoring more or less completely worked out in detail, but still with the possibility of significant modifications. The latter are usually incorporated through the substitution of individual pages with revisions for those originally included.[7]

As to the terminology used in the present study, it is useful to elaborate on the paradigm outlined above. First ideas involve early plans of movements, which include descriptive titles and key designations. It is difficult to ascertain with absolute certainty when these early plans occurred in the composition of a work, since Mahler used them before beginning to compose and also returned to such lists while completing various movements. As to sketchbooks, which also contain first ideas, Mahler was observed using them for this work,[8] but none with material for the Fourth Symphony is known to survive.

After pursuing early ideas in plans of movements and in his sketchbooks, Mahler would take up the preliminary sketches in which he would work on more extensive passages of the new work. This stage can be difficult to define because of the varying degree of detail that was worked out before the short score. Nevertheless, preliminary sketches usually are found on large-size paper (in contrast to the smaller sketchbook pages), often a single leaf torn from a bifolio sheet, with the number of staves for each system variable and the music relatively discontinuous. When Mahler took these sketches into the next stage of work, he would number them in the order he wanted them to occur in the movement, and so the numbers inscribed on the extant sheets do not necessarily reflect the order in which he composed them.

---

[7] Edward R. Reilly, 'An Inventory of Musical Sources', *News about Mahler Research*, 2 (1977), 3.

[8] Natalie Bauer-Lechner, *Erinnerungen an Gustav Mahler*, ed., and annotated Knud Martner (Hamburg: Karl Dieter Wagner, 1984), 61; English trans., *Recollections of Gustav Mahler*, ed. and annotated Peter Franklin, trans. Dika Newlin (New York: Cambridge University Press, 1980), 64–5. For an overview of Mahler's sketchbooks, see James L. Zychowicz, 'Sketches and Drafts of Gustav Mahler', 183–212.

Next, Mahler prepared the short score or *Particell*, which he composed on the same kind of paper as he used for preliminary sketches. In general, the short score is a comparatively continuous draft inscribed throughout on three- to four-stave systems. While it was still subject to revision, the short score represents a continuous draft of the entire movement for a symphony rather than the kind of isolated passages found earlier in the preliminary sketches. Unlike the earlier sketches, however, Mahler achieved in the short score the kind of uniformity and continuity that is absent from earlier sketches.

After the short score, Mahler would compose the draft score (*Partitur-entwurf*), the first orchestral score, written on a series of bifolios. The music is completely continuous and fully orchestrated in this phase of composition. He sometimes even substituted pages at this stage, and it is common to find alterations in the form of an intermittent insertion page (often marked 'Ein-lage' and sometimes followed by the manuscript page to which it refers). At times, he might even revise the form of movements at this phase of composi-tion. After completing the draft score, he would proceed to the fair copy (*Reinschrift*), that is the autograph full score. While Mahler usually inscribed the draft score on oblong (*Querformat*) sheets like those used for the prelimin-ary sketches and the short score, he generally composed the fair copy on up-right (*Hochformat*) sheets of higher-quality paper.

In general, Mahler brought the details necessary for performance into the fair copy, and would even revise this manuscript at various points before the publication of the work. Yet the refinement of details did not end with the published score, and extended throughout his life. To identify Mahler's revisions after the completion of the fair copy, the principles suggested by Reilly provide the basis for this survey, continuing the numbering used above:

6. Copyists' manuscripts (frequently identified by the German term *Stich-vorlag*), with autograph corrections by Mahler, prepared as a basis for the en-graver of the score.

7. Printers' proofs with autograph corrections and modifications.

8. Printed score with revisions marked by Mahler, or by a copyist for him. Such revisions appear to form an intermediate stage before a new edition was actually undertaken.

9. Printed scores with revisions, used or intended as the basis for a new edition of a work.[9]

A distinction exists between copyists' manuscripts and what Reilly calls *Stichvorlage*. The latter are technically printers' proofs but in Mahler's case they can also apply to copyists' manuscripts. In addition, to this list may be

---

[9] Reilly, 'An Inventory', 4.

added orchestral parts that Mahler corrected in the performance of his works. In some cases such sets of orchestral parts have not survived, and those that exist do not always contain revisions. While an original orchestral part might contain a number of corrections, not all of them may be Mahler's or even from his time.

The sources after the fair copy differ significantly from the earlier sketches. For the most part, the earlier manuscripts show Mahler writing for himself, where he would be as explicit as he needed. An earlier sketch often served as an aide-mémoire for the composer himself and did not need to contain all the detail that he would add later. On the other hand, Mahler intended his later corrections for others, specifically other conductors and, ultimately, his publisher. These refinements took the work to a more finished form, as he became more precise with the instrumentation and expression of the music in the score.

Sketches for the Fourth Symphony

Except for sketchbooks,[10] manuscripts from every stage of composition exist for the Fourth Symphony, as shown in Table 1.1. While some manuscripts are probably lost, enough materials exist to suggest the evolution of the work from the preliminary sketches, to the short score, draft score, and the fair copy of the symphony. As such, these documents provide a rare glimpse of the composer as he worked through each stage of composition for a work that reportedly had a difficult genesis.

An analysis of the extant sketches for the Fourth Symphony makes it possible to gain a clearer idea of how Mahler approached composition as the work took shape from fragmentary to more continuous ideas, and grew from one- and two-line sketches to full score. In proceeding from one phase of composition to another, he shaped his ideas and gave them continuity. It is often possible to find resemblances with the completed work even in the preliminary sketches, but the differences lie in detail rather than substance.

For Mahler, each stage of composition was a means of giving increasingly clearer shape to a work. In taking his ideas from the preliminary sketches to the short score, he did not change the substance of the music as much as elaborate on it, and this included adding transitions and developing textures that he had not pursued earlier. The differences at this stage of composition include passages that he either chose not to use or those he added later, once he saw the work in its fuller form. Thus the short score contains various insertions found on the bottoms of pages, or as separate leaves and inserted at various points.

---

[10] For a discussion about the nature of Mahler's sketchbooks, see Zychowicz, 'Sketches and Drafts of Gustav Mahler', 183–212.

TABLE 1.1. *Sketches for Mahler's Fourth Symphony*

Stage of Composition	Location	Comments
First ideas: verbal plan	US-CIpl, Fine Arts Collection	Plan for a six-movement 'Symphonie Humoreske' (Symphonic Humoresque)
First ideas: sketchbooks (*Skizzenbücher*)	None extant	Despite Bauer-Lechner's allusions to their existence, any sketchbooks that Mahler used for the Fourth Symphony are no longer extant
Preliminary sketches (*Vorentwürfe*)	US-STu, MLM 8, 633	Single-page sketch for part of first-movement exposition
	CH-CObodmeriana	Single-page sketch for the first-movement development section
	US-Cn, Case MS Vm 1001 M21 S4	Two pages of sketches for the first-movement development section
	Private source	Two pages of sketches for the first-movement development section
	A-Wigmg	Single-page sketch for the recapitulation
	A-Wn, Mus. Hs. 39.745	Sketches for the second movement (complete set)
	US-NYpm	Single-page sketch for the third-movement second theme
	A-Wn, Mus. Hs. 4366	Single-page sketch for the 'Presto' variation (recto)
Short score (*Particell*)	US-NYpm	Short score for the third movement (complete manuscript)
	Private source	Short score for the first-movement exposition
Draft score (*Partiturentwurf*)	A-Wigmg	Bifolios 2, 3, and 5 for the first movement
	A-Wn, Mus. Hs. 30.898	Insertion page ('Einlage') for bifolio 10 of the first movement
	C-Lu	Fair-copy-like draft for the second-movement opening
	A-Wn, Mus. Hs. 4366	Insertion page ('Einlage') for bifolio 5 of the third movement (verso)
	F-Pbmgm	Bifolio 7 of the third movement
Fair copy (*Reinschrift*)	A-Wgm, MS XIII.35824	

Even at this point Mahler was not yet finished with refining the detail of a work like the Fourth. As he took the short score into the draft score, he realized in the latter his notes on scoring from the various earlier sketches where he delineated the instrumentation. With each part written out as a separate line, the draft score resembles the fair copy, except for its physical appearance in oblong format (*Querformat*). Mahler would revise the draft score when he took it into the fair copy, which is always in upright format (*Hochformat*). Yet these two kinds of score are closely related, with an almost note-for-note correspondence between the draft score and fair copy, and when they occur, differences are insubstantial. The final measures of the third movement, for example, are slightly shorter in the draft score than in his later revision, as he lengthened the notated passage to allow the movement to conclude appropriately for its segue into the Finale.

Even later in the fair copy, Mahler was not always content to leave the music unmodified. A page of a fair-copy Mahler manuscript may contain a number of revisions in pencil inscribed over the inked layer, and sometimes even these have been superseded by other markings in blue pencil (the *Blaustift* that he often used to revise manuscripts) to reflect yet another level of work. He would sometimes cross out a stave and substitute another version above or below it. Similarly, he would sometimes divide otherwise evenly rastered bars and insert additional music in the fair copy.

From the earliest sketches to the fair copy Mahler's critical judgement took him from rough outlines to clearer detail, such that the content of the music and its presentation in the orchestration often merged. As early as the preliminary sketches he would indicate a desired instrument or articulation, and retain that detail in the finished work. This kind of association with timbre early in the compositional process is critical to understanding Mahler's often solid conception of his music as he worked out the detail, not the substance of a work, in the various stages of sketches. As he took his ideas into more advanced drafts, he was meticulous about what some have termed secondary parameters,[11] which include orchestration, doublings, barring, dynamics, phrase markings, etc. Such concern for detail extends beyond the preparation of the fair copy, to encompass printers' proofs and even later revisions of the published score.

In the latter his changes reflect his rethinking of certain places based on the practical experience of performances, as well as development as a composer. For Mahler this was an ongoing process: on 8 February 1911, several months before his death, when he referred to his latest revision on the Fifth Symphony, he confessed to the conductor Georg Göhler that 'it had to be almost completely reorchestrated. . . . I simply can't understand why I still had to make such mistakes, like the merest beginner.'[12] Assuredly, Mahler was not completely finished with revising the Fifth Symphony—or even the Fourth—at that time. Had he lived longer, he probably would have returned to both of them and possibly pursued further modifications. For Mahler, the accumulated knowledge and experience as a composer and a conductor

[11] Robert G. Hopkins, *Closure and Mahler's Music: The Role of Secondary Parameters* (Studies in the Criticism and Theory of Music; Philadelphia: The University of Pennsylvania Press, 1990), 1–3.

[12] Gustav Mahler, *Briefe*, ed. Herta Blaukopf (Vienna: Zsolnay, 1982), 403–4; *Selected Letters of Gustav Mahler*, ed. Knud Martner, trans. Eithne Wilkins, Ernst Kaiser, and Bill Hopkins (New York: Farrar, Straus & Giroux, 1979), 372.

allowed him to enhance the presentation of his music in the revisions he made years after completing the fair copy.

The Fourth Symphony among Mahler's Works

In considering his position on revisions late in life, Mahler's comments about the Fifth Symphony may be applied to the Fourth, which exists in a fair copy that he revised, and corrections he made on the first published edition. In addition, he returned to the Fourth at least twice more afterwards. While Mahler is known for the degree to which he revised his works after publication, the scrutiny extended to the Fourth can be attributed to two factors: (i) while the initial reception of the symphony was not completely unfavourable, the public and the critics did not seem to understand the music as Mahler intended it;[13] and (ii) the work itself contains elements that reflect a change in style from his earlier symphonies, particularly the Second, and he wanted to make certain that the differences came through clearly. Even later in his life Mahler was aware of a style change around the time of the Fourth. In commenting about the Fifth Symphony in the letter to Göhler cited above, he also states that 'it is clear that all the experience I had gained in writing the first four symphonies completely let me down in this one—for a completely new style demanded a new technique'.[14]

In some ways, the 'new technique' Mahler applied to the Fifth Symphony has its roots in the Fourth, which already differs in style from the first three symphonies. The Fourth Symphony comes at the end of his 'Wunderhorn' period, the time during which he composed the Second and Third Symphonies, as well as many of his settings from *Des Knaben Wunderhorn*.[15] With this symphony Mahler moved from the world of his earlier works and began to compose music that did not rely on explicit programmes, such as the detailed ones he wrote for the Second Symphony, or even the Third, for which two of the six movements even have sung texts and the Scherzo has its basis in the song 'Ablösung im Sommer'. Mahler also gave each movement of the Third a title and, in one score, even made programmatic comments above certain places in the music.[16] In contrast to the Third Symphony, the Fourth lacks any kind of explicit and published programme, and the only sung text occurs in the Song-Finale 'Das himmlische Leben'.

The Fourth Symphony also exhibits a different approach to texture that seems to anticipate some aspects of the later symphonies. As Hans Redlich

---

[13] Bauer-Lechner, *Erinnerungen*, 210–14; *Recollections*, 182–5.

[14] Mahler, *Briefe*, 404; *Selected Letters*, 372.

[15] Donald Mitchell examines this phase of Mahler's work in *Gustav Mahler: The Wunderhorn Years— Chronicles and Commentaries* (Boulder, Colo.: Westview Press, 1976; repr. Berkeley: The University of California Press, 1980).

[16] These annotations occur in the fair copy currently among the holdings of the Pierpont Morgan Library, Lehmann Deposit. Filler discusses this source in 'Editorial Problems', 170–2.

stated in his study of Bruckner and Mahler, 'despite its affinity with the preceding *Wunderhorn* symphonies, it [the Fourth] stands at the crossroads...its
musical idiom already shows the first-fruits of a remarkably self-critical process of contrapuntal discipline and structural logic'.[17] While this is evident in a
comparison of the Fourth with his other, earlier symphonies, it also differs
from the previous symphonies in its scoring for a much smaller orchestra.
In contrast to the Second and Third Symphonies, the Fourth shows a tend-
ency towards purer tone colours, a characteristic that results from the thinner
textures used throughout the work. This also anticipates some of the cham-
ber-music sonorities of the later works, such as *Das Lied von der Erde*.

'Das himmlische Leben' and the Fourth Symphony

The song 'Das himmlische Leben' (1892), which Mahler had composed almost a decade earlier, is at once the source and goal of the Fourth Symphony.
After attempting for years to include the song in a large-scale work, Mahler
conceived the Fourth Symphony with 'Das himmlische Leben' at its core.
Elements of the song pervade the symphony, with motifs from it found in
the three movements which precede 'Das himmlische Leben'. Because of
this, any history of the Fourth Symphony must include an examination of
the Song-Finale 'Das himmlische Leben'. As shown in Table 1.2, the inclusion
of this song in a study of the Fourth extends the history of the symphony back
to 1892, when Mahler set a text from the anthology *Des Knaben Wunderhorn*,
'Der Himmel hängt voll Geigen' ('The world through rose-coloured glasses').

'Das himmlische Leben' was originally part of a set of *5 Humoresken* for
voice and orchestra, one of the earliest settings that he made from *Des Knaben
Wunderhorn*. Mahler did not include 'Das himmlische Leben' among his sets of
Wunderhornlieder, but considered using the song as the final movement of the
Third Symphony. Towards such an end he made thematic connections

TABLE 1.2. *Manuscripts of 'Das himmlische Leben'*

Manuscript	Location	Comments
6 *Wunderhornlieder*	D-B	Piano draft of the song, dated 10 Feb. 1892
5 *Humoresken*	A-Wgm	Orchestral draft of the song, dated 12 Mar. 1892
['Das himmlische Leben']	Private owner, location unknown	'Intermediary' copyist's manuscript with corrections in Mahler's hand
Symphony No. 4	A-Wgm, MS XIII.35824	Fourth Symphony, movement four (fair copy)

[17] H. F. Redlich, *Bruckner and Mahler* (London: J. M. Dent & Sons. Ltd., 1955; rev. edn., London: Dent, 1963), 193.

between movements of this symphony and the song, as may be seen in the sketches for an instrumental variation of the song in the first movement.[18]

Eventually Mahler decided not to use 'Das himmlische Leben' in the Third, and instead planned a six-movement Fourth Symphony subtitled 'Humoreske'; as in some of the plans for the Third, he intended to use this song as the final movement. He did not pursue this *Symphonic Humoresque* according to the plan, but proceeded to compose the Fourth Symphony with 'Das himmlische Leben' as its point of departure in composition and point of arrival in the work itself.

Plan of this Study

The present study of Mahler's creative process in the Fourth Symphony involves an examination of each stage of composition and the relevant manuscripts for it. While not all the materials for the symphony have survived, enough exist to give a clear idea of the systematic process Mahler used when he composed this work. In terms of methodology, I have adopted the framework cited above that Edward R. Reilly proposed for his catalogue in progress of Mahler manuscripts, and which I subsequently employed in my own work. By using such a framework it is possible to appreciate how Mahler approached the composition of symphonic music, which emerged in greater detail at each phase.

As a point of departure, the present study includes an exploration of the structure of the Fourth Symphony, which extends from the essential musical forms to structural processes at the core of the music. In addition, it is important to understand the gestation of the Fourth Symphony from the time when Mahler composed the song 'Das himmlische Leben' and intended to use it in a large-scale work. Those efforts, although unrealized, are essential to understanding the place of that song in the completed Fourth Symphony. The impulse to undertake a work with 'Das himmlische Leben' at its core took root in the Fourth Symphony, which Mahler began at a time when he found it difficult to compose.

In terms of the actual genesis of the Fourth Symphony, each chapter of the present study concerns a discrete phase of work, from early ideas as found in the six-movement plan for the Symphonic Humoresque, to the extant preliminary sketches, the short score, the draft score, and the fair copy. While all materials before the completion of the fair copy could be regarded simply as sketches, Mahler's strategy in composition resulted in various kinds of manuscripts. It is as though he composed the music in layers, from fragmentary ideas that suggest the outlines of the longer work to increasingly continuous and detailed sketches. Thus, the short score differs qualitatively from the

---

[18] Williamson, 'Mahler's Compositional Process', 338–40.

sketches that preceded it, and the draft score reveals yet another level of complexity that took Mahler closer to the fair copy of the Fourth.

By exploring the Fourth Symphony from the inside, so to speak, it is possible to gain a different view of the work than occurs in the analyses of the music that treat the work as a single, almost static conception. Mahler's ideas about the Fourth developed gradually, and he also allowed his later ideas about this symphony to emerge in the revisions he took up at various times after the publication of the work. The idea of a single text for the Fourth blurs in terms of this manuscript study, which involves a survey of the autograph corrections Mahler left for the score. The attempts of various editors to deal with the resulting choices has left the Fourth in a difficult state. From the perspective of compositional process, it may be that the current ideas about editing Mahler's music may have to give way to approaches that take into consideration the origins of the music. Only then will the resulting score reflect more comprehensively the composer's intentions in bringing the work to completion.

Most importantly, Mahler's sketches are particularly rich documents that diverge in detail, rather than substance, from the completed work. Several sketches reveal places where he considered multiple approaches to a passage, and at some point he chose one or another solution or later found some other way to handle a difficult transition. From the perspective of the completed work the choices sometimes seem obvious, yet Mahler had to determine for himself the compositional alternatives as he proceeded through each phase of the creative process.

As much as the extant sketches reveal the richness of the composer's thought at these points, one can only wonder about the content of the sketches that are no longer extant and the ones Mahler himself destroyed en route to completing a masterful work like the Fourth Symphony. As with other creative artists who worked so diligently at bringing their work to completion, it is possible only to wonder at the many possibilities.

2. *Structural Considerations*

A Symphony of Normal Dimensions

While completing the draft score of the Fourth Symphony in Summer 1900, Mahler began to discuss the music in detail with his confidante Natalie Bauer-Lechner. After telling her the key of the work—G major—and the approximate performance time—45 minutes—he confessed that in composing the Fourth 'I only wanted to write a symphonic Humoresque, and out of it came a symphony of normal dimensions'.[1] While he was nowhere explicit about what constituted for him 'normal dimensions', the result was a concise symphony in four movements for a smaller orchestra than his earlier works.

In a sense, the Fourth Symphony is Mahler's bow to the conventional symphony. While it is one of two symphonies that he completed in four movements, he also composed the first three movements in forms traditionally associated with the classical symphony, as emerges in analyses by Stephan,[2] La Grange,[3] and Floros.[4] The first movement is a sonata in G major (Table 2.1),[5] the second a Scherzo in C minor (Table 2.2), and the third a slow movement (Adagio) cast as a set of double variations in G major (Table 2.3). Mahler himself acknowledged his reliance on traditional symphonic form while he was composing the Third Symphony,[6] and claimed that the only difference between his music and the works of Haydn, Mozart, and Beethoven lay in the sequence and dimensions of the movements. Notwithstanding this clarification, he regarded traditional symphonic structure as an inviolable principle for his own music, even though he increasingly found ways to extend its parameters.

In the Fourth Symphony, however, Mahler deviates from textbook conventions in the key relationships with the Song-Finale, through which he expands the tonality, which begins in G major and ends in E major (see

---

[1] Bauer-Lechner, *Erinnerungen*, 162; *Recollections*, 151.

[2] Stephan, *Gustav Mahler: IV. Symphonie G-Dur*, 8–26.

[3] Henry-Louis de La Grange, *Gustav Mahler*, i (Garden City, NY: Doubleday & Co., 1973), 811–23; rev. edn., *Gustav Mahler: Chronique d'une vie*, i: *Vers la gloire 1860–1900* (Paris: Fayard, 1979), 1053–67.

[4] Constantin Floros, *Gustav Mahler*, iii: *Die Symphonien* (Wiesbaden: Breitkopf & Härtel, 1985), 102–24.

[5] It may be argued that elements of Sonata-Rondo form are present in the first movement, as held by Edward W. Murphy in 'Sonata-Rondo Form in the Symphonies of Gustav Mahler', *Music Review*, 35 (1974), 52–62 at 59.

[6] Bauer-Lechner, *Erinnerungen*, 64; *Recollections*, 66.

TABLE 2.1. *The structure of the first movement*

Sonata

Section	Bar	Tonality
Exposition		
Introduction ('Schellenkappe')	1	B minor
Area 1		G major
a	4	
b	8	
a (varied)	18	
b (varied)	22	
c	32	modulates to D major
Area 2		D major
a	38	
b	47	
Closing area	8	
'Schellenkappe'	2	B minor
Area 1 (varied repetition)	77	G major
Coda	91	
Development		
'Schellenkappe' and Area 1 (a)	102	B minor
	109	E minor
	117	A minor
'Das himmlische Leben' motif	123	A major
	145	C sharp minor
'Schellenkappe' and Area 1 (a)	155	E flat minor, A flat minor
Closing area	167	F minor
'Schellenkappe' and Area 1 (abc)	185	B flat minor
Area 2 (a) and Closing area	209	C major
'Cry of Panic'	221	(with G pedal)
'Der kleine Appell'	225	(modulatory)
Area 1 (a) (false reprise)	234	
Recapitulation		
Area 1 (b)	239	G major
'Das himmlische Leben' motif	252	
Area 1 (c)	257	
Area 2		
a	263	
b	272	
Closing area	283	
'Schellenkappe' and Area 1 (abc)	298	
Coda (of Exposition)	323	
Coda (based on Area 1 themes)	340	

TABLE 2.2. *The structure of the second movement Scherzo with two trios*

Section	Bar	Tonality
Scherzo		
Introduction	1	C minor
Area A	7	C major
Area B	34	
Area A	46	C minor
Coda (Introduction)	64	
Trio 1		
Area C	69	F major
Area D	94	
Coda (Introduction)	109	
Scherzo		
Area A	110	C minor
Area B	145	C major
Area A	157	C minor
Area B	185	C major
Transition	201	modulatory
Trio 2		
Area C	203	F major
Area D	254	D major
Coda (Introduction)	275	
Scherzo		
Area A	281	D major
Area B	314	C major
Coda (A with Introduction)	329	

Table 2.4).[7] In contrast to the larger size of the Second and Third Symphonies, he treated each movement more succinctly and made the Fourth the shortest of all his symphonies. The orchestra is likewise smaller when compared with his other symphonies. By refraining from using low brass and extensive percussion in the Fourth Symphony, Mahler created the impression of an eighteenth-century orchestra. Yet with woodwinds *à 3*, four horns, three trumpets, and harp, the orchestra is hardly the kind of ensemble found with Haydn or Mozart.

Mahler also called attention to a change in his style with the completion of the Fourth Symphony. Abandoning the larger forms and gestures that occurred in his early symphonies, he attempted to employ a different means of expression in the Fourth. He touched upon this matter when he commented

---

[7] Hefling regards the relationship between G and E as critical to the tonal structure and discusses the 'constellation of keys' around E major that Mahler uses in this symphony. Stephen E. Hefling, '"Variations *in nuce*"', 115–18.

TABLE 2.3. *The structure of the third movement*

Double variations

Section	Bar	Tonality
Theme 1		
Period 1		
phrase 1	1	G major
phrase 2	9	
phrase 3	17	
Period 2		
phrase 1	25	
phrase 2	37	
phrase 3	45	
Concluding period	51	
Theme 2		
Period 1	62	E minor
Period 2	76	
Concluding period	91	D minor
Theme 1 (varied)		
Period 1	107	G major
Period 2	131	
Concluding period	151	
Theme 2 (varied)		
Period 1	179	G minor
Period 2	192	C sharp minor
Concluding period	205	F sharp minor
Theme 1 (varied)		
Variation in $\frac{3}{4}$	222	G major
Variation in $\frac{3}{8}$	238	G major
Variation in $\frac{2}{4}$	263	E major
Variation in $\frac{4}{4}$	287	G major
Coda		
'Das himmlische Leben' fragments	315	E major
Ewigkeit motif	326	G major (ending on D)

that 'the inadequacy of the players [for the première] was all the more notice-able because of the subtlety of the instrumental parts'.[8] In comparison with his earlier music, the Fourth Symphony requires more intimate, ensemble-like playing for the shifting sonorities that occur in the work. He avoided the thicker textures associated with his first three symphonies to use timbres consisting of increasingly pure tone colours rather than mixtures. Individual instrumental lines became clearer through his use of single players on a part, thus

---

[8] Bauer-Lechner, *Erinnerungen*, 182; *Recollections*, 202.

TABLE 2.4. *The structure of the fourth movement*

Strophic variations

Section	Bar	Tonality
Introduction	1	G major
Strophe 1	12	G major
Interlude ('Schellenkappe')	40	G major
Strophe 2	57	E minor
Interlude ('Schellenkappe')	76	G major
Strophe 3	80	G major
Interlude		
('Schellenkappe')	115	G major
(Introduction)	122	E major
Strophe 4	142	E major
Postlude (Introduction)	174	E major

anticipating the chamber-music-like sonorities of his late works, particularly *Das Lied von der Erde* and the Ninth Symphony. In composing the Fourth Symphony, however, Mahler was not attempting to write an overtly neoclassical work but chose a more classical idiom to reinforce the sound and meaning of the Song-Finale, which he had long intended to use as the culmination of one of his large-scale works. He moved beyond the larger canvasses of the first three symphonies, which required different means to achieve the ends he intended for each of them. With the Fourth, however, he became more concise formally. In composing the first three movements, he achieved a subtle integration of elements that would lead to the Song-Finale rather than away from it.

Mahler composed the Finale first as the song 'Das himmlische Leben', a setting from *Des Knaben Wunderhorn* that he had already completed in 1892. When he decided to use the song in the Fourth Symphony, it became the *raison d'être* for the work, and he consciously worked towards that Finale. Thus, as the symphony unfolds thematically, it also moves towards its source rather than away from any generating idea. Initially, Mahler connected the logic of this conclusion to the programmatic ideas he had for the work, and some aspects of the structure of the first three movements result from the composer's desire to link them to the Song-Finale. He evoked a 'timeless' idiom by suggesting the Classical era in the first movement and maintaining a symphony of classical proportions in the subsequent two movements. Even though Mahler composed the symphony in this manner, the primary feature of the Fourth Symphony is by no means the reversion to the Classical style. Rather, his choice of this style follows from the impulse to arrive at a symphony that describes in some sense celestial existence as expressed verbally in the song 'Das himmlische Leben'.

Towards this end, Mahler established a high degree of integration between the movements by placing song fragments in each of the three movements

TABLE 2.5. *'Das himmlische Leben' and the thematic content of the Fourth Symphony*

Movement and section	Bars	Analogue in the song
1 'Schellenkappe'	1–3	'Schellenkappe', bb. 40–7
'Schellenkappe'	72–4	'Schellenkappe', bb. 40–7
'Schellenkappe'	102–4	'Schellenkappe', bb. 40–7
Development (flute)	126 ff.	Opening vocal melody, bb. 12–16
Development (grace notes in flute)	132	Introduction, bb. 1–4
Development (flute)	135	Opening vocal melody, bb. 12–16
'Schellenkappe'	155–7	'Schellenkappe', bb. 40–7
Development (grace notes in flute and horn)	186–7	Introduction, bb. 1–4
Development (repeated eighth notes)	225–8	Accompaniment in Strophe 1, bb. 25 ff.
Development (sixteenth notes in bassoon)	226–9	Accompaniment in Interlude, b. 48
Recapitulation (low strings)	249–50	'Sollt' ein Fasttag', b. 98 (accompaniment)
'Schellenkappe'	285	'Schellenkappe', bb. 40–7
'Schellenkappe'	298–9	'Schellenkappe', bb. 40–7
2 Introduction	5–7	'Schellenkappe' (sixteenth notes), bb. 40–7
Main theme (violin)	6–8	Introduction, bb. 1–4
Trio (oboe)	78–83	'Cäcilia mit ihren Verwandten', bb. 158–63
Trio theme (violin)	212–16	'Cäcilia mit ihren Verwandten', bb. 158–63
Trio (violin)	242–5	Introduction to Strophe 4, bb. 128–9
Trio (violin)	254–61	Introduction to Strophe 4, bb. 125 ff.; also bb. 153–7 (accompaniment)
3 Second Theme (wide leaps)	63 ff.	'Sankt Ursula', bb. 150–3
Theme 1 (varied) (clarinet)	151–4	Interlude, b. 48 (accompaniment)
Theme 1 (varied) (violin and bass parts)	290–5	Chorale, bb. 36–8
Coda	320–1	Introduction, bb. 1–4
Coda	321–3	Opening vocal melody, bb. 12–16

that precede the Finale (Table 2.5). Motifs from one movement occur in others, such as the opening bells, the 'Schellenkappe', as Mahler called them,[9] which he used cyclically in the first and last movements of the symphony. Similarly, other fragments of the song emerge elsewhere in the first movement, and also in the second and third movements. Thus, this 'symphony of normal dimensions' may be the result of the limitations he placed on himself with regard to the organic unity and thematic cohesiveness he desired in this work. To have let the Fourth Symphony expand, as he claimed had happened with the Second and Third, would have weakened the integration he wanted to achieve in this piece.

As to other structural relationships, the two inner movements have in common their reliance on the variation principle. The third movement is a set of

[9] Bauer-Lechner, *Erinnerungen*, 202; *Recollections*, 182.

double variations (Table 2.3), and Mahler told Bauer-Lechner that he felt these variations to be 'the first real ones he had written'.[10] At the same time the thematic content of the Scherzo gives the impression of stemming from a single idea that pervades the movement and contributes to a sense of variations on a theme. Even the trios derive from the primary thematic material of the Scherzo, unlike the Scherzo of the Third Symphony, where Mahler had created more contrast between the sections. With the Fourth Symphony the second movement is at once a Scherzo and a variation movement, as Mahler himself attested in his comments to Bauer-Lechner (again, at the première of the work): 'Will they find out, I wonder, that the third movement consists of variations—and the second, too?'[11]

At another level, the degree of unity that Mahler achieved in the Fourth Symphony influenced the larger structure of the work. When he complained about the accidental interchange of the two middle movements in February 1901, he must have been concerned about the extensive allusion to the song in the Coda of the third movement. Were the slow movement to occur before the Scherzo, the overall effect would not be the same. The Coda of the Scherzo, with its outburst in E major that anticipates the key in which the symphony ends, would be anticlimactic if the slow movement were to follow it. Given the more extended song fragments that occur in the Coda, the strong connection between this movement and 'Das himmlische Leben' would have been interrupted by the Scherzo and the significance of the song quotations might have become obscured, if not lost entirely.

Thematic Relationships between the Movements

By placing fragments of 'Das himmlische Leben' in the three movements that precede its complete statement at the end of the Fourth Symphony, Mahler goes beyond the kind of cyclic unity usually found in nineteenth-century music. In order to integrate the Song-Finale into the symphony, he intended to reveal the song gradually by leading to it through increasingly more explicit fragments. In allowing these to pervade the work before the Finale, he strengthened the function of 'Das himmlische Leben' as the goal and source of the symphony.

Yet at one time Mahler had planned to use the song 'Das himmlische Leben' as the culminating movement of the Third Symphony and wanted to incorporate it into that work in a similar way. He must have recalled these plans for the Third when he composed the Fourth Symphony, where the song was to have a comparable function. Unlike his previous attempts to incorporate songs into his symphonic works, including the Third Symphony, Mahler

[10]   Bauer-Lechner, *Erinnerungen*, 163; *Recollections*, 152.
[11]   Bauer-Lechner, *Erinnerungen*, 202; *Recollections*, 182–3.

Ex. 2.1. The 'Schellenkappe' idea in the 1st movt.: (*a*) 'Schellenkappe', 'Das himmlische Leben' (DHL), bb. 40–1, and Fourth Symphony, 1st movt., bb. 1–2; (*b*) DHL,
bb. 12–14 (upper stave) and Fourth Symphony, 1st movt., bb. 126–30 (lower stave);
(*c*) DHL, bb. 1–4 (upper stave) and Fourth Symphony, 1st movt., bb. 131–3 (lower
stave); (*d*) DHL, bb. 48–9 (upper stave) and Fourth Symphony, 1st movt., bb. 185–8

achieved in the Fourth Symphony a level of integration without parallel in his
earlier music.

The 'Schellenkappe' idea in the first movement (Ex. 2.1) functions as a uni-
fying device and also a quotation from 'Das himmlische Leben'. The idea is
almost secondary to the song, occurring as part of an interlude and not in
the principal vocal melody. Yet by placing the 'Schellenkappe' at the beginning

Ex. 2.1 contd.

of the first movement and returning to it through the sonata, it becomes a motto for the work. When the 'Schellenkappe' 'returns' in the Song-Finale, Mahler achieves cyclic unity between the first and last movements.

A more subtle use of thematic material from 'Das himmlische Leben' in the first movement is the dotted-eighth- and sixteenth-note figuration of the 'new theme' introduced in the development section. While not a literal statement of the opening vocal melody of the song, this idea (which functions as an *Anklang*) is sufficient to suggest a passage from 'Das himmlische Leben'. Nevertheless, a more explicit quotation of the song occurs near the end of the development section. At bar 225, the repeated eighth-note accompaniment characteristic of the song begins, and in the next bar Mahler quotes the sixteenth notes in the bass that are found in bar 48 of the song. He uses similar figuration in the bass at bar 229 and returns to the repeated eighth-note figure at bar 231, which blends into the accompaniment to the first theme at bar 234.

Mahler does not refer to the song again until the recapitulation, where the 'Schellenkappe' returns at bar 298. At this point it is not clear whether the subsequent sixteenth-note figure is a reference to 'Das himmlische Leben' or to material previously used in the movement, since it resembles both. It is thus possible to regard the figuration as belonging to both the song and to the thematic material of the movement, and consequently contributing a more organic unity to the music. Further, when fragments of the song recur in the movement, they eventually become absorbed in its thematic content, and the content thus functions, at times, as both a suggestion of 'Das himmlische Leben' and a structural unit of the sonata form in this movement.

However, references to 'Das himmlische Leben' are not so distinct in the second movement. As shown in Ex. 2.2, a correspondence exists between the sixteenth-note figure that is part of the 'Schellenkappe' motif and the sixteenth notes of the solo violin melody in the second movement. A similar relationship may be observed between the latter and the opening of the song,

Ex. 2.2. Quotation of 'Das himmlische Leben' in the 2nd movt.: (*a*) 'Das himmlische Leben' (DHL), b. 41 (upper stave) and Fourth Symphony, 2nd movt., bb. 4–6 (lower stave); (*b*) DHL, b. 1 (upper stave) and Fourth Symphony, 2nd movt., bb. 6–8 (lower stave); (*c*) DHL, bb. 58–61 (upper stave) and Fourth Symphony, 2nd movt., bb. 221–16 (lower stave); (*d*) DHL, bb. 125–7 (upper system) and Fourth Symphony, 2nd movt., bb. 254–61 (lower system)

Ex. 2.2 contd.

(*d*)

with the arpeggiated tonic chord common to both. Further, Susanne Vill points out a quotation of bars 158–63 of the song in bars 213 ff. of the Scherzo.[12] This is a relatively remote connection when compared with the quotation in the first movement and the song fragments in the Coda of the third movement. It specifically involves chromatic motion on the second syllable of the word 'Verwandten', which the composer placed in the chromatic passage found in the first violin. Mahler even suggests—perhaps subconsciously—the relationship between the violin line and its vocal source with the marking 'singend' (*cantabile*).

Another quotation occurs near the end of the Scherzo, where the flute and violin parts at the beginning of the section in E major in the song (bb. 125 ff.) have an analogue in the violin and clarinet parts at bars 254–61 of the Scherzo. The figuration in the low strings and harp at this point in the second movement even resembles the triplet accompaniment found in bars 153–7 of the song. A similar subtle quotation may be found in the third movement. Stephen Hefling points out a place in the preliminary sketches for the second theme where Mahler quotes bars 152–3 of the song, the vocal melody for 'Sankt Ursula selbst dazu lacht' ('St Ursula herself smiled') in a modulation to E minor.[13] (See Ex. 2.3(*a*).) While the quotation in the completed work is not as literal as it is in the sketches, it survives in the accompaniment figure (bassoon), as well as later in the section, in the wide leaps in accompaniment (harp and cello) at bars 76–9.

[12] Susanne Vill, *Vermittlungsformen verbalisierter und musikalische Inhalt in der Musik Gustav Mahlers*. Frankfurter Beiträge zur Musikwissenschaft, 6 (Tutzing: Hans Schneider, 1979), 320.

[13] Hefling, 'Variations', 116–17.

Ex. 2.3. Quotation of 'Das himmlische Leben' in the 3rd movt.: (*a*) 'Das himmlische Leben' (DHL), bb. 151–3 (first stave) and *Particell* sketches for the 3rd movt., iv, line 6, bb. 11–14 (second stave), and Fourth Symphony, 3rd movt., bb. 62–3 (third stave); (*b*) DHL, b. 48 (upper stave) and Fourth Symphony, 3rd movt., bb. 151–4 (lower stave); (*c*) DHL, bb. 1–4 (upper stave) and Fourth Symphony, 3rd movt., bb. 318–22 (lower stave)

A more distinct quotation of the song occurs at bars 151–4 of this movement, where the bass figuration as found in bar 48 of 'Das himmlische Leben' occurs in augmentation in the clarinet part (see Ex. 2.3(*b*)). Yet Mahler placed the clearest quotation of material from the song in the Coda of the third movement, where he anticipates the key in which the symphony ends, E major (b. 315), and uses a bass accompaniment resembling the repeated perfect fourths that occur at the end of the song. He quotes the introduction of the song in the horns (bb. 318–21) and follows this with the dotted-eighth and sixteenth-note figure taken from the opening vocal melody of the song (bb. 321–2). (See Ex. 2.3(*c*).)

In addition to the relationships that exist internally between the movements, Mahler intended to link the Fourth Symphony with his first three symphonies. Bauer-Lechner reports in summer 1900 that he

> emphasized the close connection of the Fourth with these [his first three symphonies], to which it forms a conclusion. In their content and structure, the four of them form a perfectly self-contained tetralogy. A particularly close relationship exists between the Third and Fourth; in fact, the latter even has themes in common with the movement of the Third called 'Was mir die Engel erzahlen'.[14]

The connection with the Third Symphony is the strongest. Having intended to use 'Das himmlische Leben' to link the movements, he quoted bars 57–62 of the song in bars 39–44 of 'Es sungen drei Engel', the fifth movement of the completed Third Symphony, thus connecting the two songs and, eventually, the two symphonies, both programmatically and thematically.[15]

As the final component of Mahler's *Wunderhorn* tetralogy, the Fourth Symphony may be regarded as an extension of the ideas the composer approached in the Third. Having described the suffering and eventual triumph of his hero in the First Symphony, Mahler explores his death and ultimate resurrection in the Second. In the Third he probes the nature of existence, and contemplates the nature of God in the last movement. In the Fourth Symphony, however, Mahler attempted to explore heavenly life, according to the eventually suppressed programme he conveyed to Bruno Walter.[16] The programme, as related by Walter, begins with an expression of the unheard-of happiness and unearthly joy of heaven in the first movement. The second movement contains the image of Death as 'Freund Hein' (the personification of death used by the poet Matthias Claudius) playing the fiddle as he takes souls to heaven. For the third movement, Mahler had in mind the beatific smile of St Ursula, the most serious of all the saints who cannot help but

---

[14] Bauer-Lechner, *Erinnerungen*, 164; *Recollections*, 154.

[15] Mahler also mentioned this relationship to Alphons Diepenbrock when he commented on the latter's programme notes for the Fourth Symphony. Diepenbrock's notes are included in Eduard Reeser (ed.), *Gustav Mahler und Holland: Briefe* (Vienna: Universal, 1980), 104–7. Mahler's letter to Diepenbrock about the notes is found on pp. 100–1.

[16] Bruno Walter, *Briefe 1894–1962* (Frankfurt am Main: S. Fischer, 1969), 48–52.

break into a smile in her contemplation of heaven.[17] As to a more specific description of the programme, Mahler told Walter that the text of the last movement should suffice.[18] This child's image of heaven as found in the song 'Das himmlische Leben' contains the only explicit text for the symphony and the logical conclusion of the work. At the same time, Mahler expected that the first three movements would be comprehensible in an absolute sense, rather than only as programme music; thus the descriptive programme is ultimately superfluous when it comes to understanding the work.

Other Relationships

In addition to connections between movements, Mahler also included ideas that connect the Fourth Symphony to other music he composed. For one, he quoted in the Fourth Symphony the *Ewigkeit* motif[19] that he had used in his Second Symphony, and thus created a link between those two compositions that could be extended to others. (See Table 2.6.) As shown in Ex. 2.4(*a*), Mahler adapted this motif from the music Richard Wagner used to accompany the words of Brünnhilde at the end of *Siegfried*, 'Ewig war ich, ewig bin ich'. The contour and textual reference contribute a sense of ascent and attainment appropriate to the meaning he wished to convey in the Finale of the Second Symphony, as he attempted to depict the life to come. (See Ex. 2.4(*b*) and (*c*).)

In the Fourth Symphony, the *Ewigkeit* motif occurs at the beginning of the third movement, at bars 45–7 (Ex. 2.4(*d*)). While a sequential passage at bars

TABLE 2.6. *Thematic relationships between the Fourth Symphony and other works*

Movement and section	Bars	Analogue in other works
1 development (trumpet call)	224–34	Fifth Symphony, movt. 1, bb. 1–13 (trumpet fanfare)
3 Theme 1	29–33	*Kindertotenlieder*, 'Nun seh' ich wohl', bb. 48–51 ('doch ist das vom Schicksal abgeschlagen')
3 Theme 1	45–7	*Ewigkeit* motif
3 Theme 1 (varied)	299–301	*Ewigkeit* motif
4 chorale-style refrain	36–9 (72–5; 106–14)	Third Symphony, movt. 5, bb. 45–8 (59–62)
4 vocal line	57–62	Third Symphony, movt. 5, bb. 39–44
4 figuration	43–4	Third Symphony, movt. 5, bb. 70–1

[17] Ibid. 51–2.

[18] Ibid. 49.

[19] For a description of this motif, see Constantin Floros, *Gustav Mahler*, ii: *Mahler und die Symphonik des 19. Jahrhunderts in neuer Deutung* (Wiesbaden: Breitkopf & Härtel, 1977), 259–60 (musical examples on p. 408).

Ex. 2.4. The *Ewigkeit* motif in the music of Mahler: (*a*) Richard Wagner, *Siegfried*, Act 3, Brünnhilde: 'Ewig war ich, ewig bin ich…'; (*b*) Mahler, Second Symphony, 5th movt., bb. 697–702; (*c*) Second Symphony, 5th movt., bb. 421–8; (*d*) Fourth Symphony, 3rd movt., bb. 45–7; (*e*) Fourth Symphony, 3rd movt., bb. 299–301; (*f*) Fourth Symphony, 3rd movt., bb. 326–32

(*a*)

(*b*)

(*c*)

(*d*)

(*e*)

Ex. 2.4 contd.

(*f*)

66–7 resembles the motif, such a resemblance is coincidental. The next overt presentation of the idea occurs in the final variation of the first theme at bars 299–301 (Ex. 2.4(*e*)), and the most obvious use of the motif is in the Coda of the third movement. After the anticipation of the Finale and the key in which the symphony ends through the E major outburst and the fragments of 'Das himmlische Leben' at the beginning of the Coda, Mahler incorporates the *Ewigkeit* motif into the latter part of this section (bb. 326 ff.) (Ex. 2.4(*f*)). With the *Ewigkeit* motif scored for violins in octaves and the other instruments subordinate to it, the idea is unmistakable.

In addition, the manner of presentation, with the motif descending in the orchestra while the other instruments sustain high pitches (bb. 326–32), underscores the sense of ascent already present in the *Ewigkeit* motif, and helps connect this Coda to the Song-Finale that follows. While Mahler returns to G major at the end of the Coda, the movement never resolves to the tonic but, instead, fades out on the dominant D major. Lacking resolution in the third movement, the chord reaches G major only at the opening of the Song-Finale, thus strengthening the connection of the *Ewigkeit* motif in the former movement with the subject of heaven found in the latter.

Yet when the *Ewigkeit* motif occurs in the Eighth Symphony, Mahler places it in a conspicuous position, by presenting the idea in conjunction with a text that is enhanced by the associations the motif brings in from the Second and Fourth Symphonies. In the first part of the Eighth Symphony, the *Ewigkeit* motif occurs at the word 'accende' and is restated twice in that part of the symphony. The motif is found throughout the second part of the Eighth, gradually expanding from fragmentary to more explicit statements through its association with the phrase 'Das Ewig-Weibliche/Zieht uns hinan' ('the Eternal Feminine draws us upward'). As in the Finale of the Second Symphony and just before the song 'Das himmlische Leben' in the Fourth, the rising contour of the motif contributes to the programmatic depiction of Faust's entry into heaven in the second part.

A different kind of connection exists between the Coda of the Fourth Symphony Scherzo and the Adagietto of the Fifth Symphony. Beyond any overt thematic relationship, he uses the timbre found in the passage from the Fourth Symphony in the entire movement of the Fifth. The latter scoring for harp and strings recalls the sonority that he had used in the Coda of the slow movement for the Fourth Symphony. At the same time Mahler adapted the thematic content of his song 'Ich bin der Welt abhanden gekommen'[20] as the basis for the fourth movement of the Fifth Symphony. The song itself contains a passing reference to the *Ewigkeit* motif, which underscores the word 'Himmel' ('heaven') at the phrase 'Ich leb' allein in meinem Himmel' ('I live alone in my own heaven').

In the Fifth Symphony, Mahler, perhaps unconsciously, makes use of another motif from the Fourth. The idea that Mahler once called the 'little call to order' ('der kleine Appell') at the end of the development section of the first movement becomes the trumpet fanfare at the beginning of the first movement of the Fifth Symphony. This idea had a long gestation with Mahler, since it occurs in the preliminary sketches for the first movement of the Fourth and appears to have been retained in subsequent drafts of the movement. This 'call to order' is in D-flat minor in the Fourth, but in C sharp minor in the Fifth. While it functions as a means of bringing the melodic fragments together in the Fourth Symphony, it serves a different purpose in the Fifth, where it signals the opening of a funeral cortège, the 'Kondukt' found in the subtitle of that movement, the 'Trauermarsch' ('funeral march'). Whether Mahler intended an overt connection between the Fourth and Fifth Symphonies through the use of this idea is a moot point.

It is also possible to find other resemblances between Mahler's Fourth Symphony and music of other composers. In an article concerning the influence of Schubert on Mahler, Miriam K. Whaples suggests that Mahler quoted Schubert's music in the Fourth. She finds affinities between the main theme of the first movement of the symphony (bb. 3 ff.) and the second theme of the first movement of Schubert's Sonata in E flat major, D. 568 (bb. 53–4) as shown in Ex. 2.5. Whaples also believes that a descending-triplet figure in bars 126, 132, 138, 168, and 174 of the song 'Das himmlische Leben' is derived from Schubert's Sonata in D major, D. 850, specifically bars 31–2 of the finale (see Ex. 2.6).[21]

On the other hand, Jon W. Finson has called attention to the same fourth-movement figure, attributing it not to a work of Schubert, but rather to a folk song.[22] Finson posits that this motif is derived from the folk song 'Der Himmel hängt voll Geigen', the very poem that Mahler sets in 'Das himmlische Leben'. Whether Mahler's source is Schubert, whose music he knew, or folk music, is a moot point. Intentional or not, the resemblance exists, thus pointing to the eclectic quality of Mahler's music. In such a way

---

[20] References to the *Ewigkeit* motif in this and other Rückert settings are subtler than the appearances of the idea in the Second and Eighth Symphonies. For a brief discussion of these references, see Zychowicz, 'Sketches and Drafts', 77–82.

[21] Miriam K. Whaples, 'Mahler and Schubert's A Minor Sonata D. 784', *Music and Letters*, 65 (1984), 255–63 at 256–7.

[22] Jon W. Finson, 'The Reception of Gustav Mahler's *Wunderhorn* Lieder', *Journal of Musicology*, 5 (1987), 91–116 at 111–12.

Ex. 2.5. Comparison of (*a*) Schubert, Sonata in E flat major, D. 568, 1st movt., bb. 53–4, with (*b*) Mahler, Fourth Symphony, 1st movt., bb. 3–7 (violin)

Ex. 2.6. Comparison of (*a*) Schubert, Sonata in D major, D. 850, last movt., bb. 31–2, with Mahler (*b*) Fourth Symphony, 4th movt., b. 128 (flute); (*c*) Fourth Symphony, 4th movt., b. 128 (violin); (*d*) 'Der Himmel hängt voll Geigen' (folk song as quoted by Finson)

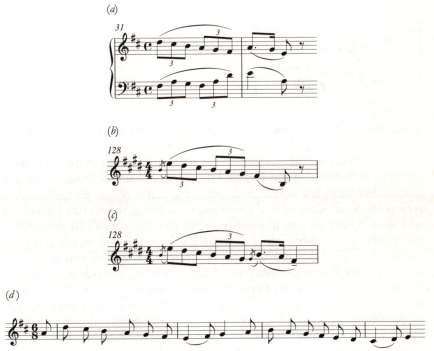

Wir g'nie-ßen die himm-li-schen Freu- den, drum tun wir das Ir- di-sche Mei - den

Ex. 2.7. Comparison of (*a*) Beethoven, *Fidelio*, Op. 72, quartet 'Mir ist so wunderbar', bb. 1–8 (reduction), with (*b*) Mahler, Fourth Symphony, 3rd movt., bb. 1–10 (reduction)

he assimilates elements from both the Romantic repertoire and popular traditions.

Such assimilation is also evident in the relationship between the opening of the third movement of the Fourth Symphony and the introduction of the quartet 'Mir ist so wunderbar' in Beethoven's *Fidelio*. While the correspondence is less exact than others, the relationship lies in the scoring of both as well as in their common disjunct bass line (see Ex. 2.7). Even though the metre differs, both pieces are in G major and in a slow tempo, and also contain a contrapuntal, rather than chordal, texture. As with other quotations, it is impossible to determine whether Mahler consciously made reference to Beethoven's music, but his familiarity with *Fidelio* suggests that it may have been an unconscious choice. The quartet from *Fidelio* may have had particular significance for him because of its musical and dramatic importance in the opera, and its epiphanic sentiment may have conveyed to him some of the open-eyed wonder that exists in the text of the Song-Finale.

Programmatic Elements

The associations of such quotations carry into the Fourth Symphony meanings outside the abstract structure of the music itself. At the same time, Mahler conceived elements of a programme for the work as he composed it, which he conveyed to members of his circle like Natalie Bauer-Lechner and Bruno Walter. He told Bauer-Lechner that he could have added descriptive titles for each movement but chose not to do so. He disclosed to Walter a programme that he decided to suppress at some point before the première of the symphony. This situation is hardly unique to the Fourth Symphony, since Mahler became increasingly reluctant to disclose explicit narrative programmes for his music.

While Mahler published programmes for his earlier symphonies, he later expressed disdain for programmes that became an end in themselves. As detailed as they are, the programmes for his first two symphonies differ from more explicit narratives that composers like Liszt used for some of their music. Mahler intended that the structure of the first two symphonies should be comprehensible without an extramusical programme, just as the Fourth Symphony could function as a piece of music on its own. By refraining from publishing a programme for the Fourth Symphony, he allowed the music to exist on its own. The only formal text he gave the symphony is the poem he adapted for the Song-Finale, where, as he told Bauer-Lechner, the child-narrator 'explains what it all means'.[23]

By refraining from publishing a programme for the Fourth Symphony, Mahler prevented the audience from investing their attention in the written word, rather than listening actively to the music. In this way he resembles Mendelssohn, who remained vague about specific narrative details, such as the ones behind the musical elements of his Overture to *A Midsummer Night's Dream*.[24] At one time Mendelssohn suggested the various ideas that he wished to portray in the Overture, but refrained from assigning to them a detailed sequence of any kind. In essence, both Mendelssohn and Mahler left the audience to make the deeper connections, thus allowing a more profound experience of the music on its own.

More importantly, Mahler's symphonies do not need detailed programmes to be understood. While the various programmes that he created for his symphonies certainly contribute a level of meaning to them, it is also possible to understand the music without any verbal text. At the same time, he did not rely on explicit programmes as the sole determinant of meaning. With Mahler programmes function at another level, since they contribute something more personal to the music. Programmes and programmatic titles often function as a kind of 'scaffolding' that Mahler used when he composed pieces like the

---

[23] Bauer-Lechner, *Erinnerungen*, 198; *Recollections*, 178.
[24] R. Larry Todd, *Mendelssohn: 'The Hebrides' and Other Overtures* (Cambridge Music Handbooks; Cambridge: Cambridge University Press, 1993), 72.

Fourth Symphony. Yet once he had completed such a work, the musical structure could stand on its own without extramusical associations. Narrative, when it occurs in Mahler's music, need not be bound to a detailed programme, but exists in the play of musical ideas that may occur within a movement or recur from movement to movement.

The structure of the Fourth Symphony is at once programmatic and yet divorced from any programme. Mahler's conversations with Bauer-Lechner and Bruno Walter reveal, however, programmatic associations that he must have had in mind as he composed the music. Beyond such private communication, however, he never elaborated on the ideas behind the Fourth to arrive at the kind of programme that he had written for the First or the Second Symphony. At the same time he confirmed a more abstract milieu for the Fourth through the Classical—and thus overtly non-programmatic—style of the first three movements.

Moreover, in the Fourth Symphony Mahler was concerned with creating a mood or a feeling more than conveying a narrative such as the one he had for the Second Symphony. He once made an analogy with the unvarying blue of the sky when he described the slow movement of the Fourth to Bauer-Lechner.[25] Such imagery is consistent with his intention to create a work that is organically unified and seamless, especially in a movement that is also a set of variations. With the entire symphony similarly closely related, he abandoned the more detailed narrative programmes of his first two symphonies and the stricter progression of thought found in the Third to create, instead, a series of linked images in the Fourth Symphony. One such image emerges in the Scherzo, which he described to Bauer-Lechner in visual terms:

the thousand little fragments of the picture are frequently subject to such a kaleidoscopic rearrangement that it's impossible to recognize it again. It's as if we saw a rainbow suddenly disintegrate into a thousand million dancing, ever-changing droplets, and its entire arc waver and dissolve. This is particularly true of the variations in the Andante [*sic*].[26]

Mahler was never so explicit about extramusical associations in the first movement, but he did explain one image, the trumpet call in the first movement (bb. 224–34), which he called 'der kleine Appell'. This supports the impression of different elements coming together at some point in a programme or in a musical structure. He further alluded to the development of motifs before the recapitulation, and told Bauer-Lechner that 'when the confusion and crowding of the troops, who started in orderly ranks, becomes too great, a command from the captain recalls them at once to the old formation under his flag'.[27]

[25] Bauer-Lechner, *Erinnerungen*, 198; *Recollections*, 178.
[26] Ibid.
[27] Bauer-Lechner, *Erinnerungen*, 164; *Recollections*, 154.

As to what these things meant to him, he once explained to Bauer-Lechner that the first three movements 'breathe the serenity of a higher world, one unfamiliar to us, which has something awe-inspiring and frightening about it. In the last movement, the child—who, though in a chrysalis-state, nevertheless already belongs to this higher world—explains what it all means.'[28]

This description fits what he had already said about the meaning of the work as a unified whole in which the movements are related to the same image. The sung text that occurs in the Finale is left for the listener to interpret on his own. In such a way Mahler breaks free from the more rigid programme that he used for his earlier symphonies. He shifts the interpretation of the work from himself, as author of the programme and composer of the music, to the perceiver. By choosing not to assign a fixed meaning to the music through an explicit, written programme, he created a work that can be highly connotative because it is not bound to a single explanatory text.

Ultimately, the interpretation of the Fourth Symphony is open-ended, and in leaving it that way Mahler hoped to avoid some of the criticism that had accompanied the reception of his earlier music. Bauer-Lechner reports that the audience at the Munich première of the Fourth Symphony expected to hear a work like the Second and, not finding one, 'unanimously clamored for verbal explanations of the meaning and content of the work'. Mahler went on to complain about the injustice of using the Second as the basis of judgement of the Fourth, claiming that the audience, 'so corrupted by program music', is 'no longer capable of understanding a work simply as a piece of music'.[29]

Mahler felt that he was part of the tradition of Mozart, Haydn, and Beethoven and, like them, wrote works that exist in both an absolute and an extramusical sense. Thus he was at odds with the rather one-sided reception of his work that demanded a fixed meaning handed down from the composer. For him, a programme was one means of interpretation, and not the sole criterion for musical judgement. While extramusical meaning could be assigned to a composition, more purely musical meaning must be divined as well.

Several aspects of the structure of the Fourth Symphony are tied to Mahler's programmatic intentions at the time of composition. Yet as a completed work, the Fourth Symphony lacks a detailed programme, and the only text associated with it is that of the song 'Das himmlische Leben'. This apparent discrepancy is important when it comes to understanding the music, but should not become a stumbling block for its apprehension. Just as he refined the content of the work in bringing the Fourth to completion, Mahler also refined his ideas about the nature of the music and the function of the programme he had considered using for the work. As a finished composition, the Fourth

---

[28] Bauer-Lechner, *Erinnerungen*, 198; *Recollections*, 178.
[29] Bauer-Lechner, *Erinnerungen*, 203; *Recollections*, 184.

is absolute music because it may be understood through sheerly musical elements; at the same time, it carries the extramusical associations hinted at in the text of the final movement. For Mahler to have been more explicit by invoking a written programme would have constrained the musical ideas and the non-verbal—ultimately non-literal—meaning that he attempted to express within the structure of the Fourth Symphony.

3.   'Das himmlische Leben' before the Fourth Symphony

In various ways the song 'Das himmlische Leben' is at the core of Mahler's Fourth Symphony, and the composer himself regarded the song as the goal and inspiration for the later work. He once told Natalie Bauer-Lechner that 'Das himmlische Leben' formed 'the tapering, topmost spire of the edifice of this Fourth Symphony'.[1] Even though the song and the symphony emerged years apart, Mahler's comment underscores the complex and successful integration between them.

Mahler composed 'Das himmlische Leben' almost a decade before he even began to conceive the Fourth Symphony and apparently found the song to be full of potential, since he attempted to incorporate the song into other compositions. At the same time, he did not use 'Das himmlische Leben' in any large-scale works before the Fourth Symphony, even though the song occurred in plans for various works in the 1890s as Mahler attempted to find an appropriate place for it in his music.

'Das himmlische Leben' is one of the Mahler's settings from *Des Knaben Wunderhorn*, and despite its function in the Fourth Symphony it retains its association with his other settings of poetry from that anthology.[2] Its presence in the fourth movement identifies the Fourth as one of Mahler's 'Wunderhorn' symphonies. Yet the song has a deeper, structural significance for the Fourth Symphony, for Mahler created thematic links between the first three movements and the Song-Finale (see Ch. 2). He once told Bauer-Lechner that ' "Das himmlische Leben" itself concealed the richest content from which entire symphony movements developed; out of all these references, it acquired an entirely special and all-encompassing meaning as the final movement of the latter [the Fourth Symphony].'[3]

Mahler composed 'Das himmlische Leben' in 1892, as indicated in the dates found on various manuscripts for the song. The score for voice and piano bears the date 10 February 1892, and the version of the song for voice

---

[1] Bauer-Lechner, *Erinnerungen*, 162; *Recollections*, 151.

[2] Note the inclusion of 'Das himmlische Leben' on pp. 22–7 of the collection *Fünfzehn Lieder, Humoresken und Balladen aus 'Des Knaben Wunderhorn' für Singstimme und Klavier*, ed. Renate Hilmar-Voit and Thomas Hampson (Gustav Mahler: Sämtliche Werke, Kritische Gesamtausgabe, 13; Vienna: Universal Edition, n.d. [1993]).

[3] Bauer-Lechner, *Erinnerungen*, 172. This passage is not translated in the English edition.

and orchestra is marked 12 March of the same year.[4] Since these dates are relatively close, it is likely that Mahler proceeded with the orchestral version soon after finishing work on the setting for voice and piano.

'Das himmlische Leben' was part of a series of settings from *Des Knaben Wunderhorn* that Mahler composed in early 1892. Despite the demanding conducting schedule of the 1891–2 season in Hamburg, he made a point of having with him his copy of *Des Knaben Wunderhorn*. In January 1892 he asked his sister Justine in Vienna to send it to him, and upon receiving the book, he told her, 'I now have the *Wunderhorn* in my hands. With that self-knowledge which is natural to creators, I can add that once again the result will be worthwhile.'[5] The extant correspondence goes no further, but it is likely that Mahler soon selected texts.

Perhaps as a result of the enthusiasm he expressed to Justine, Mahler composed these various settings within a relatively short period,[6] which was, incidentally, after a time when he found it particularly difficult to compose. (He also completed the Fourth Symphony after a period in which he expressed a similar frustration.) In February or March 1892 he wrote to Justine about the planned songs, telling her that he had 'found a good place for the *Wunderhorn* [settings], and it is now part of my symphony, nothing less than the *Third*'.[7] He probably was referring to texts he had just set or intended to complete, but precisely how he would use them is unclear. Most important is his expressed wish to use these songs—or even other *Wunderhorn* texts—in a later symphony.

The *Wunderhorn* songs that Mahler composed at this time were, for him, a set of *Humoresken*, as he called them, and they differ in length and character from his earlier *Wunderhorn* settings. In April 1892 he told Justine that these songs are 'stranger still than the former ones, [since] they are all "humor" in the best and truest sense of the word'. Referring to their potential, he continues, 'it is really an exhilarating prospect for me to write a whole library for my drawers!'[8] In this exuberant exaggeration, Mahler expressed his belief that he had accomplished something meaningful with these songs.

It is significant that Mahler called these pieces 'Humoresken', not 'Lieder' and 'Gesänge', as he did the earlier *Wunderhorn* settings. By referring to the set-

---

[4] The version for voice and piano is in the manuscript of '6 Wunderhornlieder' (D-B); the orchestral version is in the manuscript of '5 Humoresken' (A-Wgm, VI.36886).

[5] La Grange, *Mahler* (1973), i. 249; *Mahler: Chronique d'une vie*, i. 377.

[6] On 28 Jan. 1892 he completed 'Der Schildwache Nachtlied' from a sketch he had begun in 1888, and proceeded to more Lieder in February: 'Verlor'ne Mühe' on 1 Feb.; 'Wer hat dies Liedlein erdacht?' on 6 Feb.; 'Das himmlische Leben' on 10 Feb.; and 'Trost im Unglück' on 22 Feb. Versions of these songs for voice and orchestra soon followed, with the score of the first, 'Das himmlische Leben', dated 12 Mar., and the last, 'Trost im Unglück', completed near the end of April, since the orchestral score of the latter is marked 'Hamburg, Dienstag, 26. April 1892. Die 5 Humoresken geendet' ('Hamburg, Tuesday, 26 April 1892. The *5 Humoresken* completed').

[7] La Grange, *Mahler* (1973), 250; *Mahler: Chronique d'une vie*, i. 378.

[8] Ibid.

tings as 'Humoresken', he used a term that could designate music predisposed to a free, rather than a more formalized, expression of a composer's emotion. Like the literary *Humoresken* from earlier in the nineteenth century, Mahler's 'Humoresken' are not limited to a single musical form. Composers appear to have used the designation 'Humoreske' when they were more concerned with personal expression rather than with the strict adherence to formal structure.[9] Despite any specific references in the text of the piece so named, the term 'Humoreske' itself also implies some connection with generalized emotion ('the humours') rather than connoting something comical. In this specific song, Mahler deals with the undifferentiated bliss of a Christian heaven and the poem he chose certainly contains comic elements within its evocation of the afterlife.

The text of 'Das himmlische Leben' is based on the poem 'Der Himmel hängt voll Geigen' ('The world through rose-coloured glasses') and is a description of heaven from the viewpoint of a child. Unlike some of the more narrative verse in *Des Knaben Wunderhorn*, the poem is a collection of images that a child might associate with heaven, from biblical characters through later Christian saints. Like the kind of afterlife Mahler suggested in his Second Symphony, the heaven described in 'Das himmlische Leben' is free from judgement and full of peace—even the 'evil' King Herod has a place there, quite appropriately as a butcher. In this child's paradise the concerns of earthly life have no place, since all the things that might be lacking on earth are plentiful and available without cost. Food and drink are free, and even the animals give themselves willingly for slaughter. This kind of heaven does not lack for music, since the saints themselves provide it.

The poem 'Der Himmel hängt voll Geigen' is found in the second volume of *Des Knaben Wunderhorn*, which was published in 1808. As to where the editors of *Des Knaben Wunderhorn* found the text, opinions differ. Zoltan Roman holds that it is a Bavarian folk song, taken from the *Almanach* of Friedrich Nicolai (Berlin, 1778),[10] while Renate Hilmar-Voit traces the poem to a pamphlet published in 1764.[11] The text appears to be derived more tangibly from a religious poem, apparently by Peter Marcellin Sturm, 'Nach Kreuz und augestandenen Leiden', which dates from between 1774 and 1778. In practice, it was associated with the Christmas season and, as Roman states, the song would have been used at the end of Christmas plays in Bavaria and Bohemia.[12]

So far as is known, no traditional melody exists for this folk song, except for an oblique reference by Jon W. Finson to an undated source.[13] Yet a

[9] Maurice J. E. Brown, 'Humoreske', in *New Grove*, viii. 788.

[10] Zoltan Roman, 'Mahler's Songs and their Influence on his Symphonies' (Ph.D. diss., University of Toronto, 1970), 58.

[11] Renate Hilmar-Voit, *Im Wunderhorn-Ton: Gustav Mahlers sprachliches Kompositionsmaterial bis 1900* (Tutzing: Hans Schneider, 1988), 60.

[12] Roman, 'Mahler's Songs', 601.

[13] Jon W. Finson, 'The Reception of Gustav Mahler's *Wunderhorn* Lieder', 112.

relationship exists between this text and the traditional source for 'Es sungen drei Engel', another *Wunderhorn* text set by Mahler. The latter setting, which Mahler composed in 1895, is based on the poem 'Armer Kinder Bettler Lied' in *Des Knaben Wunderhorn*; it too appears to have a connection with a folk song. While the origins of 'Armer Kinder Bettler Lied' may extend to the thirteenth century, Roman traces the text to the *Mainzer Cantual 1605*. Several melodies have been associated with the text, but one in particular seems to have an affinity with Mahler's setting.[14]

Two Versions of 'Das himmlische Leben'

The music of the early version of 'Das himmlische Leben', which Mahler composed for voice and piano (the one dated 10 February 1892), is found in the manuscript assigned the siglum G[1] by Erwin Ratz in the *Revisionsbericht* of the critical edition of the Fourth Symphony. So far as is known, this version is not a piano reduction, as Ratz indicated, but rather the draft for voice and piano from which Mahler composed the later version for voice and orchestra. This manuscript is part of a collection entitled '6 Wunderhornlieder' for voice and piano, and this set contains versions for voice and piano of all of the *5 Humoresken* for voice and orchestra that Mahler subsequently completed.[15] While the manuscripts for these songs occur on various kinds of paper, he inscribed them all in upright format ('Hochformat'), a style associated with his fair copies, thus suggesting at least later drafts rather than earlier, more tentative, sketches.

In addition, the piano draft of 'Das himmlische Leben' is the only song in this set to contain indications for orchestration, and the manuscript itself appears to have been handled more than the others. While it is possible that the physical condition of the manuscript and its appearance may be the result of improper storage or mishandling during—or even after—Mahler's lifetime, it is equally plausible that he used this manuscript as a working copy rather than a final draft, and included it with the other *Wunderhornlieder* almost as an afterthought.

The tentative aspect of this manuscript becomes clear in the notation itself, since at one point Mahler seems to have been composing the work rather than copying it from an earlier draft. At bars 150–1, the words 'Sanct Ursula' are marked with a question mark above the stave, and it is possible to discern two layers of composition under it. As evident from the published version, the second syllable (the 'su' of 'Ursula') would have occurred on the second beat, and thus the intention would have resulted in a more syllabic rather than

---

[14] Roman, 'Mahler's Songs', 602.

[15] To those five earlier *Humoresken* Mahler added in 1893 'Rheinlegendchen – für höhe Stimmlage' (marked 'Steinbach Mittwoch 9. August 1893') ('Steinbach, Wednesday, 9 August 1893') to comprise the set of six pieces.

melismatic figure at this point. Such a difference is more indicative of a draft to which Mahler returned and revised than a more finished piece.

On the other hand, the orchestral score for 'Das himmlische Leben' is part of the manuscript of *5 Humoresken*, five songs that Mahler composed in January and February 1892, and this manuscript is clearly a fair copy. In addition, the paper for all the songs is the same upright, 20–stave variety, and it bears the colophon 'Joh.[hann] Aug.[gust] Böhme, Hamburg, No. 12'. The uniformity of the fair copy is underscored by the specific ordering of the songs in this set, with each numbered and followed by the subtitle 'Eine Humoreske'.

After completing the piano draft for each of the '5 Humoresken', Mahler proceeded to orchestrate them, but he did not do so in the sequence in which they appear here, as is evident in the two dates in the manuscript: 'Trost im Unglück', the third song, is marked 'Hamburg, Dienstag 26. April 1892/Die 5 Humoresken geendet' ('Hamburg, Tuesday, 26 April 1892/The *5 Humoresken* completed'). At the end of 'Das himmlische Leben', the fourth song, Mahler wrote 'Hamburg, 12. März 92' ('Hamburg, 12 March 1892'). This shows that he orchestrated the fourth and fifth songs before the third, and ordered the entire set at some point after completing all five scores.

'Das himmlische Leben' also exists in another orchestral score, which comprises an intermediary stage of work between the 1892 score and the form of the song found in the completed Fourth Symphony (1901). This intermediary score is part of a set of music manuscripts by sold in 1984 by the firm of J. A. Stargardt (Marburg).[16] The first part of the set consists of a copyist's (Otto Weidig) manuscript of a full score for 'Das himmlische Leben', with corrections in the composer's hand. The second part of the set is a similarly corrected version of the song for voice and piano.

The first page of the orchestrated score of this intermediary manuscript is reproduced in the 19–20 June 1984 catalogue for the Stargardt auction house. An examination of the page reproduced in facsimile reveals some revisions that distinguish it from the 1892 version. In the later version, the texture in the string parts is thinned through the alteration of the tenths in the cello to fifths (the tonic and dominant pitches). In addition, the marking 'sehr gemächlich' found in the 1892 piano score is changed to 'heiter behäglich' in the intermediary score. Since these changes are already present on the first page, it is likely that similar differences exist throughout the version.

This intermediary score probably dates from 1893, when Mahler's orchestral *Humoresken* were performed at a concert of the 'verstärkte Laub'sche Kapelle' in Hamburg on 27 October 1893.[17] At this performance these songs were listed as 'Balladen und Humoresken aus *Des Knaben Wunderhorn*', with

[16] J. A. Stargardt, *Katalog 631* (Marburg: J. A. Stargardt, 1984), 268. The catalogue is for an auction held on 20–1 June 1984, and the identity of the current owner is maintained as private.

[17] Knud Martner, *Gustav Mahler im Konzertsaal* (Copenhagen: Knud Martner, 1985), 33.

'Das himmlische Leben', 'Verlor'ne Mühe', and 'Wer hat dies Liedlein er-dacht?' referred to as 'Humoresken', and 'Trost im Unglück', 'Rheinlegend-chen', and 'Der Schildwache Nachtlied' as 'Balladen'. (The three 'Humo-resken' were sung by Clementine Schuch-Prosska and Paul Bulß sang the three 'Balladen'.) Despite the fact that the three 'Balladen' were performed a month later on 17 November 1893, in Wiesbaden, Mahler did not include the other 'Humoresken' at that time. So far as is known, 'Das himmlische Leben' was not performed again until it was used in the Fourth Symphony, which was given its première in 1901.

Most importantly, the intermediary score represents a stage between the initial composition and orchestration of the song and its revision for inclusion in the Fourth Symphony almost a decade later. Through evidence of this score, it is apparent that Mahler did not remain satisfied with what he had completed in 1892, and continued to work on the piece. While he left the con-tent of the song intact, he refined the details of the score to fit an evolving concept of the work. He would continue to return to 'Das himmlische Leben' even after completing this intermediary score, when he considered using the song in his Third Symphony.

'Das himmlische Leben' and the Third Symphony

Eventually Mahler revised the set of *5 Humoresken*, which became 'Humores-ken und Balladen aus *Des Knaben Wunderhorn*' when the song 'Rheinlegend-chen' was added to the original set of five for a performance in October 1893. This group of settings from *Des Knaben Wunderhorn* was at the core of the collection of *Wunderhorn* lieder that Mahler published in 1899. At that time he retained five of the six songs performed in 1893 and added five new ones, along with the alto solo from the Second Symphony, 'Urlicht', and an arrangement of the *Wunderhorn* setting from the Third Symphony, 'Es sungen drei Engel', for voice and piano. He did not include 'Das himm-lische Leben' with these *Wunderhorn* lieder or any other collection of vocal works, either with piano or with orchestra.

Nevertheless, 'Das himmlische Leben' exerted an influence on Mahler's work after it was removed from the original group of songs. Among the earl-iest plans for the Third Symphony is a movement bearing the title 'Was das Kind erzählt' ('What the child tells'), and in the later plans of movements Mahler specifically mentions the song 'Das himmlische Leben'.[18] While he does not equate the descriptive title with the song, when the latter occurs, it is as the final (seventh) movement, the same place as the movement entitled 'Was mir das Kind erzählt'.

---

[18] For a list of the various plans of movements for the Third Symphony, see La Grange, *Mahler* (1973), 796–801; *Mahler: Chronique d'une vie*, i. 1036–40.

As Mahler worked through the various plans for the Third Symphony, he appears to have become increasingly concerned about the structure of the work and the order of movements. At the end of summer 1895, he appears to have been certain about using seven movements in the Third, including the song 'Das himmlische Leben'. In fact, after listing the title and order of movements in a letter to Arnold Berliner on 17 August 1895, he stated that all the movements were complete except for the first,[19] and he reiterated this in a letter to Friedrich Löhr on 29 August 1895.[20] Filler suggests that Mahler probably revised the order of movements for the Third Symphony in autumn 1895. Based on the numbering of the movements of the fair copy, as well as information found in the memoirs of Bauer-Lechner, Filler also believes that Mahler reassessed the placement and inclusion of 'Das himmlische Leben' at this time. The song appears to have been considered as the second movement of the Third Symphony before he withdrew it entirely from that work the next year.[21]

In several of the seven-movement plans for the Third Symphony, the song 'Das himmlische Leben' is found after the Adagio, an instrumental movement that Mahler intended to depict the experience of divine love. Proceeding beyond the more general references to heaven with 'selige Stadt' ('holy city') and 'Seligkeit' ('Blessedness') as found in the earlier movement 'Es sungen drei Engel', 'Das himmlische Leben' contains more concrete images of heaven in its text. As the second movement of the Third Symphony, however, the function of 'Das himmlische Leben' would occur out of sequence and interrupt the progression of thought that existed with the other movements. Moreover, this placement would impair Mahler's programme and confuse the structure of the symphony. At best 'Das himmlische Leben' would foreshadow the implications of heaven that would be explored later in the text of 'Es sungen drei Engel' and the Adagio-Finale that Mahler once titled 'Was mir die Liebe erzählt'. Since he had already removed the song from its previous position as the final movement, he could find no other suitable place for 'Das himmlische Leben' in the Third Symphony, and so it seems logical that he struck it from the work.

While Mahler withdrew the song 'Das himmlische Leben' from the Third Symphony, it nevertheless influenced the content of other movements of the Third. As the one-time goal of the symphony, the song was important for Mahler when he began to develop ideas for the first[22] and fifth movements. It may be argued that he never completely removed the music of 'Das himmlische Leben' from the Third Symphony, because some thematic links with the song remain in the finished work. What exists may not have met his

[19] Mahler, *Briefe*, 126; *Selected Letters*, 163–4.
[20] Mahler, *Briefe*, 128; *Selected Letters*, 165.
[21] Filler, 'Editorial Problems', 77–8.
[22] John Williamson, 'Mahler's Compositional Process', 338–40.

expectations, since he complained to Bauer-Lechner at the end of June 1896 that 'nothing came of the profound interrelationships between the various movements which I had originally dreamed of [for the Third Symphony]'.[23] However, some, less 'profound' but still perceivable, relationships exist between 'Das himmlische Leben' and the first, fourth, and fifth movements of the Third Symphony.

As to connections between 'Das himmlische Leben' and the fifth movement, 'Es sungen drei Engel', Mahler linked the two settings more directly by quoting text and music. Both the fourth and fifth stanzas of 'Es sungen drei Engel' contain references to 'die himmlische Freud' ', a phrase important to the first and final stanzas of 'Das himmlische Leben' and the music accompanying the phrase is the same in both songs. Mahler virtually quotes the entire passage found in bars 57–62 of 'Das himmlische Leben' in bars 39–44 of 'Es sungen drei Engel'.

More specifically, the vocal line at bars 42–4 of the latter song resembles that found at bars 69–71 of 'Das himmlische Leben' (see Ex. 3.1). The chorale-like music at bars 45–7 of 'Es sungen drei Engel' is also a quotation of bars 72–4 of 'Das himmlische Leben'. He also used the ascending sixteenth-note figure found at bar 48 of 'Das himmlische Leben' in bars 39 and 41 of 'Es sungen drei Engel', and the grace-note figure found in bar 58 of the earlier song occurs in bar 40 of 'Es sungen drei Engel' as well. Since Mahler intended to establish thematic links among the movements of the Third Symphony, the similarities between these passages are striking, and it is clear that the music of 'Das himmlische Leben' influenced Mahler when he composed 'Es sungen drei Engel'.

Mahler also attempted to form a clear link with 'Das himmlische Leben' through allusion in the first movement of the Third Symphony, and the sketches for this movement contain an extensive quotation from the song. This manuscript includes a note by Alma Mahler in which she identifies them as the first sketches for the Third Symphony; she writes in the dedication: 'III. Symphonie/erste Skizze/drei Seiten/von Gustav Mahlers/Hand' ('Third Symphony/first sketches/three pages/in Gustav Mahler's/handwriting').[24] These three pages of sketches are written on a single bifolio leaf, occupying both sides of the first sheet and one side of the other; the 24–stave paper is in *Hochformat* (upright). The manuscript is not dated, nor does the bifolio bear an imprint (*Schutzmarke*) that might be used to date it.

It is debatable whether these are truly the first sketches for the Third Symphony. Most likely they are not, as argued by Peter Franklin,[25] Susan Filler,[26] and John Williamson.[27] These sketches probably date from 1896, when

[23] Bauer-Lechner, *Erinnerungen*, 56; *Recollections*, 59.
[24] A-Wn, Mus. Hs. 22.794.
[25] Peter R. Franklin, 'The Gestation of Mahler's Third Symphony', 445–6.
[26] Filler, 'Editorial Problems', 134–41.
[27] John Williamson, 'Mahler's Compositional Process', 338–40.

Ex. 3.1. Quotations of 'Das himmlische Leben' (DHL) in 'Es sungen drei Engel' (ES): (*a*) ES, bb. 43–4 and DHL, bb. 70–1; (*b*) ES, bb. 45–7 and DHL, bb. 72–4; (*c*) ES, b. 39 and DHL, b. 48; (*d*) ES, b. 40 and DHL, b. 58

Mahler was working on the first movement, and while they may not be the first sketches for the Third Symphony, they may be among the initial ones for its first movement. The first and third pages contain music that Mahler later incorporated into the completed movement. On the second page, however, music ultimately found in the Third Symphony continues into a passage

Ex. 3.2. Quotations of 'Das himmlische Leben' in (a) Third Symphony, 'Erste Skizze', Österreichische Nationalbibliothek, Musiksammlurg, Mus. Hs. 22794, sts. 8 and 13; (b) Fourth Symphony, 4th movt, bb. 125–30 (melody only)

that contains an allusion to 'Das himmlische Leben', as shown in Ex. 3.2. The latter passage itself becomes fragmentary and continues with music that Mahler also eventually used in the Third Symphony (page 3). While he rejected the entire section containing material related to 'Das himmlische Leben', the existence of this sketch demonstrates his intention, however brief or fleeting, to incorporate 'Das himmlische Leben' into the Third Symphony by quoting it instrumentally.

Mahler probably composed these sketches while he still planned to include 'Das himmlische Leben' in the Third Symphony as either the seventh or, possibly, the second movement. By quoting music from 'Das himmlische Leben' in the first movement, he would would create a cyclic link between that movement and others in which he had used fragments of the song. By placing such quotations before the Finale, he also provided a means to unify the symphony through increasingly literal statements. Moving from indistinct to more concrete quotations of the song, Mahler would allow the song to take shape aurally and gradually crystallize during the course of the symphony. Yet he ultimately chose not to include 'Das himmlische Leben' in the Third Symphony and abandoned such links as the ones found in the first-movement sketch.

The importance of 'Das himmlische Leben' for the structure of the Third Symphony is indisputable. Since the song is part of various plans of movements Mahler made for this work, it is clear that 'Das himmlische Leben' was at one time its programmatic and thematic goal. As Mahler realized these plans as completed movements, fragments of the song emerged in the music, thereby creating a level of unity within the symphony. It is in the link between the fifth movement and 'Das himmlische Leben' that another level of integration may be perceived. Through the connection with 'Es sungen drei Engel', Mahler ultimately found a means of establishing a direct relationship between the songs, so that he could later allude to this connection and call his first four symphonies 'a perfectly self-contained tetralogy'.[28]

Later, while working on the Fourth Symphony, Mahler told Bauer-Lechner about the particularly strong connections between it and the Third. At another level, connections also exist between the Second through Fourth Symphonies as 'Wunderhorn' symphonies that contain in some form song texts from *Des Knaben Wunderhorn*, either used directly or quoted instrumentally in each work. Besides possessing a common source in *Des Knaben Wunderhorn*, the Third and Fourth Symphonies also have the same programmatic impulse behind them. In some of the plans of movements for the Third Symphony, Mahler considered progressing beyond the movement he used as the Finale of the completed work, proceeding to the song 'Das himmlische Leben' to describe heaven. Yet even after much consideration of its structure, he

---

[28] Bauer-Lechner, *Erinnerungen*, 164; *Recollections*, 154.

could not successfully place the song within the Third Symphony, and eventually decided not to include it. It seems likely that the desire to incorporate 'Das himmlische Leben' as the Finale of a symphony, an impulse Mahler failed to realize in the Third, emerged early in his plans for the Fourth Symphony.

4. Early Plans: Mahler's 'Symphonie Humoreske'

Among the earliest autograph materials for the Fourth Symphony is the plan of movements that Mahler made for a Fourth Symphony with the subtitle 'Symphonie Humoreske'.[1] Such a plan would serve as a point of departure when he actually began to work on the music. Mahler himself confirmed this as his initial conception of the work when he later admitted to Bauer-Lechner that he 'only wanted to write a symphonic Humoresque [*eine symphonische Humoreske*]'.[2] This early plan is for a six-movement work with programmatic titles for each movement, and this conception bears a subtle relationship to the completed Fourth Symphony. Mahler eventually abandoned this plan for the Fourth Symphony as a 'Symphonie Humoreske', but some of its elements were part of his early thoughts on this new composition.

It is not unusual to find Mahler working through plans of movements like this one. Upon beginning large-scale works he sometimes created lists of movements, often with possible titles, tempo indications, and even keys. Plans also exist for the Third and Eighth Symphonies, and Mahler may have created similar lists of movements when he began other symphonies. In contrast to what he would compose in the various later stages of work, such early plans are sketches in the roughest sense, since they often emerged before he began to focus on the content of a new piece. Moreover, plans of movements usually predate the earliest notated musical ideas for a work, which occur in sketchbooks or in the preliminary sketches.[3] (Rarely, however, did he work through a number of such plans in the course of finishing work on a symphony, as he did with the Third.)

More specifically, this plan for the Fourth Symphony is a list of six movements that includes three songs with texts from *Des Knaben Wunderhorn*. Writ-

---

[1] Gustav Mahler, 'Symphonie Nro. IV (Humoreske)' (US-CIpl, Fine Arts Collection). The page is a 20-stave leaf in upright format, 30.5 by 22.5 cm. There are no other markings on the page except for a few lines at the bottom, presumably in the hand of the critic Paul Bekker (1882–1937), which read: 'Handschrift von Gustav Mahler/zum Geschenk erhalten von Frau Alma Mahler, Wien 13/I/1919' ('Manuscript of Gustav Mahler/received as a present from Frau Alma Mahler, Vienna, 13 January 1919').

[2] Bauer-Lechner, *Erinnerungen*, 162; *Recollections*, 151.

[3] One exception is the plan for the Eighth Symphony, as discussed below. In one plan of movements for the Eighth, Mahler notated the opening of the first part. See Alfred Rosenzweig, 'Wie Gustav Mahler seine "Achte" plante: Die erste handschriftliche Skizze', *Der Wiener Tag*, 4 June 1933.

ten in the manner of a title-page on a single sheet of manuscript paper, it reads as follows:

Sympbhonie Nr. IV
(Humoreske)

Nro I Die Welt als ewige Jetztzeit—G-dur
Nro II Das irdische Leben—Es-moll
Nro III Caritas—H-dur (Adagio)
Nro IV Morgenglocken—F-dur
Nro V Die Welt ohne Schwere—D-dur (Scherzo)
Nro V Das himmlische Leben!—G-dur

Symphony No. 4
(Humoresque)

No. 1 The World as Eternal Now—G major
No. 2 Earthly Life—E flat minor
No. 3 Love—B major (Adagio)
No. 4 Morning Bells—F major
No. 5 The World without Burdens—D major (Scherzo)
No. 5 Heavenly Life!—G major

The duplicate roman-numeral 'V' on the six-movement plan appears to be a slip of the pen on Mahler's part. Most likely he intended the two movements to follow, one from the other, rather than serve as alternative fifth movements for his projected Fourth Symphony. In this early plan, the symmetry of starting and ending in the same tonality is important to his conception of the work at this stage.

Mahler probably wrote this plan while he was still working on the Third Symphony. Most likely it emerged in summer 1896, when he worked through a similar one for the Third Symphony. Paul Bekker called attention to these plans of movements for the two symphonies, and referred to yet another one for the Third.[4] The two plans for the Third belong to a number of lists that Mahler created as he worked out the structure of that symphony. Ultimately his plans reflected the difficulty he was having with the place of the song 'Das himmlische Leben' and determining a satisfactory concluding movement. He eventually decided to remove 'Das himmlische Leben' from the Third Symphony and use it elsewhere. Rather than serve as the final movement of the Third that might appear to be tacked on to the structure like an afterthought, 'Das himmlische Leben' became the starting point for the Fourth Symphony.

---

[4] Paul Bekker, *Gustav Mahlers Sinfonien* (Berlin: Schuster & Loeffler, 1921; repr. Tutzing: Hans Schneider, 1969), 144. He discusses the plans for the Third Symphony on pp. 106–7. Later he refers to finding the latter plans in the collection of Alma Mahler (p. 358), but their current provenance is unknown.

Bekker further points out that the plan for the Fourth Symphony should be understood in the context of the other two plans, as Mahler's evolving conception of the Third Symphony must have influenced his ideas for the Fourth. Both plans for the Third that Bekker cites have a final movement entitled 'Was mir das Kind erzählt'. In various early plans for the Third Symphony, Mahler had interchanged the descriptive title 'Was mir das Kind erzählt' with the song title 'Das himmlische Leben' as the seventh or final movement of that work, when he intended to use that song as the conclusion of his Third Symphony.[5] So far as is known, no plans of movements contain both the movement title 'Was mir das Kind erzählt' and the song title 'Das himmlische Leben', but the connection between the two is implicit nonetheless.

Of the two plans for the Third Symphony that Bekker cites, the second bears a closer relationship to the plan of movements for the Fourth, with parenthetical remarks and also names of movements ('Adagio', for example). For Bekker this internal evidence suggests that the Third and Fourth Symphonies are 'twin works'.[6] While it is impossible to prove beyond doubt that the plans for the Third and Fourth Symphonies emerged at precisely the same moment, they still appear to be closely connected. Mahler must have composed the plan for the Fourth Symphony before he gave the Third Symphony its final shape, since it contains a movement entitled 'Morgenglocken', which refers to the setting of 'Es sungen drei Engel' that eventually became the fifth movement of the completed Third Symphony.

The existence of both 'Es sungen drei Engel' and 'Das himmlische Leben' in this plan also reinforces the strong relationship between the two songs. Further, the projected use of the three *Wunderhorn* songs, 'Das irdische Leben', 'Es sungen drei Engel' (as the 'Morgenglocken' movement), and 'Das himmlische Leben', in a single work confirms the idea that Mahler once expressed to his sister Justine about composing a symphony based on his own *Humoresken* with texts from *Des Knaben Wunderhorn*. The inscription of this plan as 'Symphony No. 4' shows Mahler's intention of writing another symphony beyond the Third. Thus, even though he appears to have abandoned the composition of large-scale works between 1897, when he accepted the post of director at the Vienna Hofoper, and 1899, when he began to work on the Fourth, his desire to continue to compose such works must have persisted. While the plan for this 'Symphonie Humoreske' bears no date, it must have emerged in 1896, since Mahler would not have considered using the 'Morgenglocken' movement in another work when he had already included it in the completed Third Symphony.

Along these lines, it is useful to consider the placement of 'Das himmlische Leben' as the last movement of the projected Fourth Symphony, which is

---

[5] La Grange, *Mahler* (1973), 798–9; *Mahler: Chronique d'une vie*, i. 1038–9.
[6] Bekker, *Gustav Mahlers Sinfonien*, 145.

similar to its sometime position as the final movement of the Third Symphony. Mahler clearly wanted to use the song in a symphony and regarded it as a final gesture and a point of arrival, rather than as an introduction or a less prominent internal movement. Without a doubt, 'Das himmlische Leben' is the concluding movement of Mahler's new Fourth Symphony.

Descriptive Titles and Pairs of Movements

The plan for a 'Symphonie Humoreske' also contains descriptive titles for the movements, and the existence of such titles in the six-movement plan seems to confirm Mahler's later statement that he could have given names to the various movements of the Fourth. While these may not have been the exact titles he could have used for the completed Fourth Symphony, he may well have had in mind ideas like these while composing the work. At the same time, the titles in this plan clearly differ from the ones used in the Third Symphony, with the formula 'Was mir...erzählt (erzählen)', and thus reflect another way of thinking.

Unlike the Third Symphony, there is no ascending order of creation or consciousness, but here, Mahler juxtaposes the harsh reality of the world with the anticipated joy of life hereafter. This duality occurs as a series of paired movements, with each pair consisting of an instrumental movement followed by a vocal one. The first movement in each pair conveys a mood through instrumental music, but the second would have been more specific in meaning, with the use of a sung text. As shown in Table 4.1, it is possible to project a progression of thought in the sequence of such paired movements.

In the first pair of movements, Mahler presents a portrait of the world as 'Eternal Now', followed by its depiction in the song 'Das irdische Leben'. The idea of an eternal present is complicated by the continual struggle for earthly sustenance, as found in the song that follows it. The next pair of movements suggests the force of divine love: the Adagio movement, 'Caritas' (that is, 'Liebe' or 'Agape' as opposed to the more carnal 'Eros'), is followed by a movement titled 'Morgenglocken', which probably refers to the song 'Es sungen drei Engel', which Mahler called 'Was mir die Morgenglocken erzählen' in his other plans for the Third Symphony. In this song the message of the

TABLE 4.1. *Instrumental and vocal pairs in the plan for a 'Symphonie Humoreske'*

Concept	Instrumental expression	Vocal description
I. A Portrait of the World	1. Die Welt als ewige Jetztzeit	2. Das irdische Leben
II. The Intervention of God	3. Caritas	4. Morgenglocken ('Es sungen drei Engel')
III. The Life Hereafter	5. Die Welt ohne Schwere	6. Das himmlische Leben

angels is unconditional forgiveness, through which it is possible to experience the fullness of divine love, and the two movements appear to share a common idea. The last pair of movements commences with a Scherzo depicting another point of view, but this time it is not the world of 'Eternal Now', but a 'World without Cares'. The implied programme suggests a transformation of life on earth, with all its cares, to a world without trouble through the intervention of divine love, and Mahler enumerates the joys of such existence in the song 'Das himmlische Leben'.

He achieves the shift in perspective from the first to the third pair of movements through the sequence of three songs. In each of them, the text points up the idea found in the corresponding instrumental movement. The first song, 'Das irdische Leben', depicts the harshness of life in the story of a child who dies while his mother admonishes him to wait until work is done before he can eat. In contrast, Mahler depicts in 'Das himmlische Leben' a heaven where food is plentiful and, unlike on earth, entirely free. The polarity between these two ideas could have been heightened by placing the first and third of these pairs of movements one after the other but, instead, he inserted another pair of movements.

In the programme of the Third Symphony, Mahler attempted to describe the various stages of existence (or consciousness) in ascending order, ending at the level of divine love (*Liebe*). He pursued a similar programme in the six-movement plan for the Fourth, where he aspired to depict the nature of heavenly existence through the ways in which it contrasts with earthly life. However, the programme inferred through this plan of movements diverges from both the one indicated by the titles posited for the Third Symphony and from later programmatic ideas about the completed Fourth Symphony, which Mahler confided to Bauer-Lechner.[7] In a sense, this six-movement plan for the 'Symphonie Humoreske' sheds light on Mahler's thought processes as he made concrete his ideas about the Third Symphony and began to conceive the content of his next large-scale work in the Fourth Symphony.

The completed Fourth Symphony clearly differs from the one Mahler projected in the plan for a 'Symphonie Humoreske', but the initial idea of conveying images of heavenly life is already present in this list of movement titles. In contrast to work outlined in this plan, the completed Fourth Symphony contains four movements, not six, none of them has a title, and there is only one vocal movement, 'Das himmlische Leben'. In commenting on the six-movement plan, Bekker suggests, however, that some of these ideas did indeed emerge in the completed Fourth Symphony. For him, the first movement of the completed Fourth bears a relationship to the projected first movement of the 'Symphonie Humoreske' on account of the key—G major—and the

[7] While references occur in several places, the most sustained discussion of this matter occurs in Bauer-Lechner, *Erinnerungen*, 162–5; *Recollections*, 151–5.

character of the music itself.[8] He goes no further than the movement titles, however, to show that Mahler did not entirely abandon some of the ideas he originally had for the new symphony.

The Six-Movement Plan and the Third Symphony

In order to understand how Mahler arrived at the structure of the completed Fourth Symphony, it is useful to consider the six-movement plan for the Fourth Symphony in the context of related plans for the Third Symphony. Mahler's apparently earliest plans for the Third Symphony contain neither 'Es sungen drei Engel' nor 'Das himmlische Leben'.[9] The first plan is for a five-movement work ending with a movement entitled 'Was mir das Kind erzählt', but not specified as 'Das himmlische Leben', while the second plan is for a seven-movement symphony ending the same way. In her memoirs Alma Mahler mentions the second plan for the Third Symphony, but does not comment on its origins.[10] Yet while it is impossible to date these plans precisely, they most likely originated in early summer 1895.

The first plan for a Third Symphony to include a movement titled 'Was mir die Morgenglocken erzählen' comes from later that summer in a plan with the Nietzsche-influenced title 'Meine fröhliche Wissenschaft' ('My Joyous Science'), which Mahler included in a letter to the physicist Arnold Berliner on 17 August 1895.[11] A number of other plans for the Third include a movement with a title related to 'Es sungen drei Engel', and to which Mahler refers as either 'Die Morgenglocken' or 'die Engel'. If Bekker's early plan for the Third—and even the early plan that Alma identifies—and the 'Symphonie Humoreske' were written in early summer 1896, Mahler probably considered them valid until mid-August, when he ultimately decided to incorporate 'Es sungen drei Engel' in the Third Symphony as the movement entitled 'Was mir die Morgenglocken erzählen', a title to which he appended 'die Engel' on another plan.

The duplication of movements found on the two plans reveals a rare instance of ambiguity in Mahler's thinking. He was considering two ways of treating an idea and organizing music he had already composed. It remained for him to decide what he wanted to do, and one solution was to preserve the thematic links between the 'Morgenglocken' movement and the song 'Das himmlische Leben' by placing both of them in another work.

---

[8] Bekker, *Gustav Mahlers Sinfonien*, 145–6.

[9] For a summary of the plans of movements for the Third Symphony, see La Grange, *Mahler*, i. 798–9; *Mahler: Chronique d'une vie*, i. 1038–9. The information in the French edition is a revision of the material found in the earlier one in English.

[10] Alma Mahler Werfel, *Gustav Mahler: Erinnerungen und Briefe* (Amsterdam: Propylaen, 1974), 64; English edn., trans. as *Gustav Mahler: Memories and Letters*, ed. Donald Mitchell, trans. Basil Creighton (3rd edn., Seattle: University of Washington Press, 1975), 38–9.

[11] La Grange, *Mahler* (1973), 796–801; *Mahler: Chronique d'une vie*, i. 1036–40.

In allowing for this possibility, Mahler was able to conceive of the Third Symphony without 'Das himmlische Leben'. At that point he probably reconsidered the structure of the Third Symphony and brought the 'Morgenglocken' movement back into it. He chose not to end the Third with 'Das himmlische Leben', and may even have considered placing that song as the second movement. By doing that, however, he would complicate unnecessarily—and possible destroy—the logic of thematic links that led to the song, since most of those connections would then come after it. He eventually decided to remove 'Das himmlische Leben' from the Third Symphony, and took up the song several years later as the goal and finale of the Fourth Symphony.

The Evolution of the Four-Movement Format

When Mahler actually decided to compose a Fourth Symphony, he may have returned to this six-movement plan for the 'Symphonie Humoreske'. Yet the structure found in the sketch would not offer much inspiration to him, since he had already used some of the ideas found in the plan. 'Es sungen drei Engel' had already been incorporated in the Third Symphony, and so he would not have used the same movement in another work. He could have used both 'Das irdische Leben' and 'Das himmlische Leben' to depict the nature of earthly and heavenly life through the polarity implicit in their texts. 'Das irdische Leben' was an important song for Mahler, as it portrayed for him the grim truth behind earthly existence.[12] At the same time, this song contrasts sharply with the description of carefree, heavenly life in 'Das himmlische Leben'. Both texts involve the perspective of the child: while the child is the victim in 'Das irdische Leben', the child becomes the key to understanding the nature of heaven in 'Das himmlische Leben'. However, the construction of a symphony around these two songs may have posed structural problems that Mahler chose not to address after working through the complex organization of the Third Symphony. It is unlikely, then, that he would have seriously considered including 'Das irdische Leben' in the Fourth Symphony when he took up the work later.

The matter of balance also arises with regard to the slow movement of the projected Fourth Symphony. If Mahler had originally planned a slow movement like the Finale of the Third, an orchestral Adagio depicting divine love, it might have been its dimensions that caused him to reject the same idea in the Fourth. On the other hand, he might not necessarily have intended an Adagio like that found in the Third, but may have conceived of another type of movement altogether. After all, an Adagio movement labelled 'Caritas' is found among the early plans for the *Eighth* Symphony. Two plans for

---

[12] Bauer-Lechner, *Erinnerungen*, 27–8; *Recollections*, 32.

that symphony resemble the one for the 'Symphonie Humoreske' and are also inscribed in the manner of a title-page, as follows:

1.   I. Hymne: Veni creator
           II. Scherzo
          III. Adagio Caritas
           IV. Hymne die Geburt des Eros

           (I. Hymn: Veni creator
           II. Scherzo
          III. Adagio: Caritas
           IV. Hymn: The Birth of Eros)

2.   I. Veni Creator
           II. Caritas
Scherzo III. Weihnachtsspiele mit dem Kindlein
           IV. Schöpfung durch Eros — Hymne

           (I. Veni creator
           II. Caritas
Scherzo III. Christmas games with the Christ Child
           IV. Creation through Eros—Hymn)[13]

In these plans the movement marked 'Caritas' is an Adagio that has its parallel in the Adagio Finale to the Third Symphony. That movement, in turn, figures in the plan for the six-movement 'Symphonie Humoreske' as the B major 'Caritas'. While the 'Caritas' movement in the plans for the Eighth Symphony contains no key designations, the fragmentary sketches on the page containing the second plan are in B minor and B major.[14] It is possible only to speculate about what Mahler had in mind for the slow movement in the plans for the Eighth or the Fourth Symphony. Yet those ideas must remain conjecture, since both were eventually superseded. The four-movement plans for the Eighth ultimately gave way to an explicit two-part composition, just as the early six-movement plan for the Fourth Symphony evolved into the four-movement structure of the completed work. At the same time, Mahler chose not to end the Fourth Symphony in the same way that he concluded the Third.

Just as Mahler must have re-evaluated his intention for the slow movement of the 'Symphonie Humoreske', he probably reconsidered the projected Scherzo, since the one indicated in the six-movement plan does not appear

---

[13] La Grange cites both plans for the Eighth Symphony in *Mahler: Chronique d'une vie*, iii. 1079–80. Mitchell refers to the second of these plans in *Songs and Symphonies of Life and Death* (Berkeley, Calif.: The University of California Press, 1985), 529–30. A facsimile of the latter was published with the article by Alfred Rosenzweig, 'Wie Gustav Mahler seine "Achte" plante'.

[14] Related to these plans is a manuscript page containing texts apparently for the Scherzo. This manuscript is among the holdings of the New York Public Library, New York City. The trio of the Scherzo would have involved vocal compositions, the first for soprano and the second for alto. Both texts are from *Des Knaben Wunderhorn*, edited by Achim von Arnim and Clemens Brentano between 1804 and 1807 (Munich: Winkler Verlag, 1957; new edn., 1984). The first is 'Schluß' (p. 875), the second 'Morgenlied' (p. 834). Mitchell makes reference to this page in *Songs and Symphonies of Life and Death*, 531–2.

to be the one in the completed Fourth Symphony. While no evidence exists to suggest that he ever referred to the Scherzo in D major in the Fifth Symphony by this or any title, the designation 'Die Welt ohne Schwere' fits the music well, as Bekker has suggested.[15] However, the Scherzo of the Fourth Symphony bears no known or implied connection with the title 'Die Welt ohne Schwere', but fits better the programmatic idea of 'Freund Hein' that Mahler described to Bruno Walter.[16] With its use of the minor mode, scordatura violin, and also the relatively dark tone colours, the Scherzo of the Fourth Symphony diverges from the more carefree kind of Scherzo suggested in the plan for the 'Symphonie Humoreske'.

As to the other movements listed in the six-movement plan, the opening movement 'Die Welt als ewige Jetztzeit' and the Song-Finale 'Das himmlische Leben' bear some consideration. With these movements as the starting and ending points, it would be natural for Mahler to compose around them 'a symphony of normal dimensions' in four movements rather than the six-movement 'Symphonie Humoreske'. The first movement in the six-movement plan is in G major, presumably in sonata form, and bears the title listed above.

More important is Mahler's choice of style for the symphony, and its potential relationship to the plan of movements or the programme he later suggested to Bruno Walter. Such a decision is wholly Mahler's and hardly dependent on any extramusical references that may have existed. As with Mahler's other music, the programme functions interdependently with the musical structure, rather than as an end in itself. Nonetheless, the 'timeless' quality of the Viennese classic style emerges in the Fourth Symphony, especially in the first movement.

In this movement Mahler evokes a 'classical' idiom not only in the outward appearances of sonata form, but also in the details of regular phrase lengths, arpeggiated figuration, ascending and descending scale passages, and motoric rhythmic patterns. Likewise, the orchestra itself resembles the classical orchestra: trombones are absent altogether, and other brass are treated conservatively. Mahler seems to have been fully conscious of these elements of classicism. In her memoirs, Alma makes a comparison with Haydn, which Mahler did not refute.[17] This suggestion of the classical style—without trying to mimic all aspects of it—appears to have allowed Mahler to capture the past in his own present, creating a 'World as Eternal Now', as implied in the title of the plan.

With 'Das himmlische Leben' as the goal and the final movement, and the opening movement (in G major), Mahler would have had to plan at least two

---

[15] Bekker, *Gustav Mahlers Sinfonien*, 145.
[16] Walter, *Briefe*, 51–2.
[17] Alma Mahler, *Erinnerungen und Briefe*, 49; *Gustav Mahler: Memories and Letters*, 24.

more movements for his new symphony. From the comments he made to Bauer-Lechner at this time, the function of classical structure was a recurring idea. Bauer-Lechner reports in an entry of 27 July 1896 that despite his extension of more accepted symphonic form in the Third Symphony, the work in his conception had strong affinities with the classical model. Towards this end, his comments about the first movement of the Third Symphony are relevant:

Now I see that without my having planned it, this movement— just like the whole work—has the same scaffolding, the same basic groundplan that you'll find in the works of Mozart and, on a grander scale, of Beethoven. Old Haydn was really its originator. Its laws must indeed be profound and eternal for Beethoven obeyed them, and they're confirmed once more in my own work. Adagio, Rondo, Minuet, Allegro—and within these forms the traditional plan, the familiar phrase structure.[18]

Even though he said this of the Third, Mahler's convictions about form are strong and his music, from the First through the Ninth Symphonies, remains bound to traditional symphonic structure. In working towards the form of the completed Fourth Symphony, he would have to compose, then, at least two additional movements, a Scherzo and a slow movement, to convey the image of the classical symphony. He would deviate from convention only in the Finale, for which he had already planned to use the song 'Das himmlische Leben'. The nature and number of movements in this work, however, dependent on the implied classicism of the first movement and carried out in the inner ones, is balanced by the thematic links that connect those movements to the concluding song.

Had he held rigidly to the six-movement plan, perhaps even with the substitution of another movement for the one entitled 'Morgenglocken', the resulting work still might not have been satisfactory. Since this plan is an early, if not the initial, conception, the number and order of movements would have been subject to revision. At the same time, the projected placement of 'Das himmlische Leben' in this outline might have been just as problematic for Mahler in the projected Fourth Symphony as it had been for the Third. Had Mahler continued in earnest with this plan, he might have revised the Adagio and Scherzo, if not completely altered them, once he had written the other movements and better defined their relationship to 'Das himmlische Leben'.

At another level, for a symphony in which he attempted to describe the afterlife, a world of 'Eternal Now' seems an appropriate beginning. The 'Freund Hein' Scherzo that Mahler eventually composed for the Fourth Symphony is more appropriate to the programme he eventually devised than the outline of the 'Symphonie Humoreske'. At the same time, the subsequent slow movement functions in a similar way, as its thematic links with the

---

[18] Bauer-Lechner, *Erinnerungen*, 64; *Recollections*, 66.

Song-Finale are critical to the structure of the work. It is as though Mahler had to work through his initial ideas in the palpable format of this outline, rather than leave them as unwritten thoughts and risk forgetting them. This six-movement plan probably served simply as an aide-mémoire that Mahler used as a point of departure for his later, more concrete work on the Fourth Symphony.

The existence of the six-movement plan, like the various plans for the Third, suggests extramusical meanings that Mahler may have left intentionally vague. He probably composed such a list of movements to determine the mood he wanted to evoke in the work. As with the plans for the Third Symphony, Mahler used the plan for the Fourth to explore some concepts, but not to compose music. When it came to his actual work on the instrumental movements—perhaps the first movement alone—he may have felt it necessary to revise the plan of movements in order to reflect his intentions more accurately.

Further Considerations

Unlike later sketches and drafts, which represent a more definite relationship between the compositional process and the completed work, the six-movement plan for the 'Symphonie Humoreske' gives evidence of more tentative thought on Mahler's part. Through this plan it is possible to see the composer exploring various ideas before beginning to sketch the actual music for the new work, and while the plan contains tantalizing details, it remains only a point of departure. While the idea of the 'Symphonie Humoreske' as found in this document may never have been translated into composition, it remains an early concept of the Fourth to which Mahler reacted when began the actual composition of the symphony.

This plan for the 'Symphonie Humoreske' also contains ideas that may be seen to reach past the completed Fourth Symphony to music composed later. (See Table 4.2.) Some of the impulses Mahler expressed in this plan may have some bearing on the Fifth, and perhaps even the Eighth Symphony. Since his preoccupation with 'Das himmlische Leben' as the focal point of a large-scale symphonic work had been present for nearly a decade before the completion of the Fourth, it is possible that ideas for later works had a similarly long gestation through a plan like this one. The concept of a Scherzo like the one in the Fifth Symphony may be connected with the idea of a Scherzo as 'Die Welt ohne Schwere', and perhaps the projected 'Caritas' movement of the Eighth may also have its origins in this plan.

The implications of the six-movement plan clearly extend beyond the Fourth Symphony itself, and even shed light on music Mahler would compose much later. Just as this document is the first indication of Mahler's intention to compose a Fourth Symphony, it also reaches back to the time when he

TABLE 4.2. *The implementation of early plans for the Third and Fourth Symphonies*

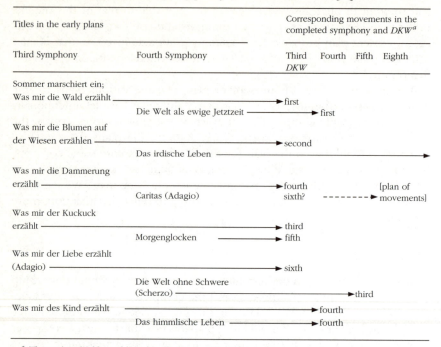

Titles in the early plans		Corresponding movements in the completed symphony and *DKW*[a]			
Third Symphony	Fourth Symphony	Third *DKW*	Fourth	Fifth	Eighth
Sommer marschiert ein; Was mir die Wald erzählt ────		──►first			
	Die Welt als ewige Jetztzeit ────		──► first		
Was mir die Blumen auf der Wiesen erzählen ────		──►second			
	Das irdische Leben ────				──────────────────────►
Was mir die Dammerung erzählt ────		──►fourth			[plan of
	Caritas (Adagio) ────	sixth?	─ ─ ─ ─ ─ ─ ─►		movements]
Was mir der Kuckuck erzählt ────		──► third			
	Morgenglocken ────	──► fifth			
Was mir der Liebe erzählt (Adagio) ────		──► sixth			
	Die Welt ohne Schwere (Scherzo) ────			──►third	
Was mir des Kind erzählt ────			──►fourth		
	Das himmlische Leben ────		──►fourth		

[a] The settings Mahler published as *Des Knaben Wunderhorn*.

was working through the number and order of the movements for the Third Symphony. Since the six-movement plan is for a symphony numbered '4' that begins and ends in G major, it is the closest documented stage before Mahler began to sketch its content. Since it must have helped him to clarify some of his ideas for both symphonies, this plan plays a crucial role in their development.

It remained for Mahler, then, to proceed with the composition of the Fourth Symphony by sketching the content in sketchbooks and taking them further in the single-leaf preliminary sketches. By that time, he was probably well beyond the kind of thought that occupied him when he pondered the broader structure of the symphony and later pursued its execution in the score. Only then could the abstract ideas found in a plan like this find expression in music. Once he decided to work on a symphony, the content would need to be addressed, which occurred in the sketchbooks and the preliminary sketches. He would then cast that material into a logical structure as he took the preliminary sketches into the short score, where many issues of content and continuity would be resolved.

5. *Preliminary Sketches*

When Mahler began to compose a symphony, he started with single-page sketches, most likely based on ideas found in sketchbooks. In general these 'preliminary sketches', as they have become known,[1] contain some of the principal ideas Mahler would take into the finished work. Preliminary sketches, by their nature, are less continuous than later ones, and they sometimes include Mahler's earliest attempts at some self-contained passages. These sketches occur on single, full-size pages, often ripped bifolio sheets,[2] which sets them apart from the work he undertook in sketchbooks.[3] Yet the content of the preliminary sketches can vary from page to page, even within the materials for a single movement.

Some commentators have disputed the concept of the preliminary-sketch stage, regarding everything prior to the fair copy or first published edition simply as 'sketches'.[4] Such a perspective negates the physical clarity that exists for other stages of work that Mahler pursued en route to more final thought. For the purpose of this discussion, the preliminary sketch is a discrete type of manuscript that represents a stage of the creative process prior to the composition of the short score. Mahler's work on preliminary sketches can encompass a varying level of detail—sometimes even on the same page—and it differs from other phases of composition that involve more continuous efforts.

Having already given some general thought to the structure in a plan of movements[5] and perhaps pursued some motifs in sketchbooks, Mahler first moved beyond isolated ideas to attempt more extended passages in the preliminary sketches.[6] While they are more extensive than the extant sketchbook

---

[1] Reilly, 'An Inventory of Musical Sources', 2–6.

[2] Mahler composed his preliminary sketches in systems of two to four staves, usually on one side of a single bifolio leaf, like some of the later short-score (*Particell*) sketches.

[3] While Mahler probably composed some ideas for the Fourth Symphony in sketchbooks, no pages survive. See Zychowicz, 'Sketches and Drafts', 183–212.

[4] Gustav Mahler, *Symphonische Entwürfe. Faksimile nach den Skizzen aus der Wiener Stadt- und Landesbibliothek und der Pierpont Morgan Library, New York*, ed. Renate Hilmar-Voit (Tutzing: Hans Schneider, 1991), [Commentary], 15. Despite Hilmar-Voit's complaints, a distinction can be drawn between stages of composition in the surviving materials before the draft score; it is not a construct invented by Edward R. Reilly and perpetuated by scholars like Filler and others. If any information is to emerge about Mahler's compositional process, it remains the task of analysts to distinguish between the sketches.

[5] Mahler also jotted down ideas for music on plans of movements, as evident in the plan for the Eighth Symphony. See Rosenzweig, 'Wie Gustav Mahler seine "Achte" plante'.

[6] As Reilly states in his description of this stage of work, it is in the preliminary sketches that Mahler began to explore 'the possibilities of developing and combining different themes and motives and, in

material, preliminary sketches are still fragmentary when compared with later materials, as found in the short score and draft score. Whereas the later short-score and draft-score stages reflect more consistent and continuous work, the preliminary sketches contain brief passages that did not necessarily emerge at the same time. Mahler no doubt reviewed the preliminary sketches before he proceeded with the short score, and often numbered them at that point to arrive at the sequence in which the material would occur in the short score.

In the full-page preliminary sketches Mahler worked through some ideas for the first time and notated other ideas as they came to him. Passages are often continuous for a system or two and then trail off. On the other hand, it is also possible to find passages that continue from one page to another. Mahler also used shorthand indications for repetitions and even left notes for instrumentation that he would pursue later. While preliminary sketches are not as continuous and detailed as the later short score and draft score, he sometimes marked articulations that were essential at that point. Almost always, he wrote on single leaves of oblong paper, and some of the extant pages contain numbers that reflect the order of ideas before the short-score stage.

The ordering of the ideas in sets of preliminary sketches results from Mahler's evaluation of the materials before he took them further, and not necessarily the chronology in which he composed the pages. As to the method of ordering of the pages, Mahler indicated the sequence with either arabic or roman numerals, with no particular preference for either system. Many of the extant preliminary sketches contain some numeral, and thus represent pages Mahler chose to take into the short score. Since he destroyed or otherwise disposed of the sketches he decided not to use, the surviving preliminary sketches are essentially only those he used to prepare the short score. Since the extant sketches are numbered and bear a relatively close relationship, they may give a somewhat unrealistic notion of the actual extent of preliminary sketches.

At another level, the extant preliminary sketches contain evidence for two distinct phases of work: (i) material Mahler developed from sketchbooks or, in some cases, set on paper for the first time; and (ii) sketch material he ordered and sometimes revised to correspond to the order of ideas found in the short score. It is likely that Mahler composed more preliminary sketches than are known to exist. At some point he reviewed the materials and decided what to take into the short score. As will be shown below, the preliminary sketch pages he chose to take forward in the composition of the Fourth Symphony bear markings that tie them to the short score, and thus represent a closer relationship with the completed work.

some cases, pointing to the sequence in which they are ultimately to appear. They were usually written in a reduced score of from two to four staves, and sometimes contain limited indications for scoring.' See Reilly, 'An Inventory of Musical Sources', 3.

While it is impossible to determine exactly the amount of ideas Mahler committed to paper at this phase of work, a number of preliminary sketch pages exist for the first three movements of the Fourth Symphony. In addition, not all the sketches are at the same level of refinement, and so it is possible to postulate—with some qualification—relatively early and later phases of work. Because some of the extant sketches appear to have emerged later in the compositional process, Mahler probably worked through more tentative drafts for various sections of the symphony, perhaps even in no longer extant sketchbooks.[7] For the fourth movement 'Das himmlische Leben', no preliminary materials are known to exist beyond the piano draft of the song.[8] Since Mahler approached the composition of songs differently than symphonic works, he would not have composed the kind of preliminary sketches for 'Das himmlische Leben' that exist for the other movements of the Fourth Symphony.[9]

First Movement

Among the preliminary sketches for the first movement are several pages that had belonged to a fuller set of materials. Of the possibly nine or more pages of preliminary sketches that existed for this movement, seven are extant. More specifically, the pages inscribed '2',[10] '3',[11] 'Pseudo 3',[12] '5',[13] '6', '7', and '8'[14] have survived (see Table 1.1 for their locations); the first page and the ones marked '4' and, most likely, '9' are no longer extant. While page '8' is the last known preliminary sketch page for the first movement, it seems

[7] For a discussion of Mahler's sketchbooks, see Zychowicz, 'Sketches and Drafts', 183–212 ('Sketchbooks at the Time of the Fourth Symphony').

[8] See the discussion of '6 Wunderhornlieder' for voice and piano in Ch. 2.

[9] An exemplary study of Mahler's approach to song composition is that of Stephen Hefling, 'The Composition of "Ich bin der Welt abhanden gekommen"', in *Gustav Mahler*, ed. Hermann Danuser (Wege der Forschung, 653; Darmstadt: Wissenschaftliche Buchgesellschaft, 1992), 96–158 at 103–8.

[10] The sketch is accompanied by a dedication, 'Skizzenblatt/aus der IV Symphonie/[signed] Alma Maria Mahler' ('Sketch page from the Fourth Symphony [signed] Alma Maria Mahler').

[11] See Tilman Seebass (ed.), *Musikhandschriften der Bodmeriana* (Cologny-Genève: Fondation Martin Bodmer, 1986), 75–6.

[12] While the two sheets of sketches for the first movement are found together, they are not closely related to each other. One is a single sheet of 20-stave paper that Mahler labelled 'Pseudo 3' and the other a single sheet of 24-stave paper numbered '6', both sheets produced by Eberle (nos. 12a and 24, respectively). They are found together because the set was a gift from Alma Mahler, as attested in her autograph dedication. Both pages contain sketches for the development section, the page marked 'Pseudo 3' consisting of bars 102–25 and page '6' consisting of bars 198–231, as shown in Table 5.3. These two sketches contain music for the beginning and the ending of the development section.

[13] Preliminary sketch pages '5' and '7' are part of the same private collection. Both pages are on 24-stave paper made by Eberle, as is evident by the colophon on page '5', which identifies the paper as no. 14, printed by 'J. E. & Co.', like a number of other sketches for Fourth Symphony.

[14] Preliminary sketch page '8' is part of a private collection, but a copy exists in the archive of the Internationale Gustav Mahler Gesellschaft, Vienna, Ph [Photocopy] 60. This sketch is reproduced by Paul Banks and Donald Mitchell, 'Gustav Mahler', in *The New Grove Turn of the Century Masters*, ed. Stanley Sadie (New York: W. W. Norton & Co., Inc., 1985), 79–181 at 126.

likely that Mahler would have continued at least to page '9' and possibly used a tenth page.

Since Mahler eventually supplemented the sketches on page '3' with a transition that he composed on the page marked 'Pseudo 3' (see below), other insertion pages may have existed at one time. It is likely that he destroyed the pages containing music he did not wish to use in this movement or music superseded by later sketches.[15] The relative neatness of a sketch like page '8' may be the result of Mahler's revising earlier work in order to arrive at this preliminary sketch page.

In addition, the physical condition of these materials suggests that they were at one time part of a complete set of materials that were later dispersed, probably by Alma Mahler herself, as suggested by dedication pages like the ones found with preliminary sketch pages '2', '3', and '6'. Despite the fact that all these pages had belonged to the set of preliminary sketches, they cannot all date from the same time, since Mahler's hand varies from page to page, as does the continuity of the materials. It is impossible to determine with certainty the exact order in which Mahler composed these pages, despite the fact that he clearly inscribed on them the order in which they were to occur in the short score.

In addition, most of the preliminary sketches for the first movement are single leaves ripped from a bifolio and written on only one side. Most of the paper was produced by the Joseph Eberle company, Vienna, as evident from the colophon (*Schutzmarke*) 'J. E. & Co.',[16] accompanied by the number indicating the type of paper, no. 12a, and the number of staves ('linig'), 20. So far as is known, no overt significance may be found in the way Mahler used such paper, since the number of staves differs from page to page, and may involve 18-, 20-, or 24-stave paper. Only in the short score and draft score would Mahler use paper with more consistency.

---

[15] As to Mahler's destruction of sketch materials, he told Natalie Bauer-Lechner about his intentions: 'G[ustav] spoke of his sketchbooks and sketch sheets: "For God's sake [see] that they aren't preserved and don't outlive me—I will see to that, and will destroy everything that is unfinished' (quoted by Hefling, 'Variations "*in nuce*"' 125). In addition, evidence of his method of selection at the sketchbook stage (as he presumably proceeded to the first large-size pages of the preliminary sketches) exist in the so-called 'Letztes Skizzenbuch' (Vienna: Österreichische Nationalbibliothek, Theatersammlung, V Ba MK 905). The pages of this sketchbook on which Mahler jotted down ideas are either crossed with an 'X' or left unmarked, with the unmarked ones containing material he decided not to take forward at that time.

[16] Susan Filler suggests that the use of Eberle paper ('J. E. & Co.') indicates the provenance of unidentified sketches as Vienna and assists in dating the material. See Susan M. Filler, 'Mahler's Sketches for a Scherzo in C Minor and a Presto in F Major', *College Music Symposium*, 24 (1984), 69–80 at 71. While it is likely that the music Mahler composed in Vienna is on paper made in that city, it is also plausible that he used whatever spare paper he had on hand for preliminary sketches, since they are already torn from two-page bifolio sheets. With the preliminary sketches for the first movement of the Fourth Symphony, dating the material is not as critical as with the abandoned 'Scherzo and Trio in C minor' that may date from the late 1890s, but may also have been composed later. It is important to realize that manuscript paper bearing the same Eberle colophon is still available in Vienna.

In the preliminary sketches for the first movement (see Table 5.1) Mahler approached the melodic and thematic content of the piece and essentially arrived at a continuity draft. The first extant manuscript, the preliminary sketch page '2', consists of a single leaf for the first movement (see Fig. 5.1),[17] which corresponds to bars 77–101 and 340–9, as shown in the table. One striking element of this page is the reference to the structure of the movement. On the middle of page '2', over the empty tenth stave, Mahler marked 'Schluß Coda?' ('Final Coda?'), referring to the two systems underneath. He repeated the question mark in the far right margin and responded to it with the affirmative 'Ja!' ('Yes!'). The marking for the 'Schluß Coda' occurs over another notation: 'erst gänzlich [unclear] und schon hier Durchführung' ('first completely [unclear] and already here the development section'). This remark goes with the caret for insertion above the double bar of the third system (analogue to b. 101), and is supported by the annotation at the end of the last system on the page, 'folgt 2. Theil' ('the second part follows'). What precedes the double bar in the third system belongs to the exposition, the 'Schluß Coda' being the final Coda of the movement, not the conclusion of the exposition or the opening of the development.

At the same time, the upper part of this page contains a sketch for bars 77–101. Since bars 304–29 in the recapitulation resemble bars 77–101 in the exposition, it may be that Mahler referred to this sketch when he composed the recapitulation. When he actually composed the recapitulation of the movement on preliminary sketch page '8' (which contains the first part of the recapitulation), the manuscript is somewhat sparse, like some continuity drafts of Beethoven. Since he had the ending of the movement already in mind on page '2', he would not need to write much more on page '8' to remind him of how he intended to conclude the movement.

The missing page '1' probably contained music for the two thematic areas of the exposition (corresponding to bars 4–37), which came before page '2'. The latter part of the first page probably included the second theme in D major, as inferred by the explicit G major key signature at the beginning of page '2'. Since Mahler used key signatures only when necessary in the preliminary sketches and not consistently at the beginning of every system, the earlier section must have been in another key. (Page '1', then, probably began in G major and contained the sketches for the first area of the exposition.)

Continuing on page '3'[18] and 'Pseudo 3', two interrelated sketch pages, Mahler proceeded with what would become the development section of the first movement. The connection between the two pages is clear from the way he circled part of the first system of page '3' and placed a caret to show an insertion in the centre of that passage. He wrote 'gilt eventuell' to the left of

---

[17] A facsimile of this sketch is also found in Floros, *Gustav Mahler*, iii. *Die Symphonien*, 332.

[18] Tilman Seebass describes this manuscript in *Musikhandschriften der Bodmeriana*, 75. He calls the sketch a *Particell* (short score), but it resembles more closely other preliminary sketches for the Fourth Symphony.

TABLE 5.1. *An analysis of sketches for the first movement*

Page	Staves	Bars	Correlation with the completed work (bars)
PAGE '2' (Stanford University Library, MLM 8, 633)			
recto	1–4	all	77–85
	6–9	all	86–95
	11–14	1–5	96–101
		6–10	340–4
	16–19	1–2	345–6
		3–4	347
		5–6	348–9
verso	blank		
PAGE '3' (Bibliotheca Bodmeriana)			
	1–5	1–6	102–7
		7–9	124–6
	7–10	all	127–36
	12–15	1–9	137–45
		10	none
	17–22	1	none
		2–9	146–53
PAGE 'PSEUDO 3' (Newberry Library, Case MS Vm 1001 M21 S4)			
	2–6	all	102–10
	7–11	all	111–20
	13–18	1–2	121–2
		3–5	123
		6–7	124–5
PAGE '5' (Private source)			
	1–5	all	184–92
	6–10	1–5	193–7
		6	201
		7	none
		8	198
	12–15	1–4	199–202
		5	204–5
		6	148/151
		7	149/152
		8–9	none
	18–21	1–2	none
		3	229–30
		4	231
		5	none
		6	196
		7	197
		8–9	Newberry Library sketches, staves 21–4
PAGE '6' (Newberry Library, Case MS Vm 1001 M21 S4)			
recto	1–6	all	198–206
	6–13	1–2	207–8

TABLE 5.1 (*contd.*)

Page	Staves	Bars	Correlation with the completed work (bars)
		3–4	209
		5–9	210–14
	14–19	all	214–25
	20–4	1–6	226–31
		7–9	none

PAGE '7' (Private source)

	2–6	1–5	226–32
		6	233–4
		7–10	235–8
	8–10	1–4	239–42
	17–22	1	232
		2	232–3
		3	233–5
		4–7	235–8
		8	238
	22–4	1	239

PAGE '8' (Internationale Gustav Mahler Gesellschaft, Ph 60)

	1–6	all	243–53
	7–10	all	254–62
	12–15	all	263–75
	16–19	all	276–86
	21–4	1–2	287–8
		3–8	analogue to bb. 272–6 above and corresponding to bb. 289–92
		9–13	293–7

the insertion mark and 'eventuell Pseudo 3' to the right of it ('allow for possible Pseudo 3'), thus showing his intention to revise music.

As sometimes occurs in the preliminary sketches, pages '3' and 'Pseudo 3' overlap, with two versions of a passage that eventually became bars 102–7 in the completed work. In taking up the revision of the passage from page '3' at the beginning of 'Pseudo 3', Mahler composed a new episode that was not part of his earlier conception. When he composed page '3', he must have intended the passage found in the first six bars of the first system (corresponding to bb. 102–7) to lead directly to the A major episode of the development section (bb. 124–53). He brought in yet another passage from 'Pseudo 3' when he took the preliminary sketches into the short score, and probably went on to use material on the no longer extant preliminary sketch page numbered '4'.

Differences between the preliminary sketches and the completed movement can sometimes be indirect, as shown in these pages. When Mahler took up the music from the end of page '3' (analogue to bb. 124–5), for example, he altered the figuration to arrive at a sequence that descends from

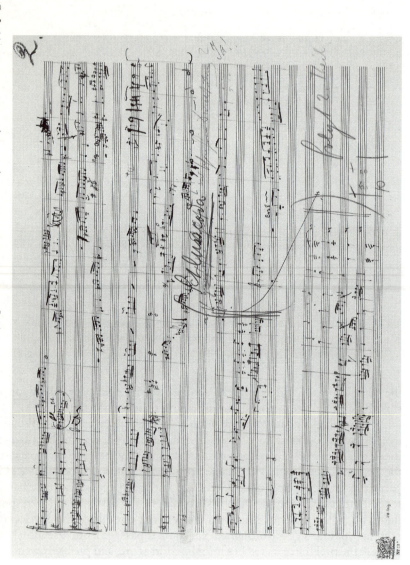

F<small>IG</small>. 5.1. Gustav Mahler, 'Skizzenblatt aus der IV. Symphonie', Stanford University Library, MLM, Box 8, 633, page '2'

G to C, then E to C. The pattern is relevant to the harmony of the movement at that point and essential to the transition to the episode in A major found on 'Pseudo 3'. Similarly, the pitch E is important to the opening of the development section on page '3', with the 'Schellenkappe' figure that opens the section and consists of E and B, not B♭ and F, as found in the completed work. Likewise, the line given to the violin in the analogue to bar 103 begins on F, which Mahler changed to C♯ in the symphony. In fact, he altered the pitch of the entire passage when he rewrote it on 'Pseudo 3.'

As shown in Table 5.1, a more direct relationship exists between much of sketch page 'Pseudo 3' and the completed work. The only point where the correlation weakens is near the end, at the apparent transition to the next section of the development (b. 123). In the last system, he begins with what would become bars 121–2 of the movement. The next three bars of the sketch are for the same passage, as shown by the curved line drawn over them, from the end of the second bar to the beginning of the fifth bar.

Before going further Mahler worked through several different ideas in this sketch page. As shown in Ex. 5.1, the second bar contains the descending eighth-note figure in the horn, along with the sixteenth-note pattern found in the symphony. He rejected the sixteenth-note figure in the second bar, went on to compose the same pattern in parallel thirds in the middle two staves, and then rejected them too after deciding to return to the same figure that he had excised earlier. In the apparent third attempt, the one Mahler connected with the curved line, he essentially composed the same music as found in bar 123 of the completed work. In essence, Mahler returned to his initial intention and rejected a more elaborate, later version of a passage he had questioned on the sketch page.

Mahler maintained at least a two-voice texture in this sketch, just as he did on pages '2' and '3'. On page 'Pseudo 3' the essential treble and bass parts are present throughout, but, unlike either of the other two sketches, the inner parts are consistent for almost all of the page. Thus, the eighth-note figuration found in the first system (and corresponding to bars 102–10) is already part of the work at this stage. As is evident from the multiple versions found on page '3', however, this was not Mahler's first attempt at the passage. Beyond the indications for instrumentation, the existence of inner parts, and even notated rests, the amount of detail that occurs on this sketch page demonstrates a more advanced conception of the music for this part of the movement.

In choosing preliminary sketch page '5', Mahler elected to include what appear to be rougher sketches when compared with page '3'. Like some of the work he pursued in sketchbooks, this page contains a continuous melodic line, interspersed with some suggestion of an accompaniment. The use of a repeated-note accompaniment figure on page '5' reflects internal consistency with other ideas for this part of the movement and also with the song 'Das himmlische Leben'.

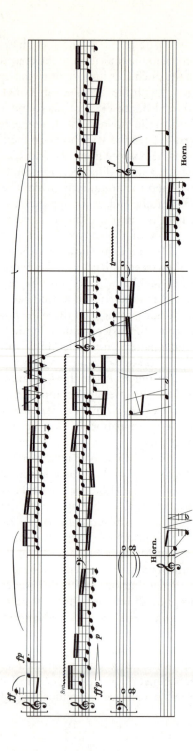

Ex. 5.1. Preliminary sketch page 'Pseudo 3' for the 1st movt, sts. 13–16, bb. 1–5 (analogue to bb. 121–3)

Mahler's indication for scoring on the second system of page '5' suggests that he wanted to use a relatively large orchestra in the passage, since he indicated third trombone (thus presuming two other trombones) and tuba, as well as a doubling with bassoon, cello, and bass. Such instrumentation would require an orchestra more like the kind required for the Second and Third Symphonies, rather than the smaller one he eventually used for the Fourth Symphony. Although he did not score the completed Fourth Symphony with low brass, in the fair copy he attempted to use the tuba to reinforce the horn in several passages of the Scherzo. Moreover, he told Bauer-Lechner around the time he completed the Fourth that while he had avoided using trombones in order to achieve a more 'classical' sound, he might have used them in the third movement.[19] His decision to avoid such scoring in the Fourth is supported by a statement he made at the rehearsal of 12 October 1901, when he explained to Bauer-Lechner that 'instrumentation is not there for the sake of sound-effects, but to bring out clearly what one has to say'.[20] Having found a way to express such an outburst with the forces he already had in mind for the score, he evidently chose to refrain from adding low brass in passages where they would contribute to volume alone.

As to the rest of the page, the relationship between the beginning of the second system and the finished work is tenuous, and the connection between this sketch and the symphony disintegrates at the end of the second system of page '5'.[21] In essence this section appears to be an attempt at continuing the passage started at the end of the previous system. Failing to compose a satisfactory continuation previously, Mahler must have decided when he worked on the short score to return to the passage beginning with the analogue to bar 198 on page '6', since that music continues from where he ended on page '5'. However, it is significant that at the end of the last bar of the third system of page '5' Mahler wrote the signature for E major, as though he intended to continue the development section in that key.

Proceeding to preliminary sketch page '6', Mahler continues the development section of the movement, and this page contains sketches for bars 198–231. While this sketch lacks a key signature, the music corresponds to the F minor section in the completed work. The page continues from an earlier one that may not have been the one inscribed '5', and so Mahler must have felt the need to provide a key signature—in fact, no key signature appears on page '5' either. Since the modulation to F minor occurs earlier in the movement, the four-flat key signature probably appeared on the no longer extant page '4'.

---

[19] Bauer-Lechner, *Erinnerungen*, 163; *Recollections*, 153.
[20] Bauer-Lechner, *Erinnerungen*, 198; *Recollections*, 178.
[21] The sixth and seventh bars are related to either bars 148–9 or 151–2, both of which have in common the repeated quarter-note figure followed by the bass theme. After that, the sixteenth-note figure bears no resemblance to what follows in either bar 150 or 153, but bears more affinity to the music in bar 201.

Sketch page '6' also shows Mahler working through ideas he eventually abandoned. The last system bears a tenuous relationship to bars 226–31 of the completed work, but this connection is not as strong as the one for the first three bars of this page. Moreover, the key signature in the final system differs from the key of the corresponding music in the symphony. Mahler had originally written 'B-moll' (B-flat minor) on stave 20, then marked 'E-moll trans[ponieren]?' ('transpose to E minor?'), demonstrating his intention to change the key of the passage. Both the B flat and E minor transpositions would create a third relation with the tonic, but the latter would have a deeper significance. The relationship between G major and E minor parallels that which exists between the two themes of the third movement, anticipating the key but not the mode of the end of Song-Finale, E major.

Several factors may have influenced Mahler's abandoning both B flat and E minor. He would have been aware of the late eighteenth-century convention of returning to the tonic at the recapitulation by means of the subdominant. By proceeding to C major at this point in his classically oriented first movement, he reinforces a tonal relationship that Hefling regards as underlying the entire symphony. The third-related key centres of G, E, and C form the basic tonal structure of the Fourth.[22] In the end, however, Mahler abandoned both key changes suggested on the sketch page.

Regarding what he retained on page '6', Mahler anticipates the recapitulation in the analogue to bar 209 by labelling the passage 'Orgelp[unkt]' ('pedal-point'). He also introduces on this page 'the little call to order',[23] which differs slightly from the way it occurs in the completed work. At the same time, the combination of various ideas before the recapitulation seems to lead to the sixteenth-note figures suggesting the 'shudder of Panic dread' that Mahler had described to Bauer-Lechner when he discussed this movement with her.[24] The music at this point seems to have been conceived purely for its sound effects. Mahler apparently wrote it hurriedly, as is evident by the ascending and descending stems without noteheads. From the approximate length of the stems and their placement on the staves, the figure seems to move through the entire orchestra at this point on page '6'.

Near the end of the page Mahler also inscribed a caret at the beginning of the penultimate measure of the third system to indicate an insertion, perhaps yet another episode before the recapitulation. He could have marked this passage after he crossed out the system below it, and possibly he intended to replace it with another passage, as is usually the case when he inscribed a caret. He eventually decided against such an insertion, since the music continues directly on preliminary sketch page '7'.

[22] Hefling, 'Variations', 118.
[23] Bauer-Lechner, *Erinnerungen*, 164; *Recollections*, 154.
[24] Bauer-Lechner, *Erinnerungen*, 163; *Recollections*, 152.

Even though Mahler crossed out the upper half of page '7', most of the sketches bear a relationship to the completed work. The first system corresponds to bars 226–38 of the symphony, while the system under it is an approximation of bars 239–42. He rewrote the music of the first two systems in the third (this passage corresponds to bars 232–8), and the literal restatement of the main theme at the top of page '7' confirms the relationship between this sketch and bars 232–9 of the symphony. The first five bars of sketch page '7' are an embryonic version of bars 226–32 of the completed work.

Preliminary sketch page '8' follows directly from page '7'. This page corresponds to bars 243–97 of the completed work, and most likely continued to a page numbered '9', which would have contained the last part of the movement. Page '8' consists of five four-stave systems in varying stages of completion. A two-voice texture occurs on the first system, while the texture is fuller on all four staves of the second. In the third system Mahler returned to two voices, continuing with only a single voice at the beginning of the last system. He returned to a thicker texture within that system, but its last two bars dissolve in an unaccompanied melody. Since Mahler did not finish the sketches for the first movement on this page (without 'etc.' or 'usw.' or any such markings that he used elsewhere) he probably used at least one other page to compose the music corresponding to bars 298–339 of the completed movement. (He had already sketched bars 340–9 on the page numbered '2' as the 'Schluß Coda').

On page '8' the music of the first system continues from the end of page '7', but the correspondence between the rest of the system and the completed work is tenuous. It is possible to find a relationship with the woodwind parts of the completed work (bb. 247–50) and a version of the passage that eventually became bars 251–3 of the symphony. Similarly the second system corresponds to bars 254–62 of the completed work except for the bass parts in the analogue to bars 257–8.

In the third system Mahler restated the second area of the exposition (bb. 38–57 of the symphony) with only the melody and bass parts. However, the bass line differs from the completed work in the second through fourth bars of the sketch and the barring of the eighth and ninth bars of the sketch differs from the symphony. Except for the $\frac{3}{4}$ bar (b. 266), the rest of the bars are in $\frac{4}{4}$, with the analogue to bar 269 in the latter metre rather than the $\frac{2}{4}$ metre found in the completed work. Two and one half beats of silence follow the melodic descent to G, as shown in Ex. 5.2. Such barring does not correspond to what occurs in the exposition, where the $\frac{2}{4}$ bar comes earlier.

In the recapitulation suggested on preliminary sketch page '2' Mahler appears to have envisaged a more literal return of the material than he actually notated on page '8'. Nevertheless, the clear idea of the form implied earlier on page '2' plays down the necessity of an explicitly written-out conclusion. As mentioned above, Mahler probably used at least one additional page to

Ex. 5.2. (*a*) Preliminary sketch page '8' for the 1st movt., st. 12, bb. 4–10 (corresponding to bb. 266–72); (*b*) Fourth Symphony, 1st movt., bb. 266–71 (flute part); (*c*) Fourth Symphony, 1st movt., bb. 41–6 (parallel passage in the exposition)

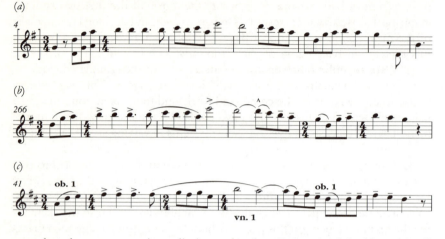

complete the movement in preliminary sketches. It remained for him to tie all these ideas together later, in the short score for the first movement.

Second Movement

The extant preliminary sketches for the Scherzo (see Table 5.2) consist of a set of numbered pages currently among the holdings of the Österreichische Nationalbibliothek. More specifically, the manuscript consists of five full-size pages, all of which resemble the preliminary sketches for the first movement, and on the same Eberle paper with the colophon 'J. E. & Co.': pages 'I' and 'II' are on no. 13, 22-stave paper; 'Einlage II' on no. 12, 20-stave paper, and pages 'III' and 'IV' on no. 18, 18-stave paper. (These pages are reproduced as Figs. 5.2–6.) While Mahler may have composed other preliminary sketches for this movement, he decided at some point to choose these pages and put them into the order in which they occur in this set before proceeding to the short score.

On the first two pages of this set, Mahler used shorthand to identify elements that he would repeat or rework later in the compositional process. The shorthand takes the form of letters labelling various sections. At the beginning of the first page, for example, he uses the upper-case letter 'A' in the left margin of the first stave, with 'Aaa' and another lower-case 'a' where the principal thematic material occurs in the third bar of the first system. He marked the next section of the sketch 'b' near the end of the first system. Likewise, he inscribed 'Bbb' over the second system, and this section continues to the double bar in the middle of the third system.

TABLE 5.2. *An analysis of sketches for the second movement (Scherzo)*
Österreichische Nationalbibliothek, Mus. Hs. 39.745

Page	Staves	Bars	Correlation with the completed work (bars)
'I'	1–4	all	5–21
	6–9	all	22–37
	11–15	1–10	38–47
		11–16	170–5
	16–22	all	176–91
'II'	1–5	1–9	192–200
		10–11	none, but corresponding to bb. 201–2
		12–16	69–73
	6–9	all	74–90
	11–16	all	91–109
	17–20	all	254–73
'III'	2–7	all	189–99
'IV'	2–7	1–10	323–32
(Coda)	2–5	10–13	335–9
	5	10–12	336–7
	6–7	10–14	333–5
	9–14	all	340–1, 343–53
	16–18	all	354–64, 341–4[a]

[a] These bars are set off with two insertion marks ('V').

After this, Mahler marked two bars that apparently begin a new section with 'a–b aber variiert' ('[sections] a–b but varied'). He evidently intended to continue with the repetition of music originally found in the sections labelled 'a' and 'b' but instead of repeating them literally in the preliminary sketches, left this reminder to combine the ideas later. He proceeds in the same system with a new section labelled 'd' (the section 'a–b aber variiert' must be 'c', although he did not mark it as such), and section 'd' continues through the fourth system of page 'I'. At that point a double bar and change of key signature signal the beginning of yet another section, extending through the first system of page 'II', which Mahler labelled 'B' (like the letter 'A' at the beginning of page 'I').

Mahler also marked places where he intended a more literal return of certain ideas. Just as the section he designates as 'B' on page 'II' of this manuscript corresponds to the first trio (bb. 69–109) of the completed work, the marking 'Wiederholung' at the bottom of the second page refers to the return of the Scherzo at the end of that section, as well as to the end of the episode sketched on the last system of the page.

As shown in Table 5.2, the letter indications on the first two pages of this manuscript indicate Mahler's initial conception of the movement, which

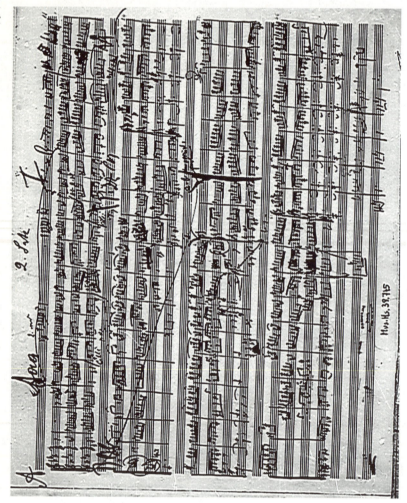

FIG. 5.2. Gustav Mahler, 'Skizze zur 4. Symphonie', Österreichische Nationalbibliothek, Mus. Hs. 39.745, page 'I'

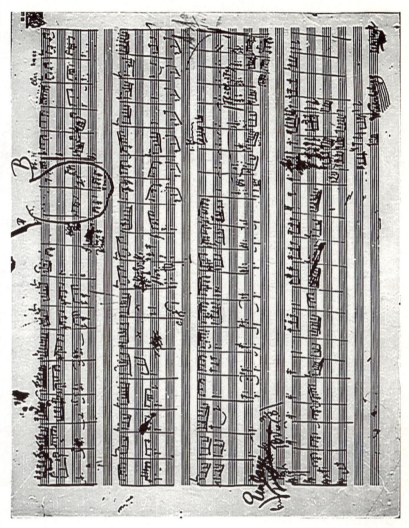

FIG. 5.3. Gustav Mahler, 'Skizze zur 4. Symphonie', Österreichische Nationalbibliothek, Mus. Hs. 39.745, page 'II'

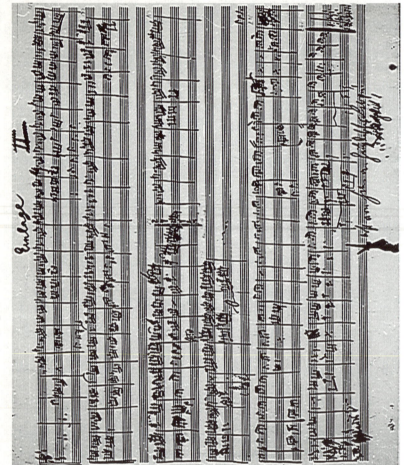

Fɪɢ. 5.4. Gustav Mahler, 'Skizze zur 4. Symphonie', Österreichische Nationalbibliothek, Mus. Hs. 39.745, page 'Einlage II'

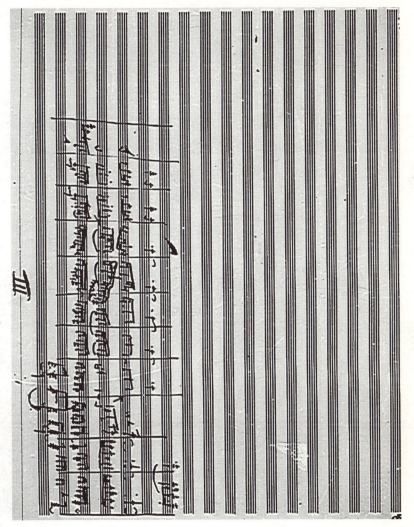

F<small>IG</small>. 5.5. Gustav Mahler, 'Skizze zur 4. Symphonie', Österreichische Nationalbibliothek, Mus. Hs. 39.745, page 'III'

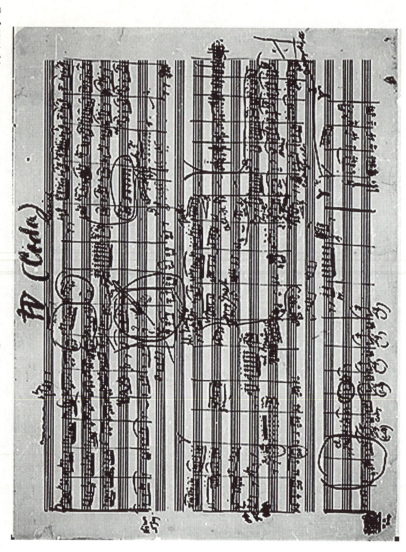

F<small>IG</small>. 5.6. Gustav Mahler, 'Skizze zur 4. Symphonie', Österreichische Nationalbibliothek, Mus. Hs. 39.745, page 'IV'

encompasses the essential thematic components of the entire movement, the Scherzo and two Trios. He planned to develop the ideas further at some point, when he would write out the sections only designated 'a–b aber variiert' as bars 48 to 68 of the completed movement. The synthesis of 'a' and 'b' material implied in that marking is evident in the completed movement, where the return of primary thematic material at bar 46 contains a mixture of elements from both the two sections.

At some point, Mahler reconsidered his initial conception of the structure of the Scherzo (Table 5.3), as is evident in his inclusion with these sketches of the insertion to page 'II' ('Einlage II'). Since the analogue to the second part of the trio (bb. 254–73) occurs on page 'II', the music found on 'Einlage II' must have been intended to precede it. Yet Mahler probably decided against this insertion some time later, since he did not follow the music as sketched on 'Einlage II' and pursued, instead, another idea related more closely to music in the first trio. Nevertheless, the chromatic idea related to the quotation of the phrase 'Cäcilia mit ihren Verwandten' from the Song-Finale is present in this sketch (fourth system). This quotation survives in the completed movement.

With the principal sections of the Scherzo already planned, Mahler did not need to compose any new thematic material for the movement. After all, he

TABLE 5.3. *A reconstruction of an early conception of the Scherzo*

Letters designated by Mahler	Bars in the preliminary sketch	Bars in the completed work	Section of the completed work
A	1–2	5–6	Introduction
Aaa			
a	3–12	7–16	Scherzo, Area A
b	13–17	17–21	Scherzo, Area A
Bbb	18–29	22–33	Scherzo, Area A
(double bar)	30–41	34–45	Scherzo, Area B
(double bar)	42–3	46–7	Scherzo, Area A
a–b aber variiert	written over an insertion mark at the end of bar 43	(48–68)	Scherzo, Area A
(double bar)	44–7	170–3	Scherzo, Area B
d	47–58	173–84	Scherzo, Area B
(key change)	59–76	185–200 (202)	Scherzo, Area A
B	77–117	69–109	Trio 1, Area C, D
Einlage II	written before the next bar	none	Trio 2, Area C
(double bar)	118–37	254–73	Trio 2, Area D
III		189–99	Scherzo, Area A
IV Coda		323–64	Coda

already had an idea of the proportions of the Scherzo on the first two pages. He did, however, sketch in detail the Coda of the movement, which corresponds directly to that part of the finished work. Unlike other preliminary sketch pages, the Coda sketch is almost as advanced as some of the short-score pages, with almost all the voices written out and the scoring essentially specified. Yet for all the details it contains, this sketch remains a preliminary sketch because it lacks the continuity usually found in Mahler's short scores.

As to more specific relationships with the completed work, the sketches for the Scherzo represent rather advanced thinking. Page 'I' contains a rudimentary form of the introduction, corresponding to the fifth and sixth bars of the completed work, but it lacks the half-step accompaniment figure found in the symphony. Mahler then sketched the substance of the first part of the Scherzo, the antecedent phrase of the first period in the first system, the consequent phrase in the second.

At the end of the second system Mahler changed the key signature from C minor to C major. The new section extends to the eighth bar of the third system. At the end of that bar, the composer adds an insertion mark ('V'), over which appears the roman numeral 'I'. The latter refers to the return of music found in the first system over which the same roman numeral is inscribed. This return is confirmed by the two written-out bars of the previous section that follow the insertion mark. Another section follows, the one marked 'a–b aber variiert' and, as mentioned above, Mahler did not explore the variation in this sketch.

The bars on the remainder of page 'I' (following 'a–b aber variiert') correspond to bars 170–91, and Mahler composed the analogue to bars 192–200 on the first system of page 'II'. As with the previous page, a close resemblance exists between the sketch and the finished work, but weakens at the analogue to bar 200. The transition found at this point in the music is tentative at best, since he circled the passage for later revision. After this passage occurs a double bar and an upper-case 'B', so that the last five bars of the first system and the entirety of the next two contain the second major division of the movement, the first trio.

The beginning of section 'B' is as indefinite as the conclusion of the previous one, and Mahler eventually retained only the bass in the analogue to bars 69–70. After working past these bars, however, he seems to have been able to express his ideas more easily. The last three bars of the first system and the entirety of the second resemble the symphony directly, the principal difference being the lack of articulation markings, a detail that would not usually occur in a preliminary sketch, even though it is part of page 'IV' in this manuscript.

Mahler sketched the second trio on the fourth system of page 'II', starting in D major where the timbre changes. He indicates harp and either second

violin or second clarinet, as evident in the numeral '2' and the letters that follow. In the symphony the second trio begins with a return of the first section
in bars 203–53, but this does not occur in the sketch. Instead, Mahler sketches
the analogue to bars 254–73, along with an insertion ('Einlage') to precede it.
While the sketch indicates a somewhat shorter second trio, he probably extended the music in the short score.

Nevertheless, the sketch for the second trio contains the essential two-
voice texture that Mahler carried into the completed work. The two main
voices in this section, which become the clarinet and viola parts in the symphony, are present here. In addition, the bass part appears to have been
changed in subsequent stages of composition. As shown in Ex. 5.3(*a*), he
eliminated the inner part in the analogue to bar 266. Even the bass part
sketched underneath—with the pitches C♯, E, and D— does not occur in
the completed work. When he revised the sketch later, he eliminated this
bass and replaced it with another, as shown in Ex. 5.3(*b*).

Ex. 5.3. (*a*) Preliminary sketch page 'II' for the 2nd movt., sts. 17–22, bb. 13–20 (analogue to bb. 266–73); (*b*) Fourth Symphony, 2nd movt., bb. 266–70 (cello part)

While the sketch for the second trio concludes at the end of page 'II', page 'III' does not continue from it. The page marked 'Einlage II' would occur at the insertion mark on the sketch page and clearly before the passage sketched in the final system of page 'II'. The repetition of the Scherzo, as suggested by the marking 'Wiederholung' at the end of the final system of page 'II', seems to have been intended to follow this latter passage. Page 'III' corresponds to bars 189–99 and contains the return of the principal thematic material for the Scherzo just before the second trio. It is a virtual revision of music already composed at the end of page 'I' and the beginning of page 'II'. In comparison with the earlier sketch, the passage on page 'III' seems closer to a short score than a preliminary sketch.

The first three bars of page 'III' correspond to the last three on page 'I', the only difference being the addition of the half-step motif that Mahler eventually introduced at the opening of the completed movement. The presence of the half-step motif on page 'III' suggests the increasing pervasiveness of the idea as Mahler worked through the sketches for the second movement.

Notwithstanding these details, the music on the page marked 'Einlage II' stands out for its lack of a counterpart in the completed movement. As an insertion page, Mahler intended the page to precede the section sketched in the fourth system of page 'II'. While he abandoned the entire episode found on 'Einlage II', the page was important enough for him to preserve—or, perhaps, not allow to be destroyed. This is all the more surprising because the sketch for the Scherzo contains a direct verbal reference to the song 'Das himmlische Leben'.

As outlined in Table 5.4, it is possible to divide 'Einlage II' into three sections differentiated by metre. The first section is in $\frac{6}{16}$ or $\frac{6}{8}$, since Mahler wrote the second metre signature under the first. At the double bar in the middle of the third system, he gives the metre signature $\frac{2}{4}$. The third section begins in the fourth system, in which Mahler apparently returns to the $\frac{3}{8}$ metre of the Scherzo, even though it lacks an explicit signature.

While Mahler is not specific about his intentions with tempo markings for this sketch, it is possible that he notated or implied such changes in metre in order to reflect a gradual increase in tempo. He began 'Einlage II' with six beats per bar, and in modulating metrically to $\frac{2}{4}$, the division of the bar changed from two groups of three to two groups of four beats per bar. When that section breaks off in the fourth system, the final metre appears to be $\frac{3}{8}$, a signature that could conceivably be taken in a single pulse per measure. The music sketched on this page progresses from six beats, to two, to one. It is as though the passage were supposed to increase in speed, like a tarantella, and thus correspond to his remarks to Bauer-Lechner. Writing about his work in mid-December 1900, she states that 'Mahler is working a few hours every morning and evening at his Fourth. From the Aussee sketches, he has

TABLE 5.4. *Structure of 'Einlage II' preliminary sketch for the second movement, Trio 2* *Österreichische Nationalbibliothek, Mus. Hs. 39.745*

Staves	Bars	Metre signature	Comments
1–3	all	$\frac{6}{16}\left(\frac{6}{8}\right)$	First variation on the primary thematic material of the Scherzo
4–6	1–2		
4–6	3–10	same	Second variation
4–6	10–16	same	Third variation
8–10	1–9	same	
8–10	10–17	$\frac{2}{4}$	Fourth variation
11–13	1–8		
14–16	1–8	$\left(\frac{6}{16}\text{ or }\frac{3}{8}\right)$	Fifth variation
14–16	10–21	same	Sixth variation (including elements of 'Das himmlische Leben')
17–19	1–21	same	
17–19	22–4	same	Segue to a more literal statement of the song as indicated by the marking on stave 20 'Erst von hier an himmlisches Leben! Deutlich! ('First here, "[Das] himmlische Leben!" Clearly!')

now laboriously reconstructed the Scherzo as he had originally planned it. At the time, it would in fact only have developed further and become much longer, ending in a tarantella.'[25]

The sketches composed at Aussee are most likely these preliminary sketches for the Scherzo, and the way Mahler 'originally planned' the movement would have been without the insertion ('Einlage') page that increased its length. The tarantella idea was a later thought that would come near the end of the movement, probably at the beginning of the second trio, and Mahler's thoughts could have been misinterpreted by Bauer-Lechner as the conclusion of the movement. Nevertheless, the movement appears to have developed in a direction that Mahler eventually found unacceptable, such that some of his dissatisfaction may be traced to this sketch page.

Most importantly, the preliminary sketch page 'Einlage II' contains clear evidence of Mahler's conscious intention to incorporate 'Das himmlische Leben' into the Fourth Symphony. While no verbal evidence of his plans to quote the song occurs in any of the extant sketches for the other movements, he wrote at the bottom of this page 'Erst von hier an himmlisches Leben! Deutlich!' ('Starting here, "[Das] himmlische Leben!" Clearly!') under the sixth system of the page. Mahler wanted to make a direct statement of at least part of the song at this point in the music, or, perhaps, even proceed to the song itself.

[25] Bauer-Lechner, *Erinnerungen*, 179; *Recollections*, 161.

In this respect, the page 'Einlage II' resembles the sketches for the first movement of the Third Symphony,[26] in which Mahler attempted to compose an instrumental development of 'Das himmlische Leben'. While the reference to the song in the sketches for the Third Symphony is an instrumental quotation, the nature of the reference in 'Einlage II' is not so clear. Since some confusion occurred with the position of the Scherzo as the second or third movement, he could have conceived the Scherzo as the movement before the Song-Finale, rather than the movement right after the first.

Since Mahler did not destroy this sketch, it is possible that he intended to refer to it later. He could have used it as a point of departure when he worked on the unfinished Scherzo and Trio movement, which appears to have emerged during this period.[27] While no overt link exists between these two works, the music on 'Einlage II' is similar to the sketches for the abortive Scherzo and Trio. The pervasive half-step motif is common to both, and both movements are in the minor mode. The triplet figure from bars 128–9 of 'Das himmlische Leben' occurs in the incomplete Scherzo as well, its first appearance being in the third system of its page '1'. Besides, the trio of the Scherzo and Trio is in $\frac{2}{4}$, while the Scherzo is in $\frac{6}{8}$, a metric relationship comparable to the ones on 'Einlage II'. While these similarities could be regarded as circumstantial, it would be imprudent to ignore them completely. These affinities are symptomatic of a style of composition and may help to establish the incomplete Scherzo and Trio as belonging to the period in which Mahler composed the Fourth, rather than placing it among his later music.

The final page of this manuscript, inscribed 'IV', contains music for the Coda of the movement, specifically bars 323–64 (see Table 5.2). This page is comprised of a network of systems from three to five staves each. The first system contains sketches for bars 323–39, but it is continuous only up to the analogue to bar 332. In the last five bars, the system divides, with the upper staves containing sketches for bars 335–9 and the lower ones for bars 333–5.

From the line that Mahler drew from the tenth to eleventh bars of the first system, it seems that he conceived the material between bars 332 and 335 after he began to compose the latter bar, adding that passage in the lower staves. This kind of discontinuity suggests that as late as the sketch for the Coda may be, it must have preceded the preparation of the short score. In addition, Mahler made some notes for scoring on this sketch. In the first system alone he designates a doubling of the bass line for horns and bassoons (beginning at

---

[26] For a discussion of this sketch for the Third Symphony, see Williamson, 'Mahler's Compositional Process', 338–40.

[27] Gustav Mahler, 'Scherzo und Trio' (Vienna, Wiener Stadt- und Landesbibliothek, MH 654/c); facsimile in Mahler, *Symphonische Entwürfe*. See also Filler, 'Mahler's Sketches for a Scherzo in C Minor and a Presto in F Major'.

b. 323). He calls for horn again later in the same system (b. 335), along with timpani, but these indications do not carry into the completed movement.

Among the other markings in the second system, Mahler suggested one passage for flute and oboe and another for bassoon. Later in the same system he gives an ascending figure to the bassoon and horn (bb. 344–5), the solo violin ('Solo-Geige') appearing for the first time in these sketches in the space directly above. He also indicates oboe, clarinet, flute, and trumpet for various figures accompanying the solo violin, and for the most part, these carry into the completed work. He even marks the trumpet in bar 346 'gestopft' ('muted') and signals the end of the solo violin part with the word 'tutti' (b. 349). In the light of such details, Mahler seems to have evolved the timbre of the movement as he worked through this preliminary sketch.

Third Movement

The preliminary sketches for the third movement of the Fourth Symphony are fragmentary at best (see Table 5.5). Yet the lack of materials and the condition of the short score suggest that Mahler may not have composed extensive preliminary sketches for this movement. The most substantive sketch is the single page for the second theme, which is found with the short score.

Since the short score itself contains many revisions, the original form of the slow movement was probably shorter than the one Mahler eventually used in

TABLE 5.5. *An analysis of preliminary sketches for the third movement*

Page	Staves	Bars	Correlation with the completed work (bars)
PAGE 'IV' (Pierpont Morgan Library)			
	1–3	1–4	62–5
		5–6	45–50
		9–13	80–4
	5–7	9–15	85–8
	9–11	1–3	62
		4–10	62–9
		11–13	69–70
		14–19	70–5
		13–16	88–93
PAGE 'EINLAGE 5' (Österreichische Nationalbibliothek, Mus. Hs. 4366)			
recto	1–3	all	263–76
	4–6	1–3	275–7
	8–12	1–2	276–7
	14–16	1–3	276 ff.
	14–17	1–3	276–7
	5–8	1–3	277
	10–13	1–3	276–8

the Fourth Symphony. He supplemented the numbered pages of the short score (written in ink) with various insertion pages (*Einlage*) in which he expanded the movement substantially. Given that such revisions occurred in the short score, it may be that relatively few preliminary sketch pages existed for the movement, and Mahler may have destroyed those when he composed the short score, since the new structure of the movement would have superseded anything he composed earlier.

The single preliminary sketch page for the second theme exists on the reverse of the first page of the short score for the slow movement.[28] This preliminary sketch differs from the other pages of the short score because it occurs on the reverse of another manuscript page and is in pencil, not ink. The presence of a sketch on the reverse of another is contrary to Mahler's habit, since he usually used one side of a single bifolio sheet for either preliminary sketches or the short score. Moreover, he appears to have composed it hurriedly, as the hand differs from the rest of the short score in its tentative and indistinct notation.

Unlike the preliminary sketches for the first two movements, it is difficult to establish as definite a correlation between this sketch and the completed work. Since it occurs on the reverse of a short-score page, it is possible that Mahler composed it after he finished the short score of the opening of the movement. Perhaps he had not even considered a second theme for his variations until he completed the short score of the first theme.

This preliminary sketch contains an early version of the second theme, which differs from the completed work in a number of ways. For one, the sketch is in G minor rather than E minor, as found in both the short score and the symphony. In addition, the sketch is remotely related to the completed work, unlike other preliminary sketches that have more direct connections with the symphony. In taking the ideas in this sketch into the short score, Mahler completely rewrote the second theme, changing the tonality and recasting the thematic material. As shown in Table 5.5, it is possible to perceive some relationships with the completed movement, but the ideas are neither in the same order nor in the same form in which they occur in the symphony.

Mahler clearly restructured his ideas in the short score, where he took an idea from one system of the preliminary sketch and transferred it to another, as is evident in the opening bar (see Ex. 5.4). Hefling has already provided a description of the revision of this sketch into the form found in the completed work. Taking into consideration the places where Mahler crossed out, circled, erased, or otherwise revised the sketch, presumably while composing it, Hefling regards the first system of the page to be the result of several layers of composition. He suggests that Mahler composed the first twelve

---

[28] For a discussion of this page, see Hefling, 'Variations', 108–9.

Ex. 5.4. (*a*) Preliminary sketch for the 3rd movt., page '1v' in the short score, sts. 1–3, bb. 1–8 (beginning of the second theme); (*b*) Fourth Symphony, 3rd movt., bb. 262–6, oboe part (beginning of the second theme)

(*a*)

(*b*)

bars, circled bars 9–12 on the first stave for revision, then recomposed bars 9–11 underneath before continuing with the rest of the system.

Following from there, it is likely that Mahler tried to begin the theme again in the first four bars of the second system and made yet another attempt at starting it in the fifth bar (after the double bar). It is in this system that he appears to have 'changed tactics'[29] by introducing the fragment of 'Sankt Ursula selbst dazu lacht' from 'Das himmlische Leben'. He probably continued on the second system, stopping only after the third bar of the third system, where he drew another double bar. The rest of that system and the entirety of the next comprise yet another part of the theme. The only interruption occurs in the last bar of the third system, where he crossed out the last bar but showed how it should continue with the arrow that connects it to the bottom of the page. The rest of the theme appears in the final system, a cadential figure occurring in the first twelve bars of what appears to be a transition to the next five.

As is evident in the use of the carets that set off the first four bars, Mahler revised this sketch. He probably intended to reconstruct the first part of the second theme with an addition in the third system and the first four bars of the fourth, as Hefling posits.[30] Mahler placed the roman numeral 'II' at the beginning of the third stave of the first system, thus setting off material that he intended to use for the second part of the theme and, indeed, the second period of the theme bears a relationship to the music so marked.

[29] Ibid. 108.
[30] Hefling, 'Variations', 108.

The material that Mahler circled in the sketch does not appear in the short score, nor does what follows it in the first system. The sketch appears to have served more as a chance for him to work through his initial ideas for the second theme, rather than a draft that he could take literally to the next stage of composition without much alteration. This preliminary sketch page represents a stage in the evolution of the movement, even though its connection with the completed symphony is weaker than sketches for other movements that emerged from this stage of composition.

Later Insertions for the Third Movement

A further preliminary sketch has survived for the third movement, and, like the other page, it suggests the tentative nature of the piece before Mahler took the music into the short score. This page, which he inscribed as 'Einlage 5', is a single bifolio leaf (see Fig. 5.7), like the other preliminary sketches, but written on both sides. The side labelled 'Einlage 5' is an insertion apparently intended for the draft score of the third movement (see below, Fig. 7.5), while the reverse is a different manuscript containing the preliminary sketches for the passage between bars 263 and 278 of the same movement.[31] (See Table 5.5.) This preliminary sketch concerns a transition that Mahler worked out in detail, and since it occurs on a page of the short score, it is unclear whether he composed this page while pursuing other preliminary sketches or worked out the transition at some later stage.

Notwithstanding its provenance, this sketch of the transition provides a glimpse of Mahler working through multiple possibilities for a single passage. It is a series of solutions for a short transition written down each side of the page—with the best solution written in the centre and boxed. The boxes that occur around the solutions in the centre extend to the sides, partially obscuring the attempts originally written on the page. It is unique for its repetitive 'working out' of a single idea that must have been difficult for Mahler.

This preliminary sketch page essentially concerns bars 263–78 of the completed movement, from which it differs with regard to tonality. While the same passage in the symphony is in E major, this sketch is in C major. In fact, the sketch progresses from C major to G major, while the passage on the reverse, like the short-score insertion for the same bars, is in E major and modulates to G major at the end. Just as Mahler altered the tonality of the second theme from G minor in the preliminary sketch to E minor in

---

[31] As to the origins of this preliminary sketch, the page numbered '5' in the short score contains the analogue to bars 222–57 and 283–95, with page '6' continuing from bar 296. Mahler probably wrote 'Einlage 5' after completing the short-score page '5' and at least starting page '6'. It seems plausible that he worked on this preliminary sketch while composing the short score, rather than composing the transition in such detail before proceeding with the short score of the movement.

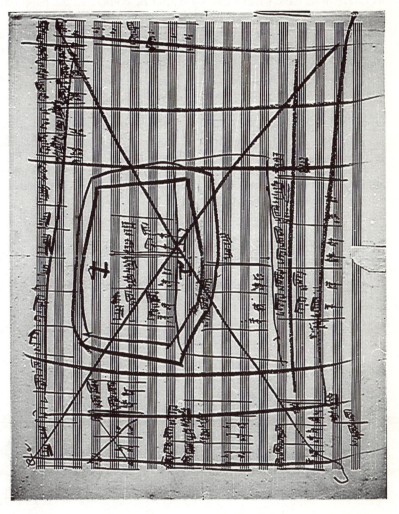

Fig. 5.7. Gustav Mahler, 'Skizze zur 4. Symphonie', Österreichische Nationalbibliothek, Mus. Hs. 4366, page 'Einlage zu Satz 4, Bogen 5' (verso)

the short score, it may have occurred to him to change the key of this passage in order to maintain the strong emphasis on E in this movement.

Mahler's intention to alter the key of this section is evident in a marking at the upper left-hand corner of the sketch, where he wrote 'C–e', which probably refers to the tonality of the sketch, C major, and his desire to transpose it to E. He must have written this soon after he composed the page, before he began working on page 'Einlage 5' of the short score.

Mahler probably wrote the first system of this page hurriedly, as is evident in the rather broad strokes of the sixteenth-note stems, as well as the slant of these notes on the second stave. This aspect is pronounced in the analogue to bar 269, which he wrote across two bars. Moreover, it is only near the end of the sketch page that he started to compose a line in counterpoint to the

Ex. 5.5. Preliminary sketch for the 3rd movt., modulation to the analogue to b. 278: (*a*) sts. 1–3, bb. 10–15 (analogue to bb. 271–8); (*b*) sts. 4–9 (far right side) (278); (*c*) sts. 4–6, bb. 1–3 (analogue to bb. 275–7); (*d*) sts. 8–12, bb. 1–2 (analogue to bb. 276–7); (*e*) sts. 14–16, bb. 1–3 (analogue to bb. 276 ff.); (*f*) sts. 14–17, four bars (analogue to bb. 276 ff.); (*g*) sts. 5–8 (near centre), three bars (analogue to bb. 277 ff.); (*h*) sts. 9–13, three bars (analogue to bb. 276–8)

(*a*)

(*b*)

Ex. 5.5 contd.

(c)

(d)

(e)

Ex. 5.5 contd.

(*f*)

(*g*)

(*h*)

principal one, having sketched a supporting line in the tenth bar of the system (analogue to b. 271), as well as adding chords to indicate the harmony.

Mahler apparently wanted to modulate at this point, but was unclear about how to achieve it. After reaching the final bar of the first system (analogue to b. 276), he rejected the attempt, and proceeded to rewrite the transition under it and also on the edge of the opposite (left-hand) side of the page. Several other solutions occurred to him, and he wrote them in the available space (see Ex. 5.5 (*a–f*)). When he had reached a satisfactory solution, he singled it out by drawing two squares around it in blue pencil. With the completion of this passage, Mahler found the transition he wanted, but it was to go to G major, not its dominant D major (Ex. 5.5 (*h*)). Thus, he also outlined the attempt below it (Ex. 5.5 (*g*)), which contains the 'correct' resolution, and labelled both solutions with a roman numeral 'I'. He drew a double square in blue pencil around the entire page, in addition to the squares around its centre. With this section worked out, it remained for him to transpose the passage from C major to E major.

This sketch shows Mahler working in greater detail than occurs in other sketches. While he may have composed this page while working on the short score, this is the kind of sketching he would pursue before bringing a passage into a later stage of work. He needed to complete this type of work before he could arrive at the kind of continuity associated with the later stages of composition.

6. Short Score

After working on the preliminary sketches for the first three movements of the Fourth Symphony, Mahler used them to prepare the more continuous short score or *Particell* of the work. At some point he organized the preliminary sketches and numbered the pages to reflect the order of ideas as he wanted them to occur in the short score. By ordering the material he had possibly composed out of sequence he had already moved beyond preliminary sketch stage. Yet not all the transitions were in place, nor had he completely thought out the structure of the symphony.

In the short score Mahler moved away from composing discrete episodes to arrive at a more continuous—and consistent— condensed score of three or four staves. He also became more explicit about the fuller conception of the piece by introducing indications for tempo and orchestration, along with articulations and phrasing. In the short score, indications for repetitions found in the preliminary sketches usually give way to the writing out of entire passages, as occurs in the short score of the slow movement. Even though he would first write out individual lines for each instrument in the next phase of composition, that is, in the draft score or *Partiturentwurf*, the short score is related more directly to the finished work than the preliminary sketches. While differences may exist between some passages, the overall shape and proportions of the work are virtually established in the short score.

Mahler also revised the short score while composing it and perhaps before he went on to compose the draft score of the symphony. For the most part, revisions of the short score take the form of insertions (*Einlagen*), which are taken into the body of the draft score. The nature of such insertions may differ, but almost all are clearly marked. It is usual to find an insertion written on a separate page and labelled 'Einlage', followed by the number of the page of the sketch to which it belongs. At times Mahler even indicated the place on the original page where the insertion should begin by marking it the same way as the separate page. Such insertions can also occur on the same page, apparently where space allowed, and there Mahler used a large caret to indicate both the insertion and the place where it was to be interpolated in the short score. In many cases he had probably decided to make the addition before he had used most of the page of the short score, rather than later in the course of work. In addition, he also altered some passages to clarify his intentions by crossing out or otherwise effacing something he wanted to change. Mahler would circle passages that he wanted to reconsider. In order to confirm the retention of a passage so marked, he would use the word 'bleibt' ('it remains' or 'stet') near the place.

As to orchestration, Mahler retained some of the details found in the earlier sketches and even introduced additional ones in the short score. Yet only a limited number of indications for instrumentation occur in the short score, and it seems logical that he had some idea of the orchestration he wanted for the other passages. He would call attention to particular instruments or timbres or combinations by marking them in the short score. Not every detail pertaining to instrumentation occurs in the short score because of its three- or four-stave format, which does not lend itself to the explicitness possible in the draft score, where each instrument has its own line.

It is also important to consider the physical appearance of the short score. As with preliminary sketches, Mahler used single pages ripped from two-leaf bifolios. It was rare for him to write on both sides of a page at this stage, the first short-score page of the third movement of the Fourth being the exception rather than the rule in this matter. In addition, he composed the short score in ink, and revised it in blue pencil (*Blaustift*), ink, or pencil.

As to the short score for the Fourth Symphony, a single leaf for the first movement[1] and the entire short score for the third are the only manuscripts extant from this stage of composition. The latter is found in a folder marked 'Skizzen aus IV' ('Sketches for the Fourth'), which probably contained the piano score for the last movement, since Mahler noted on the folder 'und Clavierauszug letzte[m] Satze' ('and the piano score of the final movement'). Since the crease on the folder that contains this manuscript is wide, Mahler probably kept the short score of the first two movements in it along with the last two.[2]

First-Movement Short Score

The single extant leaf for the short score of the first movement contains the first two pages (bb. 1–76), as shown in Table 6.1.[3] The paper is that of J. E. & Co. (Joseph Eberle & Co.) no. 12a, 20-stave variety, written on both sides, with the printer's colophon found at the bottom of the first page. Continuous for this part of the movement, the manuscript contains four four-stave systems on each page, as well as continual indications of orchestration. In

---

[1] This single-page manuscript exists in a private collection.

[2] Hefling, 'Variations', 103.

[3] This page is accompanied by the dedication 'Skizzenblatt aus der IV. Symphonie/Alma Mahler' ('Sketch page from the Fourth Symphony/Alma Mahler'). Since this dedication resembles those on the sketches for the Fourth in the Stanford University Library and Newberry Library, as well as the so-called 'First Sketches' for the Third Symphony in the Österreichische Nationalbibliothek and others, it is possible that Alma dispersed these sketches at the same time.

TABLE 6.1. *An analysis of short-score sketches for the first movement*

Private Source

Page	Staves	Bars	Correlation with the completed work (bars)
'I' r[a]	1–4	all	1–11
	6–9	all	12–21
	11–14	all	22–30
	16–19	all	31–8
'I' v	1–4	all	39–50
	6–9	all	51–60
	11–14	1	61
		2–3	62
		4–7	63–6
	16–19	all	67–76

[a] This page bears the dedication 'Skizzenblatt aus der IV. Symphonie/Alma Maria Mahler'.

addition, Mahler's hand is regular and neat, thus reinforcing the consistency that he attempted at this stage of the compositional process.

This leaf for the first movement resembles the opening of the short score of the third movement. Like the latter, it bears a close relationship with the completed work except for the third system of the second page ('I' verso), where the correspondence with the symphony begins to disintegrate. While the first bar of the third system is analogous to bar 61, the next is related to, but not the same as, bar 62. As shown in Ex. 6.1, bar 62 is in $\frac{2}{4}$, not $\frac{4}{4}$, and the harmony is clearly A major. The bar in the following passage of the short score extends for eight beats—two bars in $\frac{4}{4}$—and moves to F sharp minor.

Mahler crossed out the first violin on stave 13 after the first two beats, and placed an arrow after the last crossed-out note of the third bar to indicate that the part continues at the beginning of the fourth bar. While he revised the harmony later, he retained the same sixteenth-note figure and bass line in the symphony as found in the sketch. He also removed the same figure in stave 12 (see Ex. 6.2), eliminating it from the analogue to bar 60 (on stave 7), and revised the rhythm of the figure under it on stave 8.

Details like these accompaniment figures concern Mahler in this sketch. He notated the figuration found in this section of the movement predominately in half and quarter notes, unlike the more refined articulations found in the completed work. At the same time, the barring of bars 41 and 42 of the short score differs from that in the symphony. Mahler reversed the metre signatures in the symphony so that the repeated notes of the theme occur in the same bar, making them consistent with the first appearance of the figure at bar 38. It is interesting to note that the $\frac{2}{4}\frac{4}{4}$ order seems to be a second

Ex. 6.1. (*a*) Short-score sketch page '1' verso for the 1st movt., sts. 11–15, bb. 1–4 (analogue to bb. 61–3); (*b*) Fourth Symphony, 1st movt., b. 62 (reduction)

(*a*)

(*b*)

Ex. 6.2. Short-score sketch page '1' verso, sts. 6–9, bb. 8–10 (analogue to bb. 58–60)

thought, since the upper numerals were originally 4 and 2, thus implying $\frac{4}{4}\frac{2}{4}$, the order eventually used in the completed work.

As to other details, this manuscript reflects a stage between the preliminary sketches and the draft score. While Mahler still used the trill sign in this sketch over the first of a group of four repeated eighth notes as a shorthand for the triplet-sixteenth notes plus three eighth notes on the first page, he wrote out the triplet sixteenths on the second. Similarly, the grupetto figure in the main theme occurs in sixteenth notes on the first page, without the extra beam to make them thirty-second notes. He did, however notate thirty-second notes on the second page. Such inconsistencies are relatively minor, and characteristic of this phase of composition, in which Mahler takes the music of the preliminary sketches further, but not to the degree of refinement found in the draft score or fair copy.

While it is more uniform and consistent than the preliminary sketches, this short-score sketch still anticipates the composition of the first orchestral draft. Certain ideas are clearly present from the start in this score, like the sixteenth-note figure for clarinet in the second bar. At the same time, the sixteenth-note figure marked—and not crossed out—for cello in the next bar is evidence of more transitional thought. It is even possible to observe Mahler's creative process at the end of the second page of the sketch, where he originally placed the entrance of the violin with the main theme in the analogue to bar 75, not 76, as occurs in the symphony. In this sketch he crosses out both the theme and the indication 'Geigen' ('violins') in bar 75, instead placing them in the next measure. A similar process is evident in the sixteenth-note figure below in the same bar, where he had originally written a descending figure. Abandoning it, he wrote on stave 20 the more static figure that occurs in the completed movement.

Structural Considerations of the Third-Movement Short Score

The short score for the third movement includes a title-page inscribed '2. Satz' ('second movement') in brown crayon with the figure '3' written over the '2' in *Blaustift*.[4] This kind of exchange of figures occurs later in the draft-score style Scherzo manuscript, which is thereby made the third, not second, movement. Thus, even in the preparation of this manuscript, Mahler may still not have established the final order of movements.

Despite any confusion about its place in the Fourth Symphony, however, the content of the slow movement is well established in the short score, as shown in Table 6.2. Nevertheless, Mahler added several bars in various places when he composed the draft score. This is especially noticeable at the end of the movement, where he extended the coda beyond what he had sketched

---

[4] See ibid. 104.

TABLE 6.2. *An analysis of short-score sketches for the third movement*
Pierpont Morgan Library, New York City

Page	Staves	Bars	Correlation with the completed work (bars)
1r	1–4	all	1–8
	6–9 (5–10)	all	19–36
	11–16	all	37–54
	18–21	all	55–63
1v[a]			
2r	1–3	all	62–72
	5–7	all	72–80
	9–12	all	81–90
	13–17	all	91–105
	18–21	all	105–6
2v	111–12		
3	1–5	all	107–21
	6–9 (10)	all	122–33
	11–15	all	134–45
	16–21	all	146–50
Einlage 3			
	1–6	all	151–65
	9–14	all	166–70
	20–1	all	171–8
	22–3	all	179–81
4	1–4	1–2	179–80
		3–12	182–91
	6–9	all	192–201
	11–15	all	202–12
	16–19	all	213–21
5	1–4	all	222–40
	6–9	all	241–57
	11–14	1–5	258–62
		5–10	none
		11–14	283–90
	16–20	1–5	291–5
		6–12	none
Einlage 5			
	1–5	all	261–73
	6–11	all	274–82
6	1–4	all	296–317
	6–9	1–16	318–33
		17–21	none
	11–18	all	334–50

[a] See Ch. 5, Table 5.5.

earlier. It seems that he began to solidify in this short score the connection between the end of this movement and the Song-Finale through the structure of the coda. In fact Mahler extended the coda further in the draft score by writing out the prolongation of the final chord, rather than retaining the fermata found in the short score.

While virtually the entire movement can be found in the short score, the ten pages of the Pierpont Morgan manuscript represent multiple stages of composition. Folio 2 verso (only in the fair copy does continuous pagination occur) contains a rough form of two bars notated more precisely on page 3, and the reverse of page 1 contains the preliminary sketch of the second theme, while the other eight pages comprise the entirety of the short score. Of those eight folios, two are insertions that Mahler apparently added after the completion of each. He must have written the page labelled 'Einlage 3' after completing folio 4, just as he probably composed 'Einlage 5' following the completion of folio 5. It is likely that he composed the short score on pages 1 to 6, reviewed his work, and added the two 'insertion' sheets later. It is possible to posit a scenario in which these six folios constitute an earlier conception of the movement, one without either of the folios inscribed as 'Einlage'. If so, this may represent Mahler's initial impulse in the composition of the movement, as shown in Table 6.3.

Exactly when Mahler composed each insertion is not as important as why he did so. Upon examining the initial conception of the movement and comparing it with the final structure, it seems that the composer added the music found on 'Einlage 3' for the sake of balance. On page 3 he varied the first and second period of the first theme but not the concluding period. It is likely that he wanted this variation of the first theme to balance the variation of the second, which follows on folio 4. Mahler would have returned to the variation of the first theme some time after completing the second, then added the variation of the concluding period in order to round out the structure of the movement.

As Hefling points out, the variation found on 'Einlage 5' is based on the preliminary sketch in C major in the Österreichische Nationalbibliothek.[5] Since both sides of that leaf end in G major, the variation is related to the passage on folio 5 where Mahler modulates to that key. This is the point at which he marked the insertion in the short score, since he circled the fourth and fifth bars of the fourth system of folio 5 to signal it.

Regarding the provenance of this passage, it is likely that Mahler completed folios 5 and 6, then composed the preliminary sketch for the variation in ink—like most of the short score—after which he would have been able to use it in the composition of 'Einlage 5', which contains all the music sketched on the earlier manuscript. 'Einlage 5' begins with a version

[5] Ibid. 117.

TABLE 6.3. *A reconstruction of an early conception of the slow movement*

Page	Staves	Bars[a]	Correlation with the completed work (bars)	Key
1r	1–4 6–9	1–18	Theme 1, Period 1, Phrases 1 and 2	G major
	(5–10)	19–36	Period 1, Phrase 3, Period 2, Phrase 1	G major
	11–16	37–54	Period 2, Phrases 2 and 3	G major
	18–21	55–63	Concluding period	G major
2r	1–3	62–72	Theme 2, Period 1	E minor
	5–7	72–80	Theme 2, Period 1 Period 2	E minor E minor
	9–12	81–90	Period 2	E minor
	13–17	91–105	Concluding period	D minor
	18–21	105–6	Concluding period (cadence)	D minor
3	1–5	107–21	Theme 1 (varied), Period 1	G major
	6–9 (10)	122–33	Period 1	G major
	11–15	134–45	Period 2	G major
	16–21	146–50	Period 2	G major
4	1–4	179–80, 181–2	Theme 2 (varied), Period 1	G minor
	6–9	192–201	Period 2	C sharp minor
	11–15	202–12	Concluding period	F sharp minor
	16–29	213–21	Concluding period	F sharp minor
5	1–4	222–40	Theme 1 (varied) $\frac{3}{4}$ Variation	G major
	6–9	241–57	$\frac{3}{8}$ Variation	G major
	11–14	283–95	$\frac{4}{4}$ Variation	G major
	16–20	291–5	(continued)	G major
6	1–4	296–317	(continued)	G major
	6–9	318–33	Coda (first part)	E major
	11–18	334–50	Coda (second part)	G major

[a] Bars corresponding to the completed movement.

of the analogue to bars 261–2, which he had begun on folio 5 of the short score.

His reason for composing this variation seems to have been less for formal balance, as with 'Einlage 3', than for tonal balance. After all, this is the variation Mahler had originally sketched in C major and marked for transposition to E major. Changing the tonality of the variation in this way, he anticipated the E major outburst in the coda of the movement—and thus the conclusion of the Song-Finale. Moreover, by using E major in the final variation of the theme in G major he balanced the E minor of the second theme, and also connected the two tonal areas of the movement in this final variation through the use of the same tonal centre.

Composing the Third-Movement Short Score

Throughout the eight pages of the short score it is possible to perceive a gradual change in Mahler's approach to the third movement.[6] The first two pages, where he sketched the first and second themes of the movement, bear a close relationship to the completed work. Upon comparing the first page with the symphony, it is possible to account for almost every note. The second page is similarly clear; the single major difference occurs in the two bars of the second system that Mahler placed in parentheses and connected with an arrow to its revision at the bottom of the page. (See Ex. 6.3.)

At the end of the second folio Mahler began to sketch the first variation of the first theme. This is confirmed by the marking *alla breve*, and figuration related to the first theme found under it. Since no clear beginning to this variation exists on the second folio, it may be that he stopped working on the short score at this point, and took it up again later. When he returned to the short score, Mahler appears to have resumed where he had left off, starting the third page with the *alla breve* indication and the key signature of a single sharp. While

Ex. 6.3. Short-score sketch page '2' for the 3rd movt.: (*a*) sts. 5–7, bb. 4–5 (analogue to b. 75); (*b*) sts. 21–3, b. 5, replacement for (*a*) (analogue to b. 75)

[6] Hefling describes the manuscript ('Variations', 103) and also provides an analysis of its contents (p. 104).

Ex. 6.4. (*a*) Short-score sketch page '2' for the 3rd movt., sts. 23–4, bb. 6–8 (analogue to bb. 107–8); (*b*) sketch page '3' for the 3rd movt., st. 4, bb. 1–2 (analogue to bb. 107–8)

(*a*)

(*b*)

it is possible to infer G major in the fragmentary sketch at the bottom of folio 2 (see Ex. 6.4), it is important to note that he established the key more convincingly at the beginning of folio 3 by supplying the harmony implicit in the bass figure. In using G major at this point, it seems that he decided to proceed with the variation of the first theme rather than continuing with the second.

The music on folio 3 corresponds to the completed work, and this may be the result of later revisions, made in pencil rather than the ink of the earlier part of the manuscript. Such pencil revisions occur in the fifth and sixth bars of stave 4, where the added bass resembles the one that is found in the completed work. It should be noted, however, that the pencil sketch in the ninth to thirteenth bars of the first stave is not part of the completed symphony. Other differences between the short score page 3 and the completed work occur in the bass line. In the ninth bar of the first system (analogue to b. 115), the last note does not occur in the finished work and the bass in the next bars was revised later. Mahler also altered the rhythm of the last bar of the same system in the symphony, where he changed the first note from a half to a quarter note followed by a quarter rest.

Such divergences continue in the seventh to tenth bars of the second system, where Mahler had not yet sketched the bass that he eventually included in the completed movement. The second system of folio 3 contains a contrapuntal development of the theme and does not involve the bass figure. When he resumed the bass in the first two bars of the third system (analogue to bb. 134–5), he composed two lines eventually eliminated from the work, as shown in Ex. 6.5. Instead of the scale motion sketched in the bass at this point, he continued with disjunct motion in bar 134, but retained the half-note motion of the sketch in the next bar. Similarly, he altered the half note in the penultimate bar of the third system to a quarter note followed by a

Ex. 6.5. Short-score sketch page '3' for the 3rd movt., sts. 11–15, bb. 1–2 (analogue to bb. 134–5)

quarter rest, as though he wanted to make it consistent with the opening of the movement.

The sketch trails off in the fourth system with only five bars, with 'Einlage 3' indicated at the end of that system. Continuing from the bass line he had written under the fourth bar of the fourth system, Mahler introduced figuration that forms the basis for yet another system (the fifth) on staves 21–4 of page 3. He used figuration from the first movement in the fourth bar of the fifth system, having recalled at that point the 'bass motif' from bars 148–9 of the preceding movement. The last three bars of the fifth system, which resemble the first three bars of the third system, represent an apparently abortive attempt to continue on this page.

Mahler began the sketch 'Einlage 3' with a clearer hand than he had left on folio 3. This manuscript contains further notes for orchestration, since he indicated doublings for horn and cello as well as viola and bassoon. In addition, he even wrote 'Cl.' for clarinet in the fifth stave, but abandoned the part in the finished movement. While the sustained pitches of the clarinet part would have enriched the timbre of the passage, Mahler may not have wanted a thicker texture at this point and must have eliminated the line at some point later in the compositional process.

He also marked the first stave of 'Einlage 3' for first violin, an indication that he carried out in the completed work. This corresponds to the marking '1. Geige' ('first violin') above the second bar of the first system, along with the indication 'G-Saite' (G string). He also designated the third bar from the end of the first system (analogue to b. 163) for '2. Geige' ('second violin') on stave 3, and also marked the clarinet for the final bar of this system (analogue to b. 165). The only other such indications on this page are the ones under the first system for bassoon (analogue to bb. 162–3) and horn (analogue to bb. 164–6); he eventually retained the latter, not the former.

In all, the entire first system and first five bars of the second system of the insert page 'Einlage 3' bear a close relationship to the completed work. In the eighth and ninth bars of the first system, however, each whole note of the bass line of the short score is changed to a quarter note followed by three beats of rest. At the beginning of the sixth bar of the second system, however, Mahler placed a single stroke just to the left of the barline; he even circled the eighth to tenth bars of this system in crayon, signalling it for revision. At the end of the second system, he also sketched the beginning of the variation of the second theme, having written the key signature of two flats and the time signature $\frac{4}{4}$ in the tenth stave, along with music eventually given to the oboe and cor anglais. He wrote the horn part in the ninth stave, but at some point circled the penultimate bar, which he eventually rejected by the time he completed the fair copy.

Having apparently abandoned the passage at the end of folio 3, Mahler had yet to compose a satisfactory transition to the variation after the one on 'Einlage 3'. The broad outlines of such a transition may be found in the sixth and seventh, as well as ninth and tenth, bars of the second system. The pitch E♭ predominates in the sketch in this system, since the transition is essentially an elaboration on that single pitch, which leads to the D in the bar before the variation of the second theme (bb. 179 ff.).

The rest of the page consists of further efforts to compose a satisfactory transition. Among these attempts is the one in staves 19–20, which is a synthesis of ideas found earlier on the page, and in which the note values are twice as short as the ones used in the completed movement. Another sketch of a transition occurs on staves 20–1, which correspond to bars 171–4 of the symphony, and which are related to a further attempt on staves 22–4. He crossed out the fourth bar of the latter, and revised the passage after a double bar. Here Mahler exercised his self-critical faculty as he worked through ideas to make them fit better.

Lacking the fullness of texture found in the earlier pages of the short score, folio 4 contains the primary melodic material and most of the two-part counterpoint of the subsequent variation. While a more direct correspondence exists between this short-score page and the symphony than 'Einlage 3' and the final work, folio 4 lacks the analogue to the horn part found in bar 179 in the first bar of the first system. In addition, the second bar differs from the completed work in that the line given to the cor anglais (stave 1) ascends rather than descends, as found in the finished movement. While the next bar, the analogue to bar 181, occurs in rudimentary form on 'Einlage 3', it has no such equivalent on folio 4, where the analogue to bar 180 proceeds directly to bar 182. Such a difference supports the hypothesis that Mahler began 'Einlage 3' after he started composing folio 4.

As he continued with folio 4, Mahler began the section as a single melodic line for a single instrument, not dividing it between two, as found in the

Ex. 6.6. (*a*) Short-score sketch page '4' for the 3rd movt., sts. 6–9, b. 1 (analogue to measure 192); (*b*) Fourth Symphony, 3rd movt., b. 192 (violin 1 and violin 2 parts)

symphony (see Ex. 6.6). A fuller texture occurs in the last five bars of the third system and continues in the fourth. In addition to the textural differences in the third system, the instrumentation diverges from that of the finished movement. Mahler indicated that contrabassoon and tuba be used in the last bar (analogue to b. 212) instead of the contrabass that he eventually used. (He retains the viola specified in the last bar, but doubles that part with cello instead of the clarinet suggested by his marking 'Cl.'.)

The timbre apparently continues in the fourth system (staves 16–20), and changes only near the end of the page. Mahler indicated the bass line in the uppermost stave of the seventh bar for cello, and may even have intended it to be doubled by clarinet, as shown by the crossed-out 'Cl.'. He also added timpani in the analogue to bar 220 (fourth system, b. 8), but did not incorporate that instrument into the completed movement.

In concluding folio 4, Mahler marked a double bar to suggest the beginning of the next variation. The new section bears the metre signature $\frac{3}{4}$ and the three notes in the bass correspond to the cello part in that part of the movement. He did not, however, indicate a key signature for the next variation, and perhaps intended to leave the music in G major.

Similarly, the second variation of the first theme on folio 5 also differs from the completed movement. He wrote the entirety of folio 5 in G major and $\frac{3}{8}$, which became in the completed work G minor at bars 222–62 and E major at bars 278–302. In addition, the $\frac{3}{4}$ metre signature at the end of folio 4 became $\frac{3}{8}$ in the completed movement. Mahler abandoned triple metre in the eleventh bar of the third system (analogue to b. 288), where he simply marked '4' as a shorthand for the $\frac{4}{4}$ in the symphony.

Among other changes made directly on this page is the tempo marking at the beginning of this sketch. Mahler had originally inscribed the section *Langsam*, writing over it *Andante*, the indication found in the fair copy. He had first written 'schneller' ('faster') near the end of the first system (analogue to b. 230), writing over it 'Alegretto' [*sic*], which he gives as 'Allegretto subito (nicht eilen)' ('Allegretto subito (don't rush)') in the symphony. Similarly, he had written 'Langsam' ('slowly') in the middle of the third system, marking 'Andante' over it, as retained in the completed work. The indication near the end of the third system, 'Poco Adagio', also occurs in the finished movement.

As to other differences, Mahler also reversed the pitches A and D in the eighth bar of the first system, altering the bass note to a single beat followed by two beats of rest, as shown in Ex. 6.7. In the second system of page 5 he rewrote the melodic line in bars 6–8. Having composed the original version of the passage a third lower, he drew a line through it and rewrote the part on the same stave starting on the pitch at which it occurs in the completed work.

Ex. 6.7. (*a*) Short-score sketch page '5' for the 3rd movt., sts. 1–4, b. 8 (analogue to b. 229); (*b*) Fourth Symphony, 3rd movt., b. 229 (cello part)

(*a*)

(*b*)

While less precise than other pages, this page contains the kind of continuity that is absent from earlier, preliminary sketches.

'Einlage 5' follows folio 5 in the manuscript, since it is intended as an insertion to the third system of that page at the circled fifth and sixth bars correspondingly marked 'Einlage'. Mahler begins the insertion where he left off by repeating the two circled bars on 'Einlage 5'. The latter page is a revision of the variation originally written in C major on the Österreichische Nationalbibliothek manuscript Mus. Hs. 4366. In taking that preliminary sketch into the short score, he transposed it to E major and clearly established the metre as $\frac{2}{4}$. In composing the short score he placed the melodic line on the second rather than the first stave of the first system, always keeping the principal thematic material in the uppermost stave of each system of the insertion page. He continued the variation in the second system, where he exchanged the upper two staves of the preliminary sketch in the first two bars and essentially rewrote the transition he had already composed (and blocked in a square labelled 'T', as discussed in the previous chapter).

The first system of 'Einlage 5' resembles the first two pages of the short score, and yet unlike some parts of those pages, it contains a number of indications for orchestration. The marking for woodwinds ('Holz') in the third bar of the first system is borne out in the symphony, but specific designations on the second stave do not carry into the completed work. Mahler went on to make additions in pencil in the first bar of the second system (analogue to b. 274), correcting what he had originally written in the third bar. He even sketched in pencil on the staves under the fourth bar, where he had circled his original version of the two treble parts, and marked them with 'Bleibt' ('let it remain' or 'stet').

The beginning of the next section, the 'Presto' at bar 5 of the second system, seems to have its basis in the concluding portion of the preliminary sketch, where the modulation to G major occurs. The bass in stave 9 is fragmentary and it is evident that Mahler wanted to incorporate the 'bass motif' from the first movement in this passage. As shown in Ex. 6.8, the 'bass motif' fits the music of this passage, but Mahler rejected it in favour of a bass more closely related to the figuration of the preceding section. Evidence of this change can be found on stave 14, near the centre of this page. Stave 16 contains another version of the bass, one related to the sixteenth-note figuration of the middle voices. Having abandoned that attempt, he sketched another bass underneath (on stave 18), and eventually incorporated it into the completed work.

Folio 6 starts with a version of the bars that Mahler had blocked off at the end of folio 5. He appears originally to have intended the analogue to bars 297–8 to be a single bar. The single vertical stroke through the connected bar of pitches A, B, C, and D shows the change from quarter notes to eighth notes. He also indicated where he wanted to establish the pitch C in the bass,

Ex. 6.8. (*a*) Short-score sketch page 'Einlage 5' for the 3rd movt., sts. 6–10, bb. 7–11 (passage with motif from the first movement); (*b*) Fourth Symphony, 1st movt., bb. 148–9 (cello and bass part), 'bass motif'; (*c*) Fourth Symphony, 1st movt., bb. 223–4 (trumpet part), 'bass motif' in the 'little call to order'

but did not write out the pedal point that begins at bar 299 of the movement. Likewise he wrote only the bass figure from F♮ to C in the analogue to bars 302–3, and failed to show the continuation of the bass C in the following bars of the short score.

Mahler sketched an entrance for harp in pencil in the analogue to bar 304 that he abandoned at some point later. In addition, he did not separate the coda with a double bar, as occurs before bar 315 of the finished movement. Neither did he indicate that the passage at the beginning of the coda is in E major, since the use of accidentals in the short score implies that he thought of the coda as still in G major.

Mahler also made an allusion to 'Das himmlische Leben' at the end of the first system of folio 8 (analogue to bb. 316–17). Here he returned to a fuller texture, and even gave more detailed indications of orchestration in the second system. After the fifth bar of the second system, however, he is not so explicit. Abandoning his notations for instrumentation, he seems to have intended the remainder of the movement for strings alone, as elsewhere in the third-movement short score, where no indications for scoring occur.

Mahler wrote in the left margin of the third system a phrase that appears to begin with the word 'Millionfach' ('a million times') and to continue with what could possibly be 'Tropfen' ('droplets'). This phrase may bear out a reference in the reminiscences of Bauer-Lechner to the fragments of the song into which he let the third movement disintegrate: 'wie wenn uns ein Regenbogen plötzlich in die Milliarden seiner tanzenden, immer wechselnden Tropfen zer-fiele und damit sein ganzer Bau zu schwanken und sich aufzulösen schiene' ('it is as if we saw a rainbow suddenly disintegrate into a billion dancing, ever-changing droplets and its entire arc waver and dissolve').[7]

Mahler scratched out part of the first five bars, yet the essence of the passage remains legible. Directly under the third system he marked its revision on the fourth system so that the first and second versions of the passage from bars 235 to 244 may be read one after the other. In the upper version of bars 234–5 he used repeated fourths in eighth notes of the bass, like those found earlier in the coda at bars 318–21. He did not include those figures in the symphony, but rewrote the ascending figure he had begun in the third stave of that system (stave 13) underneath in the fourth system (staves 16–18). After sketching the descending melodic line in the eighth to eleventh bars of the fourth system, he concluded the movement in the third system. While it contains the harmony and bass motion for the last bars of the movement, the short score only goes up to the analogue to bar 350. In the short score the movement ends on a D major chord, with its prolongation suggested by a fermata in the final bar of the third system instead of being written out, as found in the concluding bars of the completed work.

In all, the short score for the third movement is one of the most complete sets of sketches of Mahler's music that survive. Beyond the continuity associated with the short score, in this manuscript it is possible to find the relatively full textures of the completed movement and also indications of scoring that look ahead to the draft score for full orchestra. In taking his ideas from the preliminary sketches into the short score, Mahler refined more sharply his conception of the movement as he brought the music closer to completion.

[7] Bauer-Lechner, *Erinnerungen*, 163; *Recollections*, 152.

7. *Draft Score*

For Mahler the draft score or *Partiturentwurf* was the first full score of a symphony with individual parts clearly specified. While he had made indications for instrumentation sporadically in the early drafts, he realized those ideas concretely and consistently only in the draft score, where he also resolved many of the issues related to the continuity of the music so that he could give the work its final shape. Most importantly, the draft score gave Mahler the opportunity to attend to the details of instrumentation, dynamics, tempos, articulations, phrase markings, and other elements that would bring the music closer to performance. While a close correspondence often exists between the draft score and short score, Mahler could still revise the structure of the work later, in the fair copy.[1]

At another level, the completion of the draft score signalled for Mahler the end of what he would deem 'work' on a symphony. Bauer-Lechner reports that he finished the Fourth Symphony—that is, the draft score—on 5 August 1900, when he wrote on the last page of the slow movement 'Dritter Satz und somit die ganze Symphonie...beendet' ('the third movement and thus the entire symphony...finished').[2] While it remained for him to produce the fair copy and eventually publish the Fourth Symphony, the draft score was the last major phase of composition before those more final stages of work. Once he had arrived at the content of the music in draft score, the more open-ended side of composition was over.

For his draft scores, Mahler normally used oblong format, and usually inscribed the manuscript in ink. When revisions occur, they may be in pencil, crayon, or ink, and precede almost immediately the preparation of the fair copy. The paper Mahler used for the manuscript of the Fourth Symphony is similar to the kind that he used for the preliminary sketches and short score, but, like the latter, often included entire bifolio leaves instead of the torn single sheets associated with early work. At times he appended to the draft score alternative or supplementary pages, which he marked as 'Einlage', like those he appended to the short score.

It is imprudent to make generalizations about the extent to which Mahler would make revisions of the draft score. Having before him the first complete

---

[1] A notable exception is the revision of the draft score for the first movement of the Ninth Symphony. See Andraschke, *Gustav Mahler IX. Symphonie: Kompositionsprozess und Analyse*, 59–67.

[2] Gustav Mahler, Fourth Symphony, Draft score pages for the third movement (F-Pbmgm); see also Bauer-Lechner, *Erinnerungen*, 165; *Recollections*, 155.

score of the composition, he was able to evaluate the structure of the work for the first time and alter it according to his musical judgement. In the draft score of the Ninth Symphony, for example, Mahler made numerous changes in orchestration, phrasing, and even the form of the movements. In the second movement of that work, he revised the draft score by altering the order of material and cutting several passages. Such a revision of structure could not have occurred before this phase of work, and this led him directly to the way he presented the movement in the fair copy. This is not the only place where he eliminated material in the draft score of the Ninth Symphony. Approximately twenty-five bars were removed from the first movement before bar 314. A less drastic excision occurs in the draft score of the last movement of the Ninth, where the ending found in the last eighteen bars of the completed work occupies twenty-five bars in the draft score.[3]

Such changes represent rethinking that may not have been possible earlier in the compositional process, when continuity was still an issue. Only in taking the work this far could Mahler take it further; after arriving at an acceptable form of the movement, he would naturally try to improve it in the draft score before giving the work a more polished presentation in the fair copy. After he took the second movement of the Ninth Symphony into draft score, he realized a way to handle its structure differently and so revised it. A similar situation occurred with the ending of the last movement of the Ninth from draft score to fair copy.[4] In both cases, revision was not inevitable, but took place after Mahler saw the work for the first time in full score.

Reconstruction

Among the holdings of the Internationale Gustav Mahler Gesellschaft, Vienna, is a set of photocopies for fourteen pages of 'sketches', which were last known to have been in the possession of Anna Mahler. The sketches are on 18-, 20-, and 24-stave paper printed by Eberle ('J. E. & Co.'), in *Querformat* (oblong), and apparently 26.5 by 31 cm. These twelve pages are part of the draft score of the first movement of the Fourth.

As shown in Table 7.1, each of the three sets of four pages constitutes a two-leaf, four-page bifolio. Each folio is inscribed in Mahler's hand with an arabic numeral on the upper left-hand corner, and each page in a hand other than Mahler's with roman numerals. With respect to the latter, the order of the first two sets is reversed: pages Ia–Id comprise the bifolio Mahler numbered '3' and pages IIa–IId the one numbered '2' (pages IIIa–IIId are for the bifolio numbered '5').

---

[3] Andraschke, *Gustav Mahler IX. Symphonie.*

[4] James L. Zychowicz, 'The Adagio of Mahler's Ninth Symphony: A Preliminary Report on the Partiturentwurf', *Revue Mahler Review*, 1 (1987), 77–113.

TABLE 7.1. *Disposition of the* Partiturentwurf *sketches*

Internationale Gustav Mahler Gesellschaft, Ph 60

Page marked on IGMG Ph 60	Bifolio number designated by Mahler	Corresponding bars in the Fourth Symphony, first movement
Ia	3	65 (last half)–74
Ib		75–83
Ic		84–92
Id		93–101
IIa	2	32–9
IIb		40–7
IIc		48–56
IId		57–65 (first half)
IIIa	5	134–42
IIIb		143–51
IIIc		152–60
IIId		161–70

These pages contain music for one-third of the first movement, and extend to bar 170. Since they belong to the same draft score, it is reasonable to assume that a bifolio numbered '1' must have existed, and its four pages contained the opening of the movement (bb. 1–31) up to the beginning of bifolio '2'. Likewise, a bifolio numbered '4' must have contained bars 102–33, which would take the movement from bifolio '3' to the beginning of bifolio '5'.

These pages were part of a much larger manuscript that is no longer intact. Since Mahler must have continued with bifolio '6' and the remaining pages of the first movement, the manuscript must have encompassed the entirety of the first movement, as well as the two subsequent ones. After all, the final bifolio of the draft score for the slow movement exists, and on it Mahler refers to the completion of the first three movements in the note at the end. Since he numbered that bifolio for the third movement '7', six bifolios must have have preceded it, and he no doubt used another set of bifolios for the second movement. His explicit written comment about the completion of the Fourth at the end of the third movement indicated the end of work on the three instrumental movements; the symphony was complete when he finished the third movement because he had already composed the Finale as the orchestral song 'Das himmlische Leben'.[5]

The draft score of the first movement would have encompassed at least ten bifolio sheets (see Table 7.2). It is possible to estimate this by calculating the number of bars found on the first five bifolios and comparing that figure with the number of bars in the completed movement. One would project what

[5] He had already prepared an orchestral score of the song for the *5 Humoresken* and probably revised that score when he prepared the 'intermediary' manuscript of the song. See Ch. 4.

TABLE 7.2. *A reconstruction of the draft score of the first movement, bars 1–170*

Bifolio number	Bars in the first movement	Number of bars (bifolio)
(1)[a]	1–31	31
2	32–65 (first half)	$33\frac{1}{2}$
3	65 (second half)–101	$36\frac{1}{2}$
(4)[a]	102–33	32
5	134–70	37

[a] The location of the first and fourth bifolios is unknown.

must have been found on '1' and '4', then determine the average number of bars on each of the first five bifolios. Following this method, each bifolio would contain an average of thirty-four bars, and based on that average, at least ten bifolio sheets would have been necessary for the first movement, for a total of 340 bars. Since the movement is 349 bars long, it is likely that Mahler used eleven sheets, the last one only partially used. In fact, the latter estimate might be supported through the evidence of a manuscript associated with the no longer extant bifolio '10'.

Among the holdings of the Österreichische Nationalbibliothek is a page of the draft score that Mahler numbered 'Einlage 10' ('Insertion page 10'), constituting a draft of bars 323–41 of the coda. Because it is unusual to find 'Einlage' pages for the fair copy, it is likely that the insertion belonged to the draft score of the first movement. Even though the number of staves per system resembles the short score, the association of this sketch with the draft score is confirmed by the list of strings in score order at the beginning of the first system. Moreover, this insertion page does not correspond to the fair copy, since the passage between bars 232 and 241 occurs on the verso side of the first page of bifolio '14' of that manuscript. Bifolio '10' of the autograph full score contains bars 221–44 of the first movement, and page 10 contains the analogue to bars 68–73.

Further, had Mahler maintained the average number of bars per bifolio as he had used for the first five bifolios, it is likely that he would have written the 'Einlage' passage (bb. 323–41) on the tenth bifolio. Based on the average of thirty-four bars for each of the bifolios after the fifth, it is possible to make the following approximation:

Bifolio	Bars
6	171–204
7	205–38
8	239–72
9	273–306
10	307–40
11	341–9 (one side of a single sheet)

Using this projection as a point of reference, one may postulate that the passage in question would have occurred on the first side of the second leaf of the eleventh bifolio. Since the beginning of that passage (bb. 323–34) occurs in the first system of 'Einlage 10' (staves 1–7) and two alternative passages follow in the next two systems, it would not be difficult to regard the first system as a reduction of the full score at that point, since it occupies about as much space as it would in the draft score. Mahler probably copied out the beginning of the passage in order to establish a context for the subsequent alternative passages. Leaving off from that point, he wrote his first version of the transition to bar 341, marking it 'entweder' ('either') on the left margin (stave 12), and the second version 'oder' ('or') lower on the same margin (stave 18).

For the third movement, a single bifolio, the last, is extant and currently found among the holdings of the Bibliothèque Musicale Gustav Mahler, Paris. In numbering this bifolio, he crossed out the original number '6' and wrote '7' instead. It is likely that the third movement occupied seven bifolios. With seven bifolios, each bifolio would contain approximately fifty bars and each page an average of twelve bars. As such, the draft score would be disposed as follows:

Bifolio	Bars
1	1–55
2	56–110
3	111–65
4	166–220
5	221–75
6	276–325
7	326–52

This projection is also supported by evidence of an insertion page, the manuscript labelled Mus. Hs. 4366 in the Österreichische Nationalbibliothek. Written on both sides, one page (recto) is a preliminary sketch for bars 263–78 of the third movement (see Table 5.5), while the other (verso), inscribed 'Einlage zu Satz 4. Bogen 5 (Adagio)' ('Insertion to the fourth [*sic*] movement, leaf 5 (Adagio)'), is a fragment that belongs to the draft score. This leaf appears to have emended the no longer extant fifth bifolio (projected above to contain bars 221–75). Based on this projection, it seems likely that the verso of 'Einlage 5' clearly belongs to the draft score of the third movement. (Again it is rare to find a single leaf inscribed on both sides and, further, to have each side belong to a different stage of composition.)

No such fragments of a draft score exist for the Scherzo. However, a bifolio draft score in the manner of a full score is among the holdings of the Mahler–Rosé Collection of the University of Western Ontario.[6] This manu-

---

[6] Mahler, 'Fragment II Mvt IV Symphony (Scherzo)', C-Lu, Music Library, Mahler–Rosé Collection.

script is the one on which Mahler transposed the solo (scordatura) violin part to give to his copyist as a model for the rest of the movement. While the page resembles a draft score in that it is fully orchestrated, it is unlike the extant pages of the draft score for the other movements because it is upright (*Hochformat*), like the fair copy, instead of oblong (*Querformat*), like the rest of the actual draft score.

While the upright format would allow for fewer bars per page, it is still possible to estimate the number of pages required for the draft score of the Scherzo based on the evidence of the extant fragments. The fair copy of the second movement occupies ten bifolio sheets, the last only half used, and the draft score would thus occupy as many pages, if not fewer. Had Mahler included a copy of 'Das himmlische Leben' with the draft score of the first three movements, it could take up eight bifolio sheets, like the version that occurs with the *5 Humoresken* (1892). It is also possible that he used the copyist's manuscript (the 'intermediary' version) of the song with the draft score of the first three movements. The 'intermediary version' of the song (discussed in Ch. 3) is thirty-three pages long, and while the description of it does not indicate the number of bifolio sheets it occupies, the draft score would have taken up at least nine bifolios if Mahler used each available page.

Given these approximations, the draft score of the Fourth Symphony would have occupied approximately thirty-five bifolio sheets, or seventy leaves, in the following disposition:

First movement: 10 or 11 bifolio sheets (20 or 22 leaves)
Second movement: 10 bifolio sheets (20 leaves)
Third movement: 7 bifolio sheets (14 leaves)
Fourth movement: 8 or 9 bifolio sheets (16 or 18 leaves)

The draft score of the Fourth Symphony would thus have occupied as few as seventy leaves (thirty-five bifolio sheets) or seventy-four leaves (thirty-seven bifolio sheets). If Mahler had included a title-page on a single bifolio sheet, the total could be increased to seventy-one or seventy-five leaves. Based on these dimensions, it seems that the draft score was most likely the set of 'sketches' listed in Otto Albrecht's *Census* of manuscripts.[7] For item 1151 Albrecht lists 'sketches' for the Fourth Symphony, describing them as seventy-three leaves, 27 by 24.5 cm., which would correspond to thirty-six bifolio sheets along with a single leaf of another bifolio and the same size paper as Eberle's. This manuscript was in the possession of Alma Mahler at the time Albrecht compiled his *Census*, presumably between the time he began his compilation in 1928 and 1953, when he published it. Its present whereabouts is unknown.

[7] Otto E. Albrecht, *A Census of Autograph Musical Manuscripts of European Composers in American Libraries* (Philadelphia: University of Pennsylvania Press, 1953), 178.

First Movement

The three extant bifolio sheets of the first movement, '2', '3', and '5', bear a close relationship to the completed Fourth Symphony. As shown in Table 7.3, a direct correspondence exists between the extant pages of the draft score and the symphony except for the barring of the passage between bars 62 and 65. In the draft score, the passage consists entirely of $\frac{4}{4}$ bars with the two beats before the last (analogue to b. 66) in $\frac{2}{4}$. The placement of the $\frac{2}{4}$ bar is reversed in the completed work, occurring after bar 61 and the rest of the passage written in $\frac{4}{4}$ (see Ex. 7.1). While this is a relatively minor difference, the revision reflects a balancing of ideas: the rhythmic figures in bar 62 parallel those in bar 64, with such symmetry also occurring in bar 65, where the rhythmic figure on the first two beats is repeated on the second. The revised barring allows for the regular placement of agogic accents that underscore the classical idiom implicit in the first three movements.

The instrumentation of these draft-score pages is thicker than that found in the fair copy. Even though the *à 2* marking for the oboes in bar 34 of the draft score becomes *à 3* in the fair copy, doublings such as those between the second violin, viola, and clarinet in bars 34–7 are eliminated in the later version. Other changes occur between the draft score and the fair copy. The two parts

TABLE 7.3. *An analysis of sketches for the first movement draft score*

Internationale Gustav Mahler Gesellschaft, Ph 60

Bifolio	Page	Correlation to bars of the completed work
2	1r	32–9
	1v	40–7
	2r	48–56
	2v	57–65 (first half)
3	1r	65 (second half)–74
	1v	75–83
	2r	84–92
	2v	93–101
5	1r	134–42
	1v	143–51
	2r	152–60
	2v	161–70

Österreichische Nationalbibliothek, Ms. 30.898

Bifolio	Page	Staves	Correlation to bars of the completed work
Einlage 10	1r	1–7	323–35
		10–16	336–40 ('entweder')
		18–23	335–41 ('oder')

Ex. 7.1. (a) *Partiturentwurf* of the 1st movt, bifolio 2, page 2v (bb. 4–8) and bifolio 3, page 1r (bb. 1–2) (violin and clarinet parts removed); (b) Fourth Symphony, 1st movt, bb. 61–6 (violin and oboe parts)

given the horn in bar 42 of the draft score, for example, occur in the clarinet and the oboe in the completed work, with the choice of woodwinds over brass perhaps reflecting a more 'classical' sound. Similarly, the flute part in bar 45 of the draft score occurs in the first violin in the completed work. Yet this does not suggest a preference for strings, since the doubling of the oboe and viola parts in bar 96 is designated for solo oboe in the fair copy.

The draft score of the first movement also contains other revisions that oc-curred to Mahler as he worked through it. He marked some alterations by crossing out either in ink or in pencil and, as earlier in the compositional pro-cess, he circles passages that he wanted to reconsider (as with the doubling of the horn by the oboe in the analogue to bars 60–2). He would also mark a pos-sible change by indicating a different instrumentation that he wanted to try later. An example of the latter occurs in the analogue to bars 73–4, where Mahler circled the flute part, having written next to it 'I. Ob[.]?' ('First oboe?'). In the fair copy he eliminated the flute, and eventually gave the part to the clarinet instead of the oboe.

As his conception of the piece evolved, Mahler reduced the number of doublings in this symphony. This gradual refinement of sound becomes clear in a comparison of the fair copy with the extant pages of the draft score, and when it came to a choice of timbre, he preferred a more transparent sound. An example of this occurs in bars 67–8, where the texture of the two melodic parts with bass may be found in the draft score for clarinet, bass clarinet, bas-soon, horn (in bass clef), viola, and cello, which he subsequently reduced in the fair copy.

A similar revision of instrumentation occurs in the analogue to bars 80–3, where Mahler attempted to blend the woodwind and string sonorities through a harmonic figure in the horns. The horn parts are practically super-fluous, since the harmony they reinforce already exists in the other voices and the rhythmic figure they carry also occurs in the bassoon and lower strings. He circled the horn parts in the draft score and deleted them in the autograph (see Ex. 7.2). Had he left the horn parts as they are in the draft score, the sub-stance of the music would not have changed, but after eliminating the horn in bar 83, it was easier for him to bring out that tone colour later at bar 87.

In addition to orchestration, Mahler first worked through tempo markings in the draft score of the Fourth Symphony. For one, the relative paucity of tempo markings in the draft score suggests that this element is a relatively later addition. In fact, the extant pages of the draft score lack any tempo markings until the analogue to bars 51–3, where he writes 'Poco rit.' followed by 'a tempo' above the score. He retains both in the fair copy, as well as in subsequent revisions of the symphony. The marking 'rit.' in bar 54 occurs in later revisions of the Fourth, but he did not mark another 'a tempo' again. He indicated 'Poco rit.' and 'A tempo' over bars 57–8, but changed these markings in the fair copy. A single 'Rit.' occurs in the fair copy, but he moved

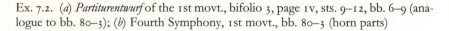

Ex. 7.2. (*a*) *Partiturentwurf* of the 1st movt., bifolio 3, page 1v, sts. 9–12, bb. 6–9 (analogue to bb. 80–3); (*b*) Fourth Symphony, 1st movt., bb. 80–3 (horn parts)

it from bar 56 to 57, and modified the marking to read 'plötzlich langsam und bedächtig (molto) meno mosso' ('suddenly slowly and deliberately (molto) meno mosso'). In making the latter change, he clearly delineates the second area and the closing of the exposition, differentiating between the two sections by giving each its own marking. The tempo marking in the fair copy is more specific, and suggests more concretely the character of the section.

At the same time, dynamics and other expression marks occur throughout the extant three bifolios of the draft score, but they are relatively few when compared with the fair copy, where Mahler is much more explicit. As with orchestration and tempo, the dynamic markings in the draft score are an approximation of the more specific indications he would make later. Some indications found in the fair copy, however, are already part of the draft score. The marking 'Schwungvoll' ('briskly'), for example, occurs in the analogue to bar 52, as does 'keck' ('boldly') in the violin part at bar 80. Performance indications such as slurs, accents, pizzicatos, and other markings are also part of the draft score.

Characteristic of this draft score is the trill sign over certain figures, and this notation connects the draft to the preliminary sketches, where it also occurs. In the fair copy Mahler replaced the trill sign with written-out sixteenth-note triplets, as at bar 82 of the first movement. Since the figure occurs regularly throughout the movement, the shorthand allowed Mahler to compose some passages relatively quickly because he did not need to write out the entire figure each time it occurred. This kind of notation is related to his use of the slash through the stem of a half or quarter note to indicate repeated eighth notes, as found in bars 89–91 of the draft score.

As mentioned above, the single sheet labelled 'Einlage 10' ('insertion to bifolio 10')[8] contains sketches Mahler used to work through a transition. More specifically, this sketch for bars 323–41 contains two ways of proceeding from the end of the recapitulation of the exposition-coda (at b. 323) to the coda for the entire movement (at b. 341), as shown in Table 7.3. As part of the recapitulation, it also corresponds to the return of material in the preliminary sketches just before the marking 'Schluß Coda' (preliminary sketch page '2').

After writing out the recapitulation of the exposition in the first system of 'Einlage 10' (staves 1–7), Mahler clearly marked his options, labelling the first solution 'entweder' ('either') on staves 10–15, and the second 'oder' ('or') on staves 18–23. In both attempts he reached the beginning of the passage that corresponds to the preliminary sketch for the 'Schluß Coda' at the end of each passage.

In preparing this transition, Mahler crossed out the first version of bar 335 (in the first system), but started each solution with the analogue to that bar, as found in the dotted-eighth, sixteenth-note figure in the bass. This suggests the version Mahler chose, since the analogue to bar 335 that belongs to the 'oder' solution is more closely related to that bar in the completed work. Yet the second bar of the 'entweder' solution diverges from bar 336 in its eighth-note motion. While the third bar of the latter option bears some relationship to bars 338–9, the resemblance ends in the last bar, where all the elements of the 'Schluß Coda' are present as a series of isolated fragments.

The 'oder' solution begins with a revision of bar 335 and bears a close resemblance to the same bar of the symphony. Mahler apparently decided to continue the eighth-note motion from the first two beats to the last two in the lower string parts, and also to sustain the chord found in the next bar. The second and third bars of this solution correspond to bars 336–8, but he appears to have revised the point from which he continued the passage in the next bars. As shown in Ex. 7.3, two layers of composition exist in this sketch, the apparent first inspiration in ink and its revision in pencil. The third and fourth bars of this solution correspond to bars 337 and 338, if the rhythm of the quarter notes is understood to follow the pencil markings in stave 20 and the figure in the third bar starts on the last three eighth notes of bar 338.

The last part of the fourth bar corresponds to bar 339 of the completed movement, when considered along with the continuation of eighth notes in this second solution. He crossed out the quarter notes, like those found in

---

[8] Mahler, 'Skizzen', A-Wn, MS 30.898. This manuscript is on Eberle's no. 18, 18-stave paper and, like other pages of the draft score, in *Querformat* (oblong).

Ex. 7.3. Draft score of the 1st movt., 'Einlage 10': (*a*) sts. 18–23, bb. 4–7, ink with pencil markings indicated (analogue to bb. 338–41); (*b*) sts. 18–23, bb. 4–7, 'original' conception of the passage—ink draft only (analogue to bb. 338–41); (*c*) Fourth Symphony, 1st movt., bb. 338–41 (reduction)

(*a*)

(*b*)

Ex. 7.3 contd.

(*c*)

the fourth bar of the 'entweder' solution, then divided the bar, keeping the last two beats silent. The fifth bar begins with two quarter-note figures marked in pencil on stave 18, the first note of the main theme starting on the second beat. The last bar of this sketch resembles bar 341 of the completed work, which corresponds to the beginning of the 'Schluß Coda' in the preliminary sketch.

Mahler called attention to the first option by circling it on this page, and this usually indicates something that he intended to revise. In this case, however, he decided to exclude, rather than include, that choice from the sketch page, since the stricken last bar of the first system and the entirety of the second do not belong to the completed work. At the same time, he did not accept the 'oder' solution without revising it by incorporating the changes he had made in pencil on 'Einlage 10'. His intention to reconsider the second option is evident in the question mark placed over the horn part in the fourth bar. Proceeding with the change he had made in pencil, including the rebarring of the fifth bar, he found a satisfactory solution for the transition to the final coda of the movement at a rather late stage in the compositional process. While he usually handled such problems in the short score, what he had already composed may not have been satisfactory when he took the material into the draft score. As with other sketches for transitions, this sketch shows Mahler at work, as he improved on an otherwise acceptable passage in this late insertion to the draft score.

Second Movement

The draft score for the Fourth Symphony would have been written on the same kind of paper throughout, as occurs in the extant pages of the draft score of the first and third movements, that is Eberle's no. 18, 18-stave paper in *Querformat* (oblong). Yet the extant Scherzo pages that may be classified as a draft score do not match the ones for the first and third movements. Rather, the manuscript of the Scherzo is another kind of draft in the manner of a full score. The difference lies in the format of the page, the manuscript in question being in *Hochformat* (upright) and on Eberle's no. 5, a watermark paper (see

F IG . 7.1. Gustav Mahler, 'Skizze zur 4. Symphonie', Österreichische Nationalbibliothek, Mus. Hs. 30.898, 'Einlage 10'

Fig. 7.1) that Mahler used for the fair copy. This paper differs in format from Eberle's no. 18, and also is a heavier, higher quality paper, more appropriate to a finished work than to a draft. Since the paper for this manuscript is the same kind used for the fair copy, it is reasonable to assume that Mahler composed it later, perhaps as a model for his copyist to follow.

This draft of the Scherzo is a single bifolio sheet with all four pages inscribed and the accompanying solo violin part (written on one page of the same paper) dated 29 December 1900. The circumstances of its composition are implicit in the dedication of the part to the violinist Arnold Rosé, in which Mahler recalls the work on this movement that he accomplished with his friend. Despite the fact that Mahler conducted the *Ring* cycle before Christmas 1900, he was ill for a performance of *Lohengrin* on 27 December, and the concertmaster Franz Schalk had to conduct in his place.[9] It was at this time that he must have worked on the Scherzo with Rosé.

In her comments about Mahler's work on the Fourth earlier that month, Bauer-Lechner recalled that he had been dissatisfied with the Scherzo. He decided only in December 1900 to use scordatura tuning for the solo violin, as is evident in Bauer-Lechner's entry for 17 December: 'He is altering the violin solo of the Scherzo by having the instrument tuned a tone higher, and rewriting the part in D minor instead of E minor. This makes it screeching and rough-sounding, "as if Death were fiddling away".'[10] As an experienced violinist, Bauer-Lechner would have understood scordatura tuning even though she seems clearly mistaken about the key in this case.[11] In the London (Ontario) manuscript, Mahler wrote the solo part in B minor, the part in the score described as 'einen halben Ton höher gestimmt' ('tuned one half-step higher'). He must have changed his mind when he copied out the solo part on the accompanying sheet, which is in five flats (B flat minor), which would require tuning a *whole* step higher. Thus, Mahler does not seem to have been wrong in his transposition as much as he seems to have been experimenting with various tunings to accomplish the effect he had in mind.

In working with Rosé, Mahler wrote out this draft score and the solo part to provide the copyist with an example of the changes he wanted, and specifically showed the tuning at the beginning of the solo part. Unfortunately, he may not have proofread this manuscript, which he mistakenly and, perhaps unconsciously, numbered as the third movement ('3. Satz (Scherzo)'). This mistake had an almost disastrous effect on the production of the fair copy.

---

[9] La Grange, 'Gustav Mahler Chronologie' (unpublished manuscript).

[10] Bauer-Lechner, *Erinnerungen*, 179; *Recollections*, 162.

[11] Peter Franklin comments in his notes on Bauer-Lechner's account that the key she indicates is wrong: 'If the soloist is to tune his strings a whole tone higher than usual, the part must clearly be notated in the key a whole tone below that of the other instruments. This passage is interesting, however, in that the final version of the movement is in C minor.... Is Natalie mistaken here, or did Mahler originally conceive the Scherzo in E minor? Mahler might have come to feel that the Romantic "point" of a Scherzo in E minor and a Finale in E major was a little too obvious.' Bauer-Lechner, *Recollections*, 222.

Since Mahler probably presented this draft to the copyist as a final one, the copyist must have taken the numbering as a revision. While Mahler corrected the order of the movements in the fair copy, he also expressed his profound fear about the fate of his music if it were left in the hands of those who could not fully comprehend his intentions.[12]

More importantly, an analysis of the contents of this draft score reveals the vastly different conception of the movement that Mahler must have had prior to the completion of the fair copy. While a correlation exists between this manuscript and the completed work (see Table 7.4), the timbre was changed drastically in the fair copy, in which Mahler exchanged the woodwind and string parts. This results in a different sound, and the resulting timbre may have precipitated a further revision. In this manuscript the string parts contain an extensive and pervasive accompaniment figure that Mahler abandoned in the fair copy. (See Ex. 7.4.)

By removing the accompaniment figure from bars 7–22 Mahler thinned the texture strikingly. In the draft score he had placed the flute, oboe, and bassoon parts in counterpoint to the solo violin, and then supported this texture with a harmonic accompaniment, thus creating a counterpoint of textures. While the full chords of the accompaniment confirm the harmonic motion of the parts above, they are otherwise inconsequential to the passage. Even though Mahler marked the accompaniment *pizzicato* and indicated a softer dynamic level for the string parts, this accompaniment nevertheless intrudes upon the other parts, which occupy the same range and tessitura. In December 1900 or soon thereafter Mahler appears to have become aware of the weaknesses in the texture, and Bauer-Lechner reported his decision to use scordatura tuning for the solo violin: 'he must alter the part-writing in the second movement. As a result of the pause between Aussee and Mayernigg, it has become too elaborate and overgrown—"like limbs without ganglia".'[13]

TABLE 7.4. *An analysis of sketches for the second movement (Scherzo), draft-score-style score*

Mahler–Rosé Collection, University of Western Ontario, London, Ontario

Bifolio	Page	Correlation to bars of the completed work
unnumbered	1r	1–6
	1v	7–15
	2r	16–25
	2v	26–33

[12] La Grange, *Mahler* (1973), 614; *Mahler: Chronique d'une vie*, ii. 67.

[13] Bauer-Lechner, *Erinnerungen*, 179; *Recollections*, 162. The entry occurs after the one dated 17 Dec. [1900].

Ex. 7.4. (*a*) Draft-score-style score for the Scherzo, page 1v, sts. 12–16, bb. 1–8 (analogue to bb. 7–14); (*b*) Fourth Symphony, 2nd movt., bb. 28–30 (accompaniment pattern); (*c*) Fourth Symphony, 2nd movt., bb. 60–3 (accompaniment pattern)

(*a*)

(*b*)

(*c*)

When a contrapuntal passage such as this has, as further counterpoint, an accompaniment scored for a full complement of strings, it certainly is overgrown and excessive. Mahler eventually decided to eliminate this accompaniment in order to clarify the texture of the passage, and returned to it only where it would support the melodic content of the movement. This accompaniment occurs in bars 27–33 of the draft-score-like pages, where he treated it differently in the fair copy. He removed the accompaniment from the analogue to bar 27, probably in order to allow the solo violin to be heard more easily, but left the accompaniment in bars 2–30, where it supports a two-voice texture. When the third voice enters at bar 31, however, he eliminated the accompaniment, just as he had done earlier in the draft. Mahler may also have used such a harmonic accompaniment throughout the original draft score, as is evident in similar passages at bars 48 ff., 84 ff., 126 ff., 160 ff., 204 ff., 221 ff., and 254 ff.

Once having decided to reverse the woodwind and string parts, Mahler revised the score extensively. In bar 4, the flute part of the London manuscript becomes the violin part of the fair copy. He revised the later version, however, marking the passage for flute in the margin and, thus, returned to his earlier idea. In bars 7–13, too, the flute in the London draft becomes the viola part of the fair copy, just as the bassoon in bars 8–10 is given to the cello in the latter. Similarly, the bassoon part in bars 11–19 of the London manuscript is given to the violin in the completed work. Likewise, the passage for two flutes and *divisi* violas in bars 22–6 of the draft is scored for two oboes in the fair copy, with the cello in the same passage scored for bassoon.

Another difference apparent in the draft score concerns the solo violin part, which is not exactly as it is found in the fair copy. (See Ex. 7.5.) In

Ex. 7.5. (*a*) Fourth Symphony, draft-score-style score for the Scherzo, page 2r, st. 11, bb. 1–7 (analogue to bb. 16–22, solo violin part); (*b*) Fourth Symphony, 2nd movt., bb. 16–22 (solo violin part)

bars 17–21 the solo violin resembles the flute in bar 14 of the draft, while in bar 18 Mahler used the flute part of the draft in the violin. In bars 19–21 of the London manuscript he gave the flute part to the solo violin and transferred the solo violin part to the first violin (section). In addition, he changed the marking at the beginning of the movement, having added 'Ohne Hast' ('without rushing') to the marking 'in gemächlicher Bewegung' ('moving comfortably') already present in the draft. He also revised the dynamic markings to reflect the change in timbre, adding such nuances as 'Sordinen auf' ('remove mutes') in bars 31–2. By adding these details Mahler brought the Fourth Symphony nearer to performance.

Third Movement

The single bifolio of the draft score for the third movement (see Figs. 7.2–4) bears a close relationship to the completed Fourth Symphony (Fig. 7.5),[14] and this draft differs from the fair copy by a single bar (see Table 7.5). Specifically, this extant bifolio corresponds to bars 326–52 of the completed work without bar 353, which Mahler extended by one bar in the fair copy. Yet the draft score differs from the latter version in subtle ways. When he took the music into the fair copy, Mahler also revised both the timbre and the texture of the movement.

For one, he removed the bass parts in bars 326–31 and added a G to make a perfect fifth above the bass C in bars 332–5 and cancelled a C written an octave lower, perhaps to change the voicing of the original sonority. Likewise, he altered the D in bar 339 from a whole to a half note in the fair copy, having entirely removed the G he had written for the cellos and basses in bars 342–3 of the draft score. (See Ex. 7.6.) He also altered the horn parts in the same section (bb. 326–31) by changing the lower two horn parts (presumably the second and fourth) from treble to bass clef. Then, instead of moving from the sonority B and D♯ to F♯ and C♯, he sustained the perfect fifth that doubles the cellos in the fair copy. In addition, the doubling of the first flute and oboe in bars 333–5 is eliminated in the fair copy, thus further reducing the relatively heavy timbre conceived for the coda in the draft score.

Mahler also intended an ascending line for harp in the analogue to bars 340–2, and even indicated the need for a second harp. This is significant for the meaning with which Mahler invested the harp in some of his music. As some have pointed out, the harp connotes for Mahler the ascension to another, higher existence— 'heaven' in this case, as implicit in the text of the final movement.[15] Yet his doubts about adding a second part at this single place are evident in the question mark that follows the notation 'II. Harfe?'

[14] Gustav Mahler, 'Fourth Symphony' (F-Pbmgm, Collection of Henry-Louis de La Grange). This manuscript is on 18-stave paper made by Eberle ('J. E. & Co., No. 18').

[15] Donald Mitchell, *Mahler: Songs and Symphonies*, 129.

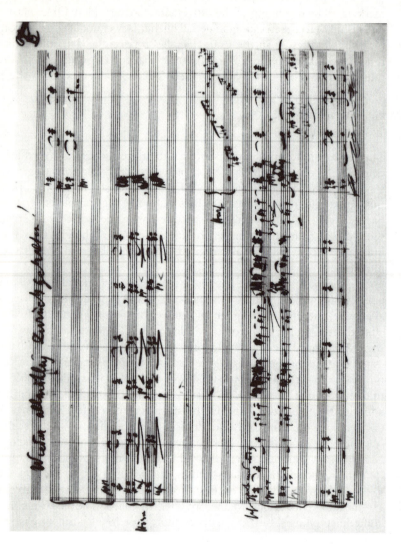
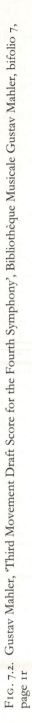

FIG. 7.2. Gustav Mahler, 'Third Movement Draft Score for the Fourth Symphony', Bibliothèque Musicale Gustav Mahler, bifolio 7, page 1r

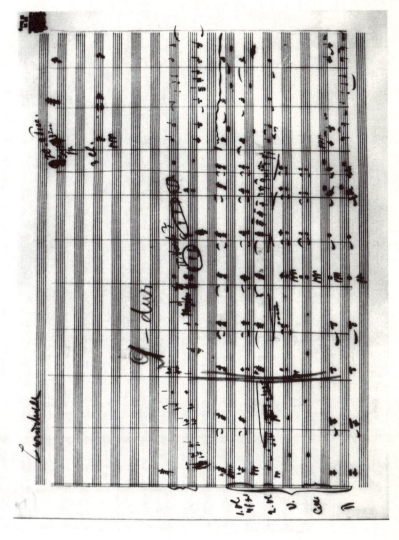

FIG. 7.3. Gustav Mahler, 'Third Movement Draft Score for the Fourth Symphony', Bibliothèque Musicale Gustav Mahler, bifolio 7, page IV

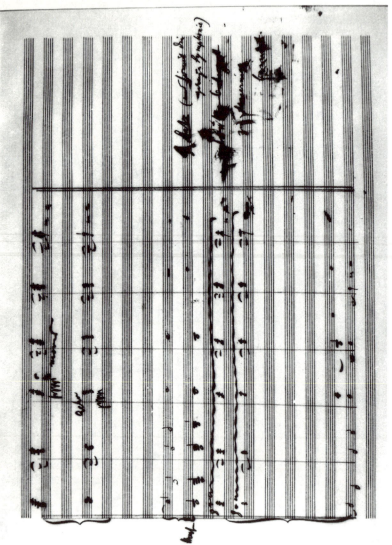

FIG. 7.4. Gustav Mahler, 'Third Movement Draft Score for the Fourth Symphony', Bibliothèque Musicale Gustav Mahler, bifolio 7, page 2r

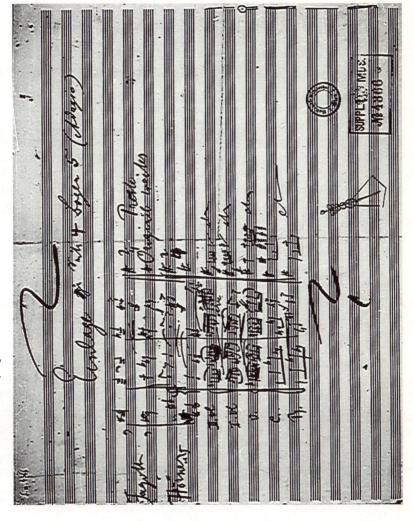

FIG. 7.5. Gustav Mahler, 'Skizze zur 4. Symphonie', Österreichische Nationalbibliothek, Mus. Hs. 4366

TABLE 7.5. *An analysis of sketches for the third-movement draft score*
Bibliothèque Musicale Gustav Mahler, Paris

Bifolio	Page[a]	Correlation to bars of the completed work
'7'	1r	326–35
	1v	336–46
	2r	347–52
	2v	blank

[a] The entire page is implied unless noted otherwise.

('second harp?'), as well as in his circling of the figure near that marking. In the fair copy and in all the subsequent revisions of the Fourth Symphony he neither used a second harp nor included that ascending figure.

Mahler also wrote 'G-Dur' ('G major') over bar 338 of the draft score, thus signalling a key change in the music. The notation might not have been completely necessary, but may have served as a reminder for the copyist, in order to ascertain that the key signature of four sharps (which should have occurred at the analogue to bar 315) is changed to a single sharp at this point in the movement.

With regard to the other page of draft score for this movement, the one that Mahler inscribed 'Einlage zu 4. Satz Bogen 5 (Adagio)' ('insertion page for the fourth movement, sheet 5 (Adagio)'), the inscription itself requires some explanation. By 'fourth movement' Mahler probably meant the last of the three movements preceding the Song-Finale, since the sheet clearly belongs to the third movement rather than to 'Das himmlische Leben' (see Table 7.6). 'Bogen 5' of the inscription must refer to the no longer extant fifth bifolio of the draft score for the slow movement.

The page marked 'Einlage 5' contains the transition to G major at the end of the passage between bars 263 and 278 of the completed work. Mahler had already determined the modulation to G major in the preliminary sketch on the reverse of this page, a variation in C major that he marked for transposition to E. It is not completely clear from this insertion page whether the passage before the double bar is in C major or E major. Mahler wrote F♯ in the bassoon part at the beginning of stave 5 and, since he employed key signatures for woodwinds (and not for trumpet, horn, and timpani), the accidental would not have been necessary if he had already modulated to E major. In the sketch for the transition on the reverse of this manuscript, however, he apparently chose the solution that begins with a C♮ in the treble, even when it was in C major (see Ex. 7.7). Although he altered the opening chord on this 'Einlage', it seems that the chord, an Italian augmented-sixth chord, would be appropriate to a passage in C major, since the chromatic motion is by half step to G, the dominant of C.

Ex. 7.6. (*a*) Draft score of the 3rd movt., bifolio 7, page 1r, sts. 5–18, bb. 1–7 (analogue to bb. 326–32); (*b*) Fourth Symphony, 3rd movt., bb. 326–31 (bassoon parts); (*c*) Fourth Symphony, 3rd movt., bb. 326–32 (cello and bass parts)

(*a*)

Ex. 7.6 contd.

(b)

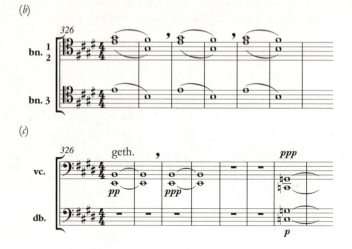

(c)

TABLE 7.6. *An analysis of sketches for the third movement* Partiturentwurf-Einlage

Österreichische Nationalbibliothek, Mus. Hs. 4366

Bifolio	Page[a]	Staves	Correlation to bars of the completed work
Einlage 5	1r		Preliminary sketches (modulation)
	1v	6–11	275–8

[a] The entire page is implied unless noted othewise.

Because the page is fragmentary and the inscription misleading in its reference to the fourth movement, it is possible that the manuscript emerged at a time when Mahler was not completely certain of his intentions and may have experimented with the passage. If he were planning to transpose the section, as suggested by the letters in the upper left-hand corner of the preliminary sketch on the reverse, he may have considered the modulation in order to determine whether he had to find yet another solution for the ending.

Upon closer examination, this insertion page resembles more closely the parallel passage as found in the short score than the later version in the fair copy. In this 'Einlage' sketch the rhythm of the bass part conforms with that notated under the system of the short score in which the same passage occurs. While a case could be made for Mahler's having proceeded directly from the preliminary sketch for the variation to this sketch, it is unlikely that he would have superseded the working-out of the passage in short score before attempting any kind of orchestral draft, even one as brief as this.

Upon comparing this 'Einlage' page with the fair copy, the differences include the use of descending sixteenth-note figuration in the analogue to bar 277, an element lacking in the insertion page, along with the continuation of the chromatically descending octaves in the bass on the beat before bar 278. Moreover, the tonality is not the same, the fair copy being firmly in E major. Thus, the string parts in the analogue to bar 276 on this 'Einlage' are a major third lower than in the fair copy. In addition, the scoring differs, too, since the bass is not used at all and the cellos are not left *divisi*. At some point later Mahler rewrote the upper cello part on this page as the viola part in the fair copy, and he expanded the unison violin part on the insertion to violins in octaves in the fair copy.

This insertion page is evidence of some difficulties Mahler must have had in deciding on a passage like this. Since the parallel passage in the fair copy

Ex. 7.7. (*a*) Short-score sketch for the 3rd movt., 'Einlage 5', sts. 6–13, bb. 4–6 (analogue to bb. 276–8); (*b*) draft score of the 3rd movt., 'Einlage zu Satz 4. Bogen 5 (Adagio)', sts. 9–13, bb. 2–4 (analogue to bb. 276–8); (*c*) reduction of final version of 3rd movt., bb. 276–8

Ex. 7.7 contd.

(*b*)

(*c*)

bears none of the signs of indecision present here, he clearly needed to work out ideas like these and refine the details of instrumentation. Evidence of the kind of indecision found on this page is completely absent in the fair copy, and this points up the importance of the draft score in bringing to completion a work like the Fourth Symphony. It would be a relatively mechanical task for Mahler to use the draft score as the basis for the fair copy, a stage that often involved a copyist rather than the composer himself when it came to preparing the actual manuscript.

Since it was the first time that Mahler was able to review the new work in full score, the draft score represents a particularly important phase of work.

He was conscious of this, as is evident in his declaration of the completion of work on the Fourth Symphony when he finished the draft score. While it was possible for him to revise various elements of the music after working on this manuscript, he was just as likely to take large parts of the score into the fair copy. In general, the draft score bears a close relationship to the fair copy, and it is relatively rare to find divergences between the two. With the Fourth Symphony, the differences between the draft score and the fair copy are in detail, rather than in substance.

8. Fair Copy

The fair copy of the Fourth Symphony is the full score that Mahler used for the première of the work and also the basis for its first publication. In the draft score he had already completed the first orchestration of the work, but it remained for him to refine the score when he took the Fourth into the fair copy. While he might change the substance of the symphony at this point, such revision was rarer than the attention he gave to the details of scoring, dynamics, and other expressive elements, which he applied more consistently at this stage of composition.

Upon completing the draft score of the Fourth Symphony, which occurred in August, Mahler proceeded to work on the fair copy of the full score during the conducting season.[1] After Mahler completed the draft score of the first three movements of the Fourth Symphony on 5 August 1900, he spent only ten more days of vacation working on the fair copy before returning to Vienna on 15 August. The opera season commenced at the beginning of September and included new productions of *Così fan tutte* (4 October 1900) and *Il trovatore* (26 October 1900). That autumn Mahler also conducted four concerts of the Vienna Philharmonic as well as the Munich première of his Second Symphony (20 October 1900). Despite this schedule, he found time to work on the fair copy a little each day, as Bauer-Lechner attests.[2]

Mahler apparently rejected the draft score of the Scherzo in mid-December and began to rewrite the movement, based on earlier sketches. In the absence of the actual draft score, it is impossible to determine whether the final version resulted from complex revisions on the draft score itself or a decision to compose a completely new one. In any case, the fair copy of the Scherzo shows no evidence of being tentative except for its number, which accidentally made it the third, rather than the second, movement.

Regarding the reversal of movements, Mahler discovered the problem on 25 February 1901, the day after he had suffered a haemorrhage. It is doubtful that he continued to work on the Fourth in February, especially since he subsequently underwent an operation on 4 March. He took a short rest in Abbazia (Opatija) on 20 March, and returned to Vienna on 6 April. During this trip he wrote to Guido Adler about his progress on the fair copy, having stated that 'I live a little in the world of my Fourth, which I am readying for publica-

---

[1] Gustav Mahler, 'Symphony No. 4' (Fair Copy), A-Wgm, XIII.35824.
[2] Bauer-Lechner, *Erinnerungen*, 179; *Recollections*, 161.

tion, and to which I will put the finishing touches tomorrow or the day after'.[3] No evidence exists to show exactly when he finished the fair copy, but it is likely that he returned to Vienna with the score complete.

The preparation of parts followed, so that Mahler could write to his friend Nina Spiegler in mid-August concerning a reading of the symphony with the Vienna Philharmonic that would take place the following October.[4] He must have still been adding 'finishing touches' to the score in late summer, since Bauer-Lechner wrote on 20 August 1901 about Mahler's concern that the Fourth was not clear enough ('noch nicht scharf genug').[5] No doubt, he returned to the score several more times before its first reading in October, as well as before its première on 25 November 1901.

The fair copy of Mahler's Fourth Symphony consists of ninety-one leaves, that is, forty-five bifolio sheets and a single ripped bifolio, comprising 182 pages in all. The paper is Eberle's no. 5, 18-stave paper in *Hochformat* (upright), a higher quality paper that bears the watermark 'J. E. & Co., Wien'. (The disposition of the manuscript is given in Table 8.1.) The bifolios of each movement are numbered, along with a continuous pagination for the entire symphony.

The date of completion of the Scherzo is given on the last page of that movement—5 January 1901—and the only other similar annotation is the undated marking 'Ende der Symphonie' on the last page of the fourth movement. As to the date of the Scherzo, it reflects relatively quick work, as Mahler inscribed in his dedication of the solo violin part '29 December 1900', as related above. He must have proceeded rapidly with his final refinements of the movement once he had worked with the violinist Arnold Rosé (who was also his brother-in-law) on the tunings for the scordatura part.

The fair copy also includes the crossed-out marking on the first page of the Scherzo: 'Anm. f. d. Dir.: 3 Achteln Schlage' (that is, 'Anm[erkung] f[ür] d[en] Dir[igenten]') ('Note for the conductor: [Beat] three eighth notes'). While this indication would militate against an excessively fast tempo, Mahler abandoned it in lieu of more conventional tempo markings in the score. One further marking exists in the fair copy. At the beginning of the Song-Finale he inscribed a list of numbers that corresponds to the number of bifolios for the symphony:

15
10
11
8
—
44

---

[3] Edward R. Reilly, *Gustav Mahler und Guido Adler: Zur Geschichte einer Freundschaft* (Vienna: Universal Edition, 1978), 35–6; *Gustav Mahler and Guido Adler: Records of a Friendship* (New York: Cambridge University Press, 1982), 96.

[4] Mahler, *Briefe*, 263; *Selected Letters*, 254.

[5] Bauer-Lechner, 'Mahleriana' (unpublished manuscript), F-Pbmgm, Collection of Henry-Louis de La Grange.

TABLE 8.1. *Disposition of the fair copy*
Gesellschaft der Musikfreunde, Vienna, XIII.35824

Movement	Bifolio	Bars
First	1	1–24
	2	25–49
	3	50–73
	4	74–98
	5	99–123
	6	124–48
	7	149–72
	8	173–96
	9	197–220
	10	221–44
	11	245–68
	12	269–93
	13	294–316
	14	317–40
	15	341–9
Second	1	1–33
	2	34–66
	3	67–101
	4	102–30
	5	131–76
	6	177–214
	7	215–260
	8	261–306
	9	307–45
	10	346–55
Third	1	1–33
	2	34–66
	3	67–96
	4	97–130
	5	131–61
	6	162–98
	7	199–234
	8	235–74
	9	275–306
	10	307–34
	11	335–53
Fourth	1	1–22
	2	23–45
	3	46–65
	4	66–89
	5	90–114
	6	115–37
	7	138–61
	8	162–84

The First Movement

The alterations in the fair copy of the first movement show the refinement of detail Mahler accomplished at this stage of composition. For the most part, he revised various doublings that were part of the draft score to clarify the sound of the movement. In taking the oboe part at bars 38–9 into the fair copy, for example, he wrote the part in the score, but crossed it out at some point later. At times, a voicing found in the draft score does not occur in the fair copy, as with the clarinet and horns at bar 42, or the bassoon at bars 48–9. Sometimes he exchanged a part in the fair copy, as with the flute at bar 45 of the draft score, which is given to the first violin in the same bar of the fair copy. Elsewhere he reinstated in the fair copy alterations he had made in the draft score, as with the clarinet and third bassoon at bar 66, both of which he had crossed out in the draft score.

Within the fair copy itself, the doubling of the flute by the oboe in the first bar is crossed out in blue pencil (*Blaustift*). Likewise, Mahler adjusted the bass and cello parts at the opening of the movement to reflect a lighter sound. He further lightened the orchestration by crossing out in pencil the bassoon which had doubled the cello and bass parts in bars 16–17. Such a differentiation continues throughout the movement, reflecting a clarification of timbre, emphasizing pure colours, with doublings gradually giving way to single instruments on a part.

Another alteration occurs in bars 86–90, where Mahler had composed a part in repeated notes for the flutes (see Ex. 8.1). He excised this in the fair copy, and replaced it with the new passage inscribed in the upper margin. The first flute part appears to be superfluous, because the harmony contained in it, along with similar figuration, is already present in the orchestra, thus thickening an already full texture. He also removed the dotted-eighth, sixteenth-note figure from bars 158–9 of the development section, as shown in Ex. 8.2. Again, he seems to have done this in order to lighten the texture. While this is not, as in the former instance, a harmonic part, it is by no means crucial at this point of the development, where Mahler emphasized other motifs. An example of such thinning of texture occurs on the first page of the

Ex. 8.1. Fourth Symphony, 1st movt., fair copy, bb. 86–90 (flute part)

Ex. 8.2. Fourth Symphony, 1st movt., fair copy, bb. 158–9 (viola and cello parts)

eleventh bifolio in bars 245–50, where he rejected a full orchestral tutti for a more transparent sound. In this passage he also removed any doublings within sections; where a string part had been doubled in the woodwinds, he eliminated the latter, leaving the string timbre by itself.

Along with such changes of tone colour, Mahler also corrected some mistakes in the fair copy. The crossed-out flute part in bar 303, like the clarinet in the next bar, is a mistake, since the copyist began to write each part a bar early. At times changes in register also occur, as in bar 319, where the third clarinet is an octave higher than found later. Mahler even inscribed some alternative and additional parts in the margins of the score, as with the harp at bars 110–11 and 160–1, where both insertions occur at the bottom of the page.

Beyond revisions of timbre, Mahler also revised tempo markings in the fair copy. The indication at the beginning of the first movement is 'Heiter behaglich; anmuthig bewegt' ('comfortably happy; moving gracefully') in the fair copy, rather than 'Bedachtig. Nicht eilen' ('Deliberately. Don't rush') that Mahler later used. Such alterations occur later in the score, such as at bar 67, where the marking 'Immer gemächlicher' ('always comfortably') in the fair copy is later revised to 'Wieder gemächlich' ('again comfortably'). A similar difference occurs at bar 119, where 'Etwas drängend' ('somewhat pressing') later becomes 'Ein wenig drängend' ('a little pressing'). In making such changes, Mahler either becomes more specific or simply phrases the marking differently; thus, it is a matter of personal preference for the original marking at bar 239, 'Wieder wie zu Anfang: Gemächlich u. behaglich' ('Again, as at the beginning: comfortably and happily') or the later 'Wieder zu Anfang: Sehr gemächlich, behaglich' ('Again as at the beginning: very comfortably, happily').

A more telling revision occurs at bar 283, where 'a tempo (sehr gemassigt)' ('a tempo [quite moderately]') becomes 'Wieder plötzlich langsam und bedächtig (molto meno mosso)' ('Again suddenly slow and deliberately [molto meno mosso]'), a more specific indication. A similar change occurs at bar 125, where the original marking is 'a Tempo—ohne Hast, jedoch etwas frischer als am Anfang' ('A tempo—without haste, yet somewhat more lightly than at the beginning'), later rendered as 'Fliessend, aber ohne Hast' ('Flowing, but without rushing').

At times, Mahler left passages in the fair copy unmarked. He added some markings some time later, such as at bar 32, where the word 'Frisch' does not occur in the fair copy. Likewise, no tempo markings occur at bar 77 ('Tempo I') or at bar 80 ('Fliessend'). By the same token, he took out some markings that were originally in the fair copy, such as the indication at bar 167 ('Nicht schleppen'). As with orchestration, the changes in tempo markings in this movement reflect a gradual refinement of that element as he brought the music closer to performance.

The Second Movement

Fewer revisions occur in the fair copy of the second movement, and the most striking difference is the scoring of six horns, tuba, bassoons, and contrabassoon in several passages. While this scoring is crossed out in the fair copy, Mahler nevertheless considered this timbre for a time. As shown in Ex. 8.3, this scoring is found with the half-step figure in the upper instruments when it occurs at bars 63–6, and also in the section between bars 67 and 101. This sonority later recurs without tuba but with an expanded horn section at bars 185–93. Such an idiosyncratic timbre does not seem to have been used for volume alone, but rather for its distinctive tone colour, creating a particularly dark timbre appropriate to the music in these passages. In revising the Scherzo in the fair copy, he omitted the tuba entirely and reduced the total number of horns to four. In the finished work the contrabassoon was left out of the movement.

Besides these revisions, Mahler also eliminated doublings in the fair copy of the second movement in the same way as he had in the first movement. In the fair copy he crossed out the flute doublings of the oboe in bars 3–4. He also eliminated a doubling of the second violin and the abortive second harp part at bars 116–17, just as he crossed out the second harp at bars 254–70, where it was to have duplicated the first harp. He also removed the

Ex. 8.3. Fourth Symphony, 2nd movt., bb. 63–6 (bassoon, horn, and tuba parts)

doublings of the second violin, viola, and bass by the clarinet, oboe, and bassoon at bars 121–9, a revision typical of the first movement.

Mahler changed only a few tempo markings in the second movement. For example, he crossed out the indication 'Recht gemächlich' ('truly comfortable') at bar 69 and eventually replaced it with 'Nicht eilen' ('Don't rush'). A further change may be found at bar 281, where he had written 'Wieder erste Bewegung, jedoch noch etwa zurückhalten' ('Like the first tempo, but held back a little'), and later simply marked the passage 'Gehalten' ('held back'). Such simplification occurs later, where he eventually dropped the indication 'Erste Bewegung zurückkehrend' ('return to the initial tempo') that occurs at bar 296 of the fair copy. As in the first movement, these revisions often reflect a turn of phrase intended to render them more precisely.

Some of the other revisions of the fair copy of the Scherzo concern the first violin part. At bar 46 he wrote 'N. B. Die 2. Spieler am I. Pulte hat den 1. Stimme zu spielen' ('NB. The second player at the first desk has to play the first part'), rephrasing the latter part to 'den Andern zu spielen' ('to play the second [part]') at some point later. He also marked the solo part 'rührig' ('energetically') at bar 184. In addition, the key of the solo violin part was changed in *Blaustift* to the 'correct' signature, just as the incorrect five sharps at bar 184 were changed to five flats.

The Third Movement

In the fair copy of the third movement Mahler continued the kind of revision found in the first two movements. The first sixteen bars were revised to remove the doubling of the sustained D in the viola, along with the doublings of the pizzicato bass line in the cello part. Such revision occurs in bars 31–46, where the first violin part had been marked for the first and second desks but changed to 'I' in pencil. Such changes in the string writing demonstrate a preference for a more transparent sonority. The relatively lush sound of a cello section in three parts, as found at the beginning, gives way to a thinner, but nonetheless effective, scoring in the revision.

Throughout the movement Mahler would exchange one timbre for another, as at bar 82, where the clarinet part was given to the flute and oboe. He also crossed out the verbal doublings of the bassoon with the contrabassoon ('mit Contr.') at the same place. There are also places in the fair copy that were left uncorrected at that stage, but revised later. Such a sonority occurs in the divided cello part at bars 238 ff., as shown in Ex. 8.4. The upper cello part comprises a fifth voice in the passage, which Mahler eventually removed to thin the texture.

More extensive changes occur between bars 263 and 274 with a paste-over found above the string parts at bars 263 to 266. While an examination of the manuscript shows that the paste-over conceals a passage already crossed out in ink, it may replace an obvious mistake rather than another version of the

Ex. 8.4. Fourth Symphony, 3rd movt., fair copy, bb. 238–41 (cello parts)

passage. On the other hand, the excision of the string parts at the bottom of the page suggests that Mahler may have originally scored the woodwinds differently and, in adding the paste-over, covered the original, perhaps simpler, woodwind parts. Since he had already rethought the orchestration of the Scherzo, he may have considered such a revision of timbre in the slow movement. He thus eliminated the doublings of the oboe, bassoon, and harp parts in the cellos and basses, choosing a woodwind timbre over a string sound sound in this passage.

As in the first two movements, differences occur with some of the tempo markings in the third movement. The indications 'Nicht schleppen' (b. 68), 'Zurückhaltend' (b. 71), and 'Fliessend' (b. 77) that Mahler later adopted do not appear in the fair copy. In addition, the marking 'Bewegt' at bar 89 became qualitatively different as 'Etwas zurückhaltend' in a later revision, just as 'Wieder langsam' at bar 93 was revised to 'Wieder a tempo'. Moreover, the marking 'Andante subito' at bar 283 is not his first choice for the section, since it obscures another indication apparently written under it.

The Fourth Movement

The revisions in the Song-Finale 'Das himmlische Leben' are similar to those in the first three movements, thus reflecting Mahler's attempt to make its orchestration conform to the rest of the symphony. While preparing the fair copy, he told Bauer-Lechner in April 1901 that he wanted to revise the orchestration of 'Das himmlische Leben' rather than stay with the more modest scoring of the orchestral *Humoresken*.[6]

As to the orchestration of 'Das himmlische Leben', the song exists in three known versions: (i) the original 1892 orchestration; (ii) the 'intermediary'

---

[6] Bauer-Lechner, 'Mahleriana' (unpublished manuscript), F-Pbmgm, Collection of Henry-Louis de La Grange. In an entry for 6 Apr. 1901 Bauer-Lechner wrote: 'Auf den Spaziergangen erzählte er mir, da er mit der Ausarbeitung des Adagios schon vor meinem Kommen fertig geworden und jetzt daran sei, "Das himmlische Leben" verändert zu instrumentieren, da er sich bei dem grösseren Orchester, das ihm durch die vorangegangenen Sätze zur Verfügung stünde, auf das bescheidene Orchester, wie er es bei den Humoresken anwende, nicht mehr zu beschränken brauche.' ('During walks with me he told me that he had already completed the instrumentation of the Adagio before my arrival; he was now working on orchestrating "Das himmlische Leben" differently, since he no longer had to restrict himself to the modest orchestra as he used in the "Humoresken"; he now had at his disposal a larger orchestra, which had been used in the preceding movements.')

version (in a private collection); and (iii) the version that occurs in the Fourth Symphony. Each version reflects a different intention on Mahler's part. It is impossible to judge the 1892 orchestration as inferior to the other two because it was intended as one of the *5 Humoresken*, not as the concluding movement of a symphony. The apparently divergent orchestration of the 'intermediary' version may reflect a similar intention for the song as either part of the later orchestral *Wunderhornlieder* or as a movement of the Third Symphony. Upon completing the fair copy of the Fourth Symphony, Mahler felt obliged to make further alterations in the orchestration of the song to make the scoring confirm with the timbre of the rest of the symphony.

Thus, the revision of the fourth movement in the fair copy shows Mahler's attempt to refine the music further, as he had done with the other movements. For example, the first three bars of the Song-Finale do not contain any string parts, as found in later revisions. He attempted later to add a viola part that would double a clarinet in bars 25–8, but crossed it out in the score. He also added the clarinet part in bars 29–30 at the bottom of the page, as an afterthought.

As elsewhere in the symphony, he eliminated doublings in the Song-Finale. In bar 47, for example, the bassoons had doubled the second violin and cello, but Mahler crossed them out in the fair copy. Similarly, the first and second clarinets and bassoon had doubled the second violin in bars 63–5, but were removed in this manuscript. In order to obtain a particular timbre, he added parts in the top or bottom margins of the score, such as the second violin in bars 96–7, the cor anglais in bar 115, the bass in bars 118–19, and the first violin in bar 125. He also exchanged some parts in this movement, having given the bass clarinet in bar 66 to the bassoon.

In addition, the flute part in bars 128–33 varies from what Mahler eventually published; in the fair copy it had doubled the second violin in bars 130–3. Because this passage lies in the lowest and less projective part of the flute register, he may have removed the doubling because of the inherent difficulties with playing the part and the thin sound that occurs when even the best of players performs the part successfully. (See Ex. 8.5.) He also used the grace-note, half-note figure (b. 124) in the cor anglais in bars 143–7; as shown in Ex. 8.6, it is found there neither transposed nor cancelled.

Although he revised them later, both violin parts in bars 161–3 are divided, doubling the clarinets in bar 162. Such *divisi* string writing may reflect the manner in which Mahler intended—or expected—the orchestra to be seated, with the first violins on one side and the seconds on the other, with the violas and cellos between. In such an arrangement, the scoring of this passage would contribute a sudden, almost 'stereophonic', fullness to the timbre.[7] Further-

---

[7] For a discussion of such a seating arrangement, see Daniel J. Koury, *Orchestral Performance Practices in the Nineteenth Century: Size, Proportions, and Seating* (Ann Arbor: UMI Research Press, 1986), 201 *passim*.

Ex. 8.5. Fourth Symphony, 4th movt., bb. 128–33 (flute part)

Ex. 8.6. Fourth Symphony, 4th movt., fair copy, bb. 143–7 (cor anglais part)

Ex. 8.7. Fourth Symphony, 4th movt., fair copy, bb. 161–3 (first and second violins)

more, the back-and-forth play between the two violin sections in the subsequent bars could be conceived in such a seating plan, especially for the imitation found in bars 168–9. (See Ex. 8.7.)

As in the other movements, Mahler also revised some of the tempo markings in the Song-Finale. However, the indication 'Tempo I' found at bar 80 of the published score is absent in the fair copy, as is any tempo at all in bar 87, where he later added 'Allmählich aber sehr unmerklich bewegter' ('gradually but imperceptibly faster'). Neither does a tempo marking occur at bar 95 of the fair copy, but the indication 'nicht schleppen', which Mahler later removed, occurs at bar 96.

Mahler also revised some of the other notations in this movement, but again, after he had completed the fair copy. It was only in the published score that he added the note at the beginning of 'Das himmlische Leben': 'Anmerkung für den Dirigenten: Es ist von höchster Wichtigkeit daß die Sängerin *äusserst* diskret begleitet wird' ('Note for the conductor: It is most important that the singer[8] [feminine] be accompanied discreetly'). Likewise, the fair copy lacks the published instruction for the singer at bar 12 ('N. B. Singstimme mit kindlich heiterem Ausdruck; durchaus ohne Parodie!'; 'NB. The voice [is to be] with childlike, joyful expression, without parody throughout!').[9] Both these markings reflect Mahler's concern for the vocal quality of the Song-Finale, something he must have intended in the music, but only expressed in the score at some point after he had completed the fair copy. The fact that he added such markings later underscores the gradual refinement of detail that took place even after the completion of the fair copy.

With regard to other instructions that occur in the fair copy, at bar 40 Mahler advises the conductor to take the 'Schellenkappe' at the same tempo as in the first movement ('Hier muß dieses Tempo genommen werden, als an den correspondierenden Stellen im ersten Satze'). A note also accompanies the fermata at the end of bar 153: '[the fermata sign] bedeutet hier nur ein kurzes Anhalten auf der Note, nicht etwa einen Fermate') ('The fermata sign signifies here a short hold on the note, not some sort of [conventional] fermata'). The same note occurs in the 1892 orchestral score, but was later excised. In removing this note, Mahler may have felt that the brevity of the fermata was self-evident, since the text of the vocal line continues in the next bar.

While the fair copy clearly superseded the version of the Fourth Symphony found in the draft score, it by no means reflects the refinement of nuance and detail that Mahler contributed to the first published score of the work. Yet the fair copy served as the basis for the parts used in the première of the Fourth, and it appears to have been the score that Mahler used for early performances of the work. As such, the revisions incorporated in the fair copy reflect the refinement of the Fourth from its completion in April 1901 probably through the Vienna première in January 1902. Moreover, Mahler must have made further revisions in the score before the first edition published by Ludwig Doblinger in 1902. This was not the final version of the symphony, since he would continue to refine the Fourth throughout the rest of his life. Nevertheless the fair copy is significant as the version of the Fourth Symphony that Mahler intended to take into performance and set alongside his other, completed works.

---

[8] Mahler specifically uses the feminine ending for the word 'singer' (*Sängerin*), which does not imply a boy soprano (*Knabe*), as some have imagined for the part.

[9] The former indication emphasizes the importance of the voice in the movement, while the latter helps describe the desired vocal effect. The voice should not become a caricature. The humour in this movement and the entire work is broad but subtle. The comic elements of 'Das himmlische Leben' are to be found in the text, not in the way it is performed.

9. Revisions of the Fourth Symphony and the Problem of Editing Mahler's Music

For Mahler the publication of a symphony rarely concluded his involvement with the work, since he continued to revise published music after he performed it. The same refinement of detail that he took from his earliest sketches to the fair copy continued after publication, as he further clarified his intentions at various times. For some works, like the Fourth Symphony, Mahler revised the score not once but several times after its première and first publication, and he left a complex series of alterations that reflect the development of his conception of the work.[1]

The revisions of the Fourth Symphony that Mahler undertook after he completed the fair copy involve qualitative choices that reflect his new understandings of timbre and expression. Towards the end of his life he confessed to having yet to learn things he eventually found to be basic, and he called himself an 'eternal beginner' even as he approached his fiftieth year. Around that time he also said that he wanted to revise his music every five years.[2] While he never realized it, that wish reveals Mahler's desire to revisit his music on a regular basis—or, perhaps, as he felt necessary—rather than leave it otherwise untouched and potentially lacking the insights that he could bring to the score through further experience.

Such is the case with the Fourth Symphony, to which Mahler returned more regularly than other works, since he revised it at least three times between its first publication in 1901 and his death in 1911.[3] In fact, the revisions on which he was working at the time of his death were not published in any edition of the Fourth until Erwin Ratz incorporated them into the critical edition in the composer's collected works in 1963.[4] Taking a cue from Mahler's own words, it would seem completely appropriate for the symphony to exist in the form he last left it. Yet the propriety of bringing into print the alterations that Mahler left unpublished is an issue that has provoked discussion and may never be resolved completely.

---

[1] For a detailed account of Mahler's revisions of this work, see James L. Zychowicz, 'Toward an *Ausgabe letzter Hand*'. For a survey of the various editions, see id., 'Sketches and Drafts', 392–403.

[2] Gustav Mahler to Bruno Walter, Dec. 1909, *Briefe*, 371; *Selected Letters*, 345.

[3] Zychowicz, 'Toward an *Ausgabe letzter Hand*', 264.

[4] Ratz, *Gustav Mahler: Symphony No. 4*.

TABLE 9.1. *Revisions of the printed score*

Source	Manuscript type	Date
A. Rosenthal, London (IGMG Ph 70)	Printed score with autograph corrections	probably 1903
Bibliothek der Grazer Musikhochschule, Graz	Printed score with autograph corrections	1905
Universal Edition, Vienna	Printed score with autograph corrections	11 Oct. 1910
Universal Edition (IGMG MS N/IV/113)	Galley proof with autograph corrections	probably 1910
Universal Edition	Printed score with autograph corrections	probably early 1911
IGMG MS N/IV/114	Printed score with corrections in another hand	after 1912

Early Revisions of the Fourth Symphony

After the publication of the Fourth Symphony in 1901, Mahler revised the orchestration at least three times in his career (see Table 9.1). In 1903 he provided the conductor Julius Buths with corrections to the first edition and included alterations in the instrumentation at specific points, but not continuously throughout the score.[5] Later in 1905 he undertook more extensive revisions for the première of the Fourth in Graz, which Robert Wickenhauser conducted.[6] These revisions were essential to the new edition published in 1906, but did not involve a thorough examination of the entire score.

Several years later, when Mahler entered into negotiations with Universal Edition in 1910 to publish 'definitive' versions of his first four symphonies,[7] he expressed the desire to arrive at the 'finally established score' of the Fourth that would incorporate all the corrections he had made since the first edition. He even made a provision for publishing the 'final version' of the Fourth Symphony based on work he was undertaking that summer.[8] He continued to revise the score in the following months and eventually completed, this last set of revisions on the Fourth Symphony.

---

[5] These corrections appear to be the ones in the revised score listed as item B¹ in Ratz's preface. See Zychowicz, 'Sketches and Drafts', 399–401.

[6] A summary of this particular revision occurs in Gösta Neuwirth, 'Zur Geschichte der 4. Symphonie', in *Mahler-Interpretation: Aspekte zum Werk und Wirken von Gustav Mahler*, ed. Rudolf Stephan (Mainz: Schott, 1985), 105–10.

[7] Gustav Mahler to Emil Freund from July 1910, letter no. 449 in *Gustav Mahler Briefe*, ed. Blaukopf, 392.

[8] Mahler to Emil Freund, 15 July 1910, no. 450 in *Gustav Mahler Briefe*, 393.

Mahler's Final Revisions

Each time Mahler revised the Fourth Symphony, he worked to clarify the instrumentation by removing doublings and what were, for him, infelicities. While he did not change the content of the work with regard to the essential musical lines, he attempted to improve its presentation in the orchestra. In making these revisions Mahler concentrated on the so-called secondary parameters, which include registral pitch, dynamics, duration, timbre, etc., to support the primary musical elements. In addition, some of his revisions most likely resulted from his performances of the Fourth with various orchestras and also represent an effort at more precise notation of both musical symbols and verbal directions.

The final revisions of the Fourth Symphony that Mahler made between 1910 and 1911 exist in two sources. When he first undertook the revision of his first four symphonies for the 'definitive version', Mahler provided Universal in summer 1910 with a marked-up proof (source 'D' in the preface to the 1963 edition). Universal subsequently incorporated those alterations in 1910 in the edition of the Fourth identified with Platten Number 2944 (the previous edition bore the Platten number 31). Mahler himself used a publisher's proof of that version of the Fourth as the basis for further revisions, which he entered between autumn 1910 and January 1911. The proof copy of the score with Mahler's final alterations (source 'E' in 1963 preface) was deposited with Universal Edition, Vienna, by Alma Mahler after Gustav's death.

Despite the fact that it took over half a century until their publication, Mahler's final revisions were not entirely forgotten, since Erwin Stein called attention to this source in an article he published in 1929.[9] Nevertheless, Universal did not publish these revisions in any reprint edition of the Fourth Symphony prior to 1963, and other publishers also ignored these alterations in their editions of the work. In fact, these final revisions were not published until Erwin Ratz incorporated them into the critical edition of the symphony for the collected works, which was the first newly edited version of the score to appear since Mahler's lifetime.

The Nature of the Final Revisions

In the revisions of the Fourth that he pursued at the end of his life, Mahler attempted to allow each line of the work to be heard clearly. Without changing the essential timbre already present in the Fourth as radically as he had the First Symphony, he made the already relatively light orchestration of the Fourth even more consistent and precise. He did not want to risk obscuring the struc-

---

[9] Erwin Stein, 'Eine unbekannte Ausgabe letzter Hand von Mahlers IV. Symphonie', *Pult und Taktstock*, 6 (1929), 31–2; English trans., 'The Unknown Last Version of Mahler's Fourth Symphony', in *Orpheus in New Guises* (New York: Rockliff, 1953), 31–3.

ture by dense scoring,[10] where balance would become an arbitrary matter for the conductor to determine. Towards this end, he strove to create an orchestration of the Fourth that would allow the work essentially to speak for itself.

Despite the qualitative judgements that surround them, these final revisions demonstrate definite tendencies on the part of the composer, and a clear logic supports the alterations. It has been generally accepted as a characteristic of his late style that Mahler thinned the orchestration to the essential colours and eliminated awkward or unnecessary doublings. Even though he revoiced some passages, he had no intention of completely reorchestrating the symphony; rather he refined what was already present in the score.

For example, he restricted the timbre of the cor anglais in this score, especially in the Song-Finale. At various points he transferred the texture previously found in the bassoon part to the lower strings, including *divisi* cellos. The flute timbre was also changed occasionally in the work, where the *tutti* sonorities found in earlier scores thin to fewer players in the final version of the work. At times the revision in scoring also required a change in rhythm, since the clear articulation that would result from a particular blend necessitated a different notation with a wind instrument, for example, than with a string instrument to achieve the same effect.

At other times, Mahler not only changed the instrumentation, but also altered the dynamic markings to make the revision effective. While dynamics operate at a less measurable degree than instrumentation, the revisions are useful in providing the conductor with some idea—albeit a relative one—of the intended intensity of the music. Again, the dynamics are by no means absolute values, but serve as approximations that are helpful to the conductor in performance. As a composer Mahler knew what he wanted to achieve, and as a conductor he was also aware of the pitfalls of performing this symphony. It is possible to ascribe these kinds of changes to the dual perspective he was able to bring to his work.

Following from the element of dynamics, Mahler also revised the rhythmic articulation of several passages. In removing one instrument in a doubling, he might change the rhythm of the remaining one. An eighth note might change to a sixteenth note followed by a sixteenth rest in order to insure clear articulation and prevent the blurring of a figure. Such changes are relatively rare, but when they occur the revisions are by no means arbitrary. In adjusting the rhythm, Mahler made the notation of his music more precise and left the conductor with a clearer idea of his intentions for the symphony.

Mahler also clarified the articulation of several passages in the score by incorporating breath marks and other phrase markings into the final revisions.

---

[10] The draft score fragment for the Scherzo cited above contains evidence of Mahler's early orchestration of the movement. In completing the fair copy, however, he completely rethought the instrumentation of this movement, which he had already complained of as being unwieldy. See Zychowicz, 'Sketches and Drafts', 353–61.

He added bowings at several points and included more consistent indications for arco or pizzicato. At times he also changed the expression markings that occur at various points in the score. In making all these revisions, he became more explicit about his intentions and used the notation to convey his expectations for performance.

Tempo markings also differ in the final version of the Fourth, but the revision of this aspect of the score is not as drastic as, for example, his changes from the draft score to the fair copy. By the time Mahler committed to paper these final revisions, his conception of tempo was fairly stable and required little adjustment. Nevertheless, he eliminated the marking 'Tempo 1. (Hauptzeitmass.)' in bar 18 of the first movement, thus leaving the conductor to find for himself the appropriate tempo for this section. He did not gratuitously remove tempo markings in this revision, since he added the indication 'Etwas fliessender' in bar 63 of the first movement to clarify the tempo of that section. At another point he replaced one tempo indication with another, such as the one at bar 115 of the first movement, where the marking 'sempre a Tempo' gives way to 'Nicht eilen', which is more specific for the passage in question.

Among the other changes that Mahler notated with these final revisions are corrections of errors and inconsistencies that had not yet been corrected in any publication of the Fourth Symphony. These alterations are by no means as critical as the emendations he made in orchestration. In fact, the 1963 edition prepared by Ratz contains several mistakes in the mechanics of the score that involve similar elements: the irregular use of system braces, the incorrect placement of clefs and key signatures, and the inconsistent use of fonts for dynamic indications and other markings. Even without these remaining mistakes corrected, Ratz's edition stands apart from the other existing ones for its unique presentation of Mahler's final thoughts on the Fourth Symphony.

Editions of the Fourth Symphony

While it bears the imprimatur of the Internationale Gustav Mahler Gesellschaft, the critical edition edited by Ratz remains one of several editions of the Fourth Symphony currently available. Redlich enumerates eight editions, not counting his own, in the introduction to his Eulenburg score for the Fourth,[11] while Rudolf Stephan lists thirteen editions in his catalogue.[12] The discrepancies in number are a result of problems in defining an edition of the work, and for the purposes of this survey, each new publication of the Fourth Symphony is listed in Table 9.2. The first edition, as stated above, was published by Ludwig Doblinger (Vienna, 1902) as a quarto (large-size)

[11] Hans F. Redlich, Introduction to *Symphony No. 4* (London: Edition Eulenburg, 1966), pp. xxiv–xxvi.
[12] Rudolf Stephan, *Gustav Mahler: Werk und Interpretation: Autographe, Partituren, Dokumente* (Cologne: Arno Volk, 1979), 67–8.

score, with Platten no. 31. This engraving served as the basis for a study score in octavo (small-size) format produced from Doblinger's plates by Mahler's new Vienna publisher, Universal, as indicated on the cover ('aufgenommen

TABLE 9.2. *Editions of the Fourth Symphony*

Publisher	Location	Edition No.	Format	Pages	Date	Comments
Ludwig Doblinger	Vienna	Pl. no. 31	quarto	125	n.d. (1902)	First edition
Universal Edition	Vienna	Pl. no. 31	octavo	125	n.d. (1905)	'in die Universal Edition aufgenommen'
Universal Edition	Vienna	U.E. 952	octavo	125	n.d. (1906)	
Universal Edition	Vienna	U.E. 2944	quarto	125	n.d. (1910)	
Universal Edition	Vienna	W.Ph.V. 214^a	octavo	188	1925	Philharmonia series; Introduction by Erwin Stein
Universal	Vienna	none	octavo	125	1925	Variant of Edition W.Ph.V. 214
Boosey & Hawkes	London	Hawkes Pocket scores no. 581	octavo	125	1943	Introduction by Fritz Stiedry
International Music Publishers	New York	none	octavo	125	n.d. (1951)	Text for Eulenburg Edition, 1966
Universal Edition	Vienna	none	octavo	125	1952	'Revised Edition' with introduction by Erwin Stein
Universal Edition	Vienna	U.E. 13823 Pl. no. 2944	quarto	125	1963	Sämtliche Werke, 4; Revisionsbericht by E. Ratz
Verlag 'Musik'	Moscow	No. 31224	octavo	158	1965	Introduction by B. Levik
Edition Eulenburg	London	No. 575	octavo	188	1966	Introduction by Hans Redlich
Universal Edition	Vienna	No. 214	octavo	188	1966	Philharmonia series; 1963 edition with introduction by Erwin Stein
Dover	New York	[Pl. no. 31]	quarto	125	n.d. (1989)	Reprint of the first edition; published with the Third Symphony

^{a} This Universal edition appears to have also served as the text for the edition published by Edwin F. Kalmus (New York, n.d.), no. 297, without the introduction by Erwin Stein.

in die Universal Edition'; taken up by Universal Edition), and probably issued in 1905.[13]

The revised edition of 1906 (see Table 9.2) is another octavo, which may be identified by the name of the publisher on the cover along with both the Universal Edition no. 952 and the original Platten number 31; in it the publisher incorporated Mahler's earliest revisions. When Universal reprinted the Fourth in 1910 as a quarto, the publisher assigned it the number U.E. 2944, and the edition published in Universal's 'Philharmonia' series in 1925 (no. 214) is actually a reprint of the previous octavo edition (no. 952). The 1925 edition differs from the earlier publication by the inclusion of a photograph of Mahler as the frontispiece and an introduction by Erwin Stein ['E. St.']. Universal subsequently reprinted this edition without an edition number.

When the head of Universal Edition Emil Hertzka, who had worked with Mahler himself, died in 1932, ownership of the publishing house passed to his widow, who left Austria in 1938 after the Nazi Anschluß. At that time she transferred the publishing rights of some music to the British publisher Boosey & Hawkes, Ltd., and another edition of the Fourth appeared in 1943, when Boosey & Hawkes reprinted the 1910 octavo as Pocket Score no. 581. (This edition includes an introduction by the conductor Fritz Stiedry.) Likewise, the International Music Company, New York, reprinted the same edition without Stiedry's introduction around 1950 in an undated publication. The rights to the Fourth Symphony reverted to Universal Edition, Vienna, after World War II, and in 1952 it reprinted the 1925 edition with the introduction by Erwin Stein.

Up to this time all the new publications of the Fourth were based in some way on editions originally published during Mahler's lifetime. Yet in 1963 Erwin Ratz broke from this tradition when he undertook a revised edition of the score as part of the newly founded Mahler Gesamtausgabe. Ratz intended his edition as an *Ausgabe letzter Hand*, which incorporates, albeit tacitly in the absence of an adequate critical apparatus, Mahler's final revisions as part of the critical score.

For the *Ausgabe letzter Hand*, which the Internationale Gustav Mahler Gesellschaft established as the editorial goal of the Mahler Gesamtausgabe, each edition required the use of materials related to Mahler's final version of a work rather than an analysis of all the extant materials and a decision to follow a strategy that addresses the specific situation for each work. Yet the *Ausgabe letzter Hand* should not be construed as the only approach that exists for editing Mahler's music. In preparing an appropriate edition, an editor would need to determine if the best version was the *Ausgabe letzter Hand* or some other form of the work that has a basis in a documented source. For some music

---

[13] Doblinger transferred some of its publishing rights to Universal Edition in 1903 for a part-share interest in the latter. See Lennart Reimers and Alexander Weinmann, 'Universal Edition', *New Grove*, xix. 453–4.

the *Ausgabe letzter Hand* would provide an optimal approach, but for other works it may be better to find some other means of establishing the text.

Nevertheless, the publication of Ratz's score opened the door for other editions of the Fourth. Universal reprinted the critical edition as a study score (quarto format) in its Philharmonia series in 1966, which replaced the earlier catalogue no. 214 (despite the inclusion of the 1925 introduction by Stein rather than the *Revisionsbericht* of Ratz). The next year the Moscow publisher Musik issued an edition of the Fourth in 1965, apparently basing its score on Ratz's new edition. The Russian publication includes an introduction by B. Levik, and with its 158 pages in octavo format, it is a new engraving, not a reprint of any of the other published scores of the work. A further, more reactionary, edition is the one published in 1966 by Edition Eulenburg, London, and with an introductory essay by Hans F. Redlich in which he discusses textual problems related to the Fourth and criticizes the Internationale Gustav Mahler Gesellschaft for publishing Mahler's final revisions in its critical edition of the Fourth:

The amendments of this 'final version' embodied in Volume IV of the Complete Edition are more drastic than any previous revision of the Symphony. Hence, they should be approached with more reverential interest tempered by caution. It remains an unsolved question whether Mahler would have published these amendments as they now stand, specially [*sic*] if he had been given time to see them in perspective. Some of these changes in orchestration . . . could not be called 'improvements of great significance' . . . by any stretch of the imagination. Clearly this 'final version' remains without Mahler's Imprimatur and, thus, lacks final authenticity. Only the musical texts of the symphony published between 1902 and 1910 carry full authenticity for posterity.[14]

In bringing 'final authenticity' into the argument Redlich begs the question: What kind of 'imprimatur' exists for an edition that reverts to an earlier one, when Mahler had clearly intended to publish a revision of the Fourth around 1910? After all, the composer made the 1910 revisions in preparation for a new edition of the Fourth along with the first three symphonies through Universal.

Redlich's conservative approach to Mahler becomes apparent in his article about the difficulties of arriving at an authoritative edition of Mahler's works.[15] At the beginning of his argument, Redlich draws a parallel between the various editions of the symphonies of Bruckner and Mahler, but fails to distinguish the former's drastic revisions of substance from the revision of detail found in the latter. Yet Redlich stops short of defining the parameters of what he would call a basic text for either composer. When it comes to dis-

---

[14] Redlich, *Symphony No. 4*, p. xxiv.
[15] Redlich, 'Gustav Mahler: Probleme einer kritischen Gesamtausgabe', *Musikforschung*, 14 (1966), 386–401.

cussing Mahler's Fourth Symphony in this article, he does not deal directly with an editorial approach that would account for Mahler's final revisions, but enumerates instead various mechanical errors in the 1963 edition. As valid as that list of mistakes may be, they do not constitute an approach to editorial practice.

Nevertheless, Redlich's responses to this and other editions of Ratz remain some of the strongest criticisms of the collected works and the efforts of the Internationale Gustav Mahler Gesellschaft. As a respected scholar of his day, Redlich was well suited to tackling the difficult task of editing the music of Mahler. After all, he had published studies of a number of composers, including Monteverdi, Wagner, Bruckner, Mahler, and Berg. He had also prepared editions of Monteverdi's music and served on the advisory committee of the *Hallische Händel-Ausgabe*. With these qualifications, his criticism of the Mahler edition carries some authority. Yet it may also result from Redlich not being part of the Mahler edition, let alone leading it. In producing editions of Mahler's First, Fourth, Sixth, and Seventh Symphonies for Edition Eulenburg, Redlich appears to have set himself up as the rival to Ratz, thus occasioning his relatively extreme critical stance.

Redlich's editions of Mahler's music are not without interest, since he makes some valid points about the difficulties with the Fourth in the introduction to his edition of that work. His editions of the Fourth, Sixth, and Seventh Symphonies are more conservative than those published by the Internationale Gustav Mahler Gesellschaft because of his unwillingness to accept revisions that the composer did not see through to publication. He criticized the Internationale Gustav Mahler Gesellschaft for having published revisions that were, in his eyes, questionable at best. He expressed his perspective further in the preface to his own edition of the Seventh, where he stated that

the present revision [of the Seventh Symphony] does not incorporate changes in orchestration and later modifications of tempo indications . . . carried out by Mahler, Mengelberg, and others during the last two years of Mahler's life. These retouches lack final authenticity. . . . They might easily have been discarded, had Mahler lived longer and had he been given opportunities to hear the symphony [the Seventh] more often and to prepare himself a revised edition of the full score. The case of far-reaching changes in the structure of Symphony VI comes here to mind, which were eventually countermanded by the composer himself who ultimately reverted to the original version. . . . They should find no place in the music text of the full score. They should rather form part of a critical appendix in which they are offered as alternative readings only.[16]

Redlich's argument can be persuasive when taken at face value, yet if one takes further his point about relying on a text that the composer has seen

---

[16] Redlich, Introduction to *Symphony No. 7* (London: Edition Eulenburg, n.d.), pp. x–xi.

into print, one would have to disallow the publication of *Das Lied von der Erde* and the Ninth Symphony—not to mention the first movement of the Tenth Symphony, or any performing edition of that work—since they were neither performed nor even revised in manuscript to the extent of Mahler's earlier music. At the same time, the matter of 'far-reaching' revisions has a qualitative slant that is clearly not germane to the editorial practice that Ratz used. It is the editorial method that sets Ratz apart from Redlich, since each editor used a different approach to support what he believed to be the best interests of the composer in his respective editions.

The Problem of Creating a Definitive Edition

The impact of the *Ausgabe letzter Hand* for the critical edition of the Fourth Symphony is important to consider, since it was to become the basic text and definitive publication of the work. The various editions of the Fourth that were published after Mahler's death essentially reprinted scores that he had seen into print. Moreover, outside of Ratz's edition the only other new publication of the Fourth clearly avoids Mahler's final alterations. In his edition, Redlich acknowledged the existence of the final set of corrections that Ratz used for the critical edition,[17] but disputed the validity of this source as the basis for a new edition,[18] since the alterations did not bear the proof of performance that established for him their authority.[19] Redlich sanctioned revisions only if Mahler had seen them in print or if he had taken the altered version into performance, and, for him, the final revisions of the Fourth Symphony did not meet either criteria.

Barring the parameters established for any single edition, however, Mahler's final revisions for the Fourth Symphony are authentic and bear the authority of any other documented source. When it came to revising the Fourth or any of his works, Mahler did not undertake alterations wilfully. The composer's own intention of arriving at a definitive text for the first four symphonies was in earnest and by no means the attempt of a dying composer to set his house in order before expiring. Rather, these final revisions reflect the approach he took in establishing the timbre for works he composed at that time in his career. The kind of transparent instrumentation

---

[17] Redlich, 'Gustav Mahler: Probleme einer kritischen Gesamtausgabe', 386–9.

[18] Mahler, *Symphony No. 4*, ed. Redlich, pp. xxiii–xxiv.

[19] Redlich dismissed the final corrections that Mahler made in score because he could not confirm the use of those revisions in performance. It is an editor's prerogative to extend such a parameter to his edition, but that judgement does not invalidate the source. If his argument is taken further, Redlich would not allow an edition of *Das Lied von der Erde* or the Ninth Symphony, since Mahler failed to see either completed work into performance. As to the Fourth Symphony, the extant document from Mahler's final performance of that work would rescind any of the later corrections, if it is taken out of context. The version of the Fourth as represented by the first violin part that Theodor Spiering used contains several handwritten revisions and paste-overs that correspond to Source D in Ratz. (Spiering's violin part is an uncatalogued item in the Gorno Music Library of the University of Cincinnati.)

that he used in the last revisions of the Fourth also occurs in his later works, particularly the Ninth Symphony and the first movement of the Tenth, where pure colours and more pointillistic instrumental effects are part of the musical substance. In such a way Mahler may be seen to extend his vision across the body of his work, to arrive at a sound that truly underscores the content of his music.

However, Ratz's edition did not include a detailed critical report, and while this absence should not detract from the editor's efforts, it certainly did not strengthen the case for the publication. Without a full critical report, the nature of the revisions is indeterminate and the uniqueness of the score has less significance. The thorough and exhaustive character of Mahler's final revisions becomes more readily apparent upon analysing the alterations. Through an analysis of the revisions, the thoroughness of the alterations emerges as he refined details on almost every page of the score to bring the Fourth to a more definitive form.[20] In so doing Mahler created a more transparent instrumentation of the work and also attempted to make the score more consistent with regard to dynamics, articulations, and other nuances. These revisions bring the score into focus in a way that had not occurred with any of the more limited alterations Mahler had undertaken earlier. While he might have returned to the score again had he lived longer, it is difficult to imagine another such thorough examination of the entire work.

As Mahler's latest thought on the Fourth, the authority of these final revisions is underscored by his contract with Universal to publish 'definitive versions' of the first four symphonies. From Mahler's compositional activity it becomes apparent that he devoted much energy to creating new works, not recasting completed ones, and it would be out of character for him to make a virtual career of rewriting his earlier music. Thus, with the Fourth, the evidence, internal and external, points to the revisions made at the end of his life as the final ones Mahler sanctioned and intended to publish. By all rights, the final revisions would seem to belong in an edition.

Yet, any edition of Mahler's music eventually falls short of addressing all the issues involved with the notation and, more importantly, the performance of a musical work. More importantly, editing music ultimately involves decisions that reflect the personality of the editor in the service of the composer. In the case of Redlich, his work should be understood in its context. Like Ratz, Redlich appears to have felt that he was preserving the true spirit of Mahler in his editions. However, by incorporating Mahler's late revisions into the 1963 score of the Fourth Symphony, Ratz seems to have done what he thought best in order to fulfil the composer's intentions. In keeping from his edition of the Fourth the very revisions that Ratz incorporated into his, Redlich seems to have been expressing a similar intent.

---

[20] In the Appendix to this study I have reviewed the final corrections and present such a critical report.

Arriving at a Text

For the Internationale Gustav Mahler Gesellschaft to use the *Ausgabe letzter Hand* as the unique basis for its critical edition of the Fourth or any of the symphonies is difficult to accept without qualification. As with other music of Mahler, the Fourth exists in several versions, from the fair copy to the first edition and revised editions. Because Mahler revised the Fourth Symphony several times, the multiple versions that exist cannot be dismissed wholesale.

The Internationale Gustav Mahler Gesellschaft determined that the appropriate editorial stance for its Gesamtausgabe was an *Ausgabe letzter Hand* (more appropriately for some editions, a *Fassung letzter Hand*), in order to present Mahler's last thoughts on his music. This position is useful when it comes to evaluating sources, but not necessarily for determining authority. Without further elucidation, even the editorial practice of an *Ausgabe letzter Hand* is insufficient. In a practical sense, the composer's last thought may be transitional and untested and would then have less consequence in editorial matters. Moreover, the pre-eminence accorded to Mahler's final thought as the basis for the single sanctioned edition of his works has obscured the possibility of using varying editorial approaches more suitable to the music and the circumstances in which the composer left it. Such an editorial perspective may better serve the music and, more importantly, the composer's intentions in this matter.

In addition to the *Ausgabe letzter Hand*, several choices exist, and it is possible to establish a reliable text of Mahler's music based on various sources: the first edition (by no means is the fair copy an option for an appropriate edition);[21] the last edition the composer saw into print; an edition prepared posthumously that incorporates his final revisions (*Ausgabe letzter Hand* or *Fassung letzter Hand*);[22] or some other version of the symphony associated with a specific performance. Notwithstanding these choices, it is important that any edition have a solid basis in the sources, which are abundant—a collation edition that involves an editor's choice of preferred readings is out of the question, given the existence of documented sources.

To sanction a single edition for this work, however, suggests a text that takes into account all the other sources. Such an edition is often the result of the traditional method of *recensio* and *examinatio* that arrives at a collation edition. This approach is useful for approaching the music of earlier times, when manuscript copies might preserve several traditions, none of which

---

[21] Jerome J. McGann, *A Critique of Modern Textual Criticism* (Charlottesville: The University of Virginia Press, 1992), 34.

[22] See Georg von Dadelsen, 'Die "Fassung letzter Hand" in der Musik', *Acta Musicologica*, 33 (1961), 1–14, and also Georg Feder, *Musikphilologie: Eine Einführung in die musikalische Textkritik, Hermeneutik und Editionstechnik* (Darmstadt: Wissenschaftliche Buchgesellschaft, 1987), 58–61.

can be connected with the composer. Yet with music found in published versions rather than transmitted in manuscript, this approach to textual criticism should give way to an approach that better serves the sources that exist in a historic context.[23]

The question remains as to the nature of an appropriate edition of Mahler's music when several, often competing, choices exist. For Ratz the so-called *Ausgabe letzter Hand* could address the problem adequately, while Redlich would support a single edition based on the last version the composer published or performed. As to the latter, the documents associated with the Fourth Symphony suggest that Mahler did not take his final manuscript revisions into performance.[24] While a case could be made for the approaches of either Ratz and Redlich, it is the responsibility of the editor to represent the composer without further clouding the situation by becoming overly dogmatic in defining an edition.

The editorial problems with Mahler's music concern the role that various kinds of revisions have in establishing the text of a work. In editing his music, it is not a matter of publishing multiple versions to reflect substantive changes, as occurs with Bruckner's music, where the cumulative weight of such changes results in multiple editions of a work like Bruckner's Third Symphony.[25] The differences that exist between the first edition of Mahler's Fourth Symphony and the alterations taken up around 1903, 1905, and 1910 are not substantial enough to merit separate publications. Rather, the revisions represent gradual refinements that make it impossible to arrive at a single reading of the 'best sources', since each source exists in its discrete historic context.

With Mahler, composition was a process to arrive at a finished score, but work on that score did not end with the completion of the fair copy or the publication of the first edition. Rather, the revisions that he undertook at

---

[23] McGann, *Critique*, 59.

[24] Based on the first violin part that belonged to the concertmaster Theodor Spiering, Mahler's final performance of the Fourth Symphony was the version published in 1906. See Zychowicz, 'Toward an *Ausgabe letzter Hand*', 268.

[25] The Bruckner edition contains three complete editions of the Third Symphony, and a variant version of one movement. Bruckner composed his Third Symphony between 1872 and 1873 and returned to it in 1874; he completed the first definitive version of the work in 1877 (published in 1878); and a revised version of the work emerged in 1889 (published in 1890). The Anton Bruckner Gesamtausgabe published three different versions of the Third Symphony: *III. Symphonie D-moll* (Wagner-Symphonie), Fassung 1873, ed. Leopold Nowak (Sämtliche Werke, III/1; Vienna: Musikwissenschaftlicher Verlag, 1977); *III. Symphonie D-moll* (Wagner-Symphonie), Fassung 1877, ed. Leopold Nowak (Sämtliche Werke, III/2; Vienna: Musikwissenschaftlicher Verlag, 1981); and *III. Symphonie D-moll*, Fassung 1889, ed. Leopold Nowak (Sämtliche Werke, III/3; Vienna: Musikwissenschaftlicher Verlag, 1959). The Gesamtausgabe also includes a variant version of the *Adagio* that stems from 1876, *III. Symphonie D-moll, Adagio 1876* (Wagner-Symphonie), Adagio Nr. 2, ed. Leopold Nowak (Sämtliche Werke zu III/1; Vienna: Musikwissenschaftlicher Verlag, 1977). See Deryck Cooke, 'The Bruckner Problem Simplified', in *Vindication: Essays on Romantic Music* (Cambridge University Press, 1982), pp. 43–71 at 55–8. See also the catalogue of works following the biographical article in *New Grove*, s.v. 'Anton Bruckner', by Deryck Cooke.

various times extend the process of composition further, and underscore the fluid nature of the text as the composer refined it. For this music the idea of a single, rigidly fixed score is antithetical to the nature of a work like the Fourth Symphony. Multiple versions differ in detail, rather than substance, as performances of the symphony could take place based on the fair copy and subsequent sets of revisions. In some cases some alterations are clearly improvements in the expression of the ideas in score and the actual scoring of the music; in other cases, some of the changes seem to be expediencies connected with a conductor or performance. In arriving at a reliable edition of the Fourth Symphony, it is important to discern such differences and analyse the final revisions. Since the last revisions emerge from an autograph source, but were not published, it is unclear whether Mahler would have continued to revise the symphony either by going further in modifying the score or by withdrawing some of the alterations.

The approach Ratz took in editing the Fourth Symphony, laudable for its time, should give way to a new edition that treats the sources even more carefully and incorporates a critical report with the score. Only through such analysis does the nature of Mahler's revisions become clear, and the nature of the score move from a rigid and fixed conception to something tied more to performance. The successful performance of Mahler's music requires the kind of attention to detail that the composer lavished on it. This becomes clear with the Fourth Symphony, where it is possible to perceive the work as it evolved into the fair copy and after, as Mahler took the score further and arrived at a transparent orchestration that should emerge in his final thoughts on the work.

Only in understanding the entire process of composition, starting with the earliest sketches and continuing through the rest of the creative process, is it possible to arrive at an edition, which may not necessarily conform to the restrictive models that exist. Mahler's music contains challenges that editors need to approach more critically, as studies of the sources reveal more about the nature of his music for the Fourth Symphony and other works. In the context of the manuscripts and other autograph materials, the situation with Mahler's music becomes clear, and this understanding should form the basis of an editorial approach that can address each work in an appropriate and individual manner.

Conclusion

Mahler's sketches and drafts for the Fourth Symphony reveal much about the genesis of this seminal work and, more importantly, contribute insights into his creative process. Through the number and variety of sketches for this particular symphony it is possible to apprehend the origins of this work first-hand rather than to rely on second-hand sources that are removed from the actual composition of the music. In a sense, it is also possible to observe the composer at work, as he proceeded from his initial, fragmentary ideas to more continuous music, sometimes struggling over transitions and other elements.

From the earliest manuscripts for the song 'Das himmlische Leben' that Mahler composed in 1892 to the last revisions of the completed work that he undertook in 1911, the materials associated with the Fourth Symphony represent the scope of his compositional process as the ideas for the symphony took shape. While no set of materials for each stage is complete, the variety of the known sketches is sufficient to suggest the amount of materials that Mahler used to complete the work. In the context of these manuscripts, it is also useful to consider his later revisions of the Fourth Symphony, which extend beyond the actual conclusion of the work as he brought the score into clearer focus by adjusting the so-called secondary parameters.

What else can the manuscripts and autograph materials reveal? Mahler himself expressed caution about investigations of Beethoven's sketches, and suggested that it is important not to invest too much in what lies at the surface. Such wariness is prudent when it comes to ascribing intentions to any composer. Yet it may also betray his own self-consciousness at revealing the methodical work through which he arrived at this symphony. The value of the sketches like those for the Fourth Symphony lies at another, deeper level, as they show Mahler's evolving conception of the work and hint at the choices he made en route to the finished composition in full score.

At another level Mahler's periodic return to the Fourth after the completion of the fair copy and the publication of the work bears some relationship to his opinion of it. He once referred to the Fourth as the stepchild of his symphonies, since it did not receive the esteem that he thought it deserved. Later, when he discussed the recently finished Ninth Symphony with Bruno Walter, he compared the new composition with the Fourth by stating that both works contained highly personal expressions. At that time he also called himself 'the eternal beginner', an expression he had used when he was completing the Fourth almost ten years earlier. Perhaps he found himself on the verge of a new approach to composition with the Ninth Symphony, just as he had been with the Fourth.

In terms of what he wrote after it, the Fourth Symphony is a crucial work among Mahler's symphonies. It marks the end of his so-called 'Wunderhorn' period and simultaneously serves as evidence of his return to the composition of large-scale works after a two-year hiatus. Aesthetically, the Fourth displays an antinomy: while it is not a programme symphony in the manner of his earlier ones, neither are programmatic associations entirely absent from it. In it he internalized his previous, more explicit conception of a programme and allowed only the Song-Finale to contain an explicit text. In addition, his quotation of the song in the first three movements not only establishes thematic unity, but also contributes a subtle programmatic dimension to the symphony through instrumental suggestions of the song. Such a procedure anticipates the later use of vocal music in the so-called middle trilogy of symphonies.

The Fourth Symphony also remains one of Mahler's most accessible works. He was conscious of the expansiveness of his earlier symphonies, particularly the Second and Third, which he admitted were twice as long as originally planned. He is uncannily concise in the Fourth, which is a four-movement work that requires a conventional orchestra and lasts less than an hour. In this work traditional forms occur: sonata, Scherzo and Trio, and theme and variations, followed by a strophic finale. The Fourth Symphony has neither an elaborate programme, as found with the Second, nor a sophisticated text, such as Nietzche's in the Third. In a sense, if it is about anything, the Fourth is simply about heavenly life, with its only overt description in a childlike poem from *Des Knaben Wunderhorn*. Nevertheless, the Fourth remains an impressive example of abstract music with a structure that allows it to exist without programmatic explanation and verbal excuses.

Emerging at a time when Mahler felt he could no longer compose, the Fourth Symphony is also evidence of the immense talent that he was eventually able to tap in the succeeding works that followed steadily through the next decade. After a difficult gestation, the resulting work exceeded in many ways the symphonic mastery already present in his earlier music. At the same time, he produced in the Fourth Symphony a work that anticipates in various ways the approach he would take to his later compositions. Mahler's accomplishment is all the more admirable in the light of the various manuscripts that reveal the kinds of details he pursued from vague ideas to the meticulous score of the completed Fourth Symphony.

Appendix: Critical Report for Mahler's Final Autograph Revisions

The following critical report contains a list of the revisions that Mahler made in the proof that Universal provided him (U.E. 2944) (Source E in Ratz's edition of the work, identified as N/IV/116 in the archive of the Internationale Gustav Mahler Gesellschaft, Vienna). This source is a proof in which Universal had already incorporated the revisions that Mahler had made on an earlier proof and submitted on 11 October 1910 (Source D in Ratz, and N/IV/112 in the archive of the Internationale Gustav Mahler Gesellschaft). Mahler entered his final improvements in Source E with a red marking pencil, and Ratz used this as the basis for his edition.

This report is arranged by movement, with the page of the score listed first, then the bar number (superscript 1 and 2 indicate first and second half), the instrument name and specific part (e.g. '1. Oboe', rather than 'Oboe'), and a description of the revision. Rather than generalize about the alterations, the report accounts for each difference bar by bar. (Except where noted, entries apply to the full bars.)

All the revisions are reported exactly as they appear in the score, including such markings as 'zu 2', which sometimes appears as 'à 2' in the critical edition. When a verbal notation in the score spans two lines, the line break is indicated with a solidus (/). Where Mahler replaced one element with another, the comments include a brief description of what had existed in the score, as well as what he marked as his revision. While it is no substitute for an examination of the source itself, this critical report should underscore the nature and extent of Mahler's final revisions on the Fourth Symphony. The alterations extend beyond a few random changes and, instead, encompass more elements than instrumentation. Where Mahler thinned the score or changed the timbre, he would also adjust dynamics and sometimes the rhythm to make certain that the passage receives clear articulation in the ensemble. These changes represent a level of clarity not possible a decade earlier, when he first published the Fourth Symphony. The almost pointillistic colour that he intended for the work emerges in these final revisions on the score.

Page	Bar	Part	Comments
First Movement			
3	4	1.2. Flutes	add 'ohne rit.' in the second half of the bar
	4	3.4. Flutes	add 'ohne rit.' in the second half of the bar
4	10	1.2. Bassoons	add crescendo marking in the second half of the bar

	10	3. Bassoon	add crescendo marking in the second half of the bar
	14	1.2. Flutes	eliminate doubling (with 3. Clarinet)
	14	3. Clarinet	add crescendo and decrescendo marking under the first and second halves of the bar; add accent to the second half note
	15	1.2. Flutes	add marking 'a 2'
5	18	All	eliminate marking: 'Tempo 1. (Hauptzeitmass.)'
	18	Cello	add marking 'ohne Ausdruck'
	20	1.2. Violins	add dynamic '*ppp*'
	20	Viola	add dynamic '*ppp*'
	20	Cello	add dynamic '*ppp*'; remove 'dim.' (at second beat)
	21–5	Viola	first 5 eighth notes: remove part (had doubled the Cello)
	24	1. Horn	change last eighth note to B
	24	1.2. Horns	eliminate doubling with 3.4. Horns
	25	Viola	add 'arco' at sixth eighth note
7	41	2.3. Clarinets	change pitch of last quarter note from B to C♯
	44	1. Horn	eliminate part (slurred half notes F♯ and G)
	44	2.4. Horns	change half rest and half note B♭ for the 2. Horn to stemmed half note A and F♯ and marking '*pp*' (first half of the bar) and B♭ and G (second half)
	44	Viola	replace half notes G and F♯ with eighth-note passage
	44–51¹	Cello (upper)	replace doubling (with lower cello part) with half notes G, F♯, and G
	45	Viola	eliminate doubling with upper Cello
	45	4. Horn	remove dynamic '*p*'
	46	Cello (upper)	add up-bow marking (last eighth note)
8	52	1.3. Horns	change dynamic '*f*' (first beat) to dynamic '*p*'; remove dynamic '*p*' (under third note)
9	63	All	add marking: 'Etwas fliessender'
	65	1.2.3.4. Flutes	eliminate doubling (with Oboe)
	65	1. Clarinet	add upper notes C on beats 2 and 4
	66	All	eliminate marking 'Etwas eilend'
	70	Cello	add down-bow markings on first and third beats; add slurs over the first and third beats
	71	Double bass	add down-bow markings on first and third beats; add slurs over the first and third beats
10	72	Double bass	add down-bow markings on first and third beats; add slurs over the first and third beats
	77	1. Oboe	remove dynamic '*pp*'; add dynamic '*p*' and 'espr.'
	79	1. Clarinet	add accent over fourth pitch
	79	1. Bassoon	add accent over fourth pitch
11	90	1. Violin	add dynamic '*p*'

	90	Viola	add to the first beat the divisi pitches G and B (up-stem) and B and D (down-stem), and markings '*p*' and 'pizz.'; add a quarter rest on the second beat
	89–90	2.3. Clarinets	correct transposition (one half step higher)
	90	1.2.3.4. Flutes	add accent to third beat
12	91	Cello	add dynamic '*p*' on first beat and decrescendo marking over last two notes (after dynamic '*sf*')
	92	Cello	add dynamic '*p*' on first beat and decrescendo marking over last two notes (after dynamic '*sf*')
	93	Cello	add dynamic '*p*' on first beat and decrescendo marking over last two notes (after dynamic '*sf*')
	102	2. Clarinet	add dynamic '*pp*' on first beat
14	114	1. Horn	(in margin) change to 1.3. Horn
	114	2. Horn	(in margin) change to 2.4. Horn
	115	All	replace marking: 'Nicht eilen' with 'sempre a Tempo' (centre above rehearsal no. 9)
	119	1.3. Horns	change 1. to 'a 2'
	119	2.4. Horns	change 2. to 'a 2'
15	120	1. Horn	(in margin) change to 1.3. Horn
	120	2.4. Horns	remove 2. and whole rest (under stave)
	124	Double bass	replace single slur over the bar with one slur over the first two beats, another from the third beat to the first beat of bar 125
	125	Cello	replace half note E and trill marking with half rest
	127	Bass clarinet	replace dynamic '*p*' with dynamic '*mf*' and add 'deutlich' over first beat
	128	1.2.3.4. Flutes	replace dynamic '*p*' with dynamic '*pp*'; add breath mark after first half note
	128	Bass clarinet	add dynamic '*pp*' (at first beat)
	129	Bass clarinet	add dynamic '*mf*' (at first beat)
	130	1.2.3.4. Flutes	replace dynamic '*p*' with dynamic '*pp*'; add breath mark after first half note
	130	Bass clarinet	add dynamic '*mf*' (at first beat)
16	133	1.2.3.4. Flutes	add dynamic '*pp*' (at first beat)
	133	1. Bassoon	replace dynamic '*pp*' with dynamic '*mf*' at first beat; add 'dim.' at third beat
	134	1. Bassoon	add dynamic '*pp*' at first beat
	134	1.2.3.4. Flutes	add breath mark before the quarter note on the third beat
	135	1. Bassoon	add dynamic '*mf*' at third beat
	136	1.2.3.4. Flutes	change dynamic '*p*' to dynamic '*pp*'
	136	1. Bassoon	add 'dim.' at third beat
	137	1. Bassoon	add dynamic '*pp*' at third beat
	138	1.2.3.4. Flutes	change dynamic '*p*' to dynamic '*pp*'

	139	1.2.3.4. Flutes	change dynamic '*p*' to dynamic '*pp*' at third beat
	142	All	remove marking: 'Immer fliessend.'
20	166–7	Cello	replace bars with whole rests (had doubled Double bass)
	167	1.2. Flutes	replace dynamic '*p*' with dynamic '*pp*'
	167	3.4. Flutes	replace dynamic '*p*' with dynamic '*pp*'
	169	1. Horn	change dynamic '*p*' to dynamic '*mf*' and add 'keck' above first beat
21	176	Glockenspiel	change dynamic '*p*' to dynamic '*f*'
23	185	Viola	replace dynamic '*f*' with dynamic '*p*'
	186	1.2. Bassoons	remove Bassoon
	186	Cello	remove part after the third eighth note
	187	1. Violin	let slur conclude on the last eighth note in this bar
24	188	1. Violin	let slur connect first two eighth notes in this bar; add dynamic '*ff*' at first beat; add down-bow on sixteenth note E♮
	194	3.4. Flutes	remove part (had doubled 1.2. Oboes)
	194	1.2. Clarinets	remove part (had doubled 1. Oboe)
	194	3.4 Clarinets	remove part (had doubled 2. Oboe)
25	195	3.4. Flutes	remove part (had doubled 1.2. Oboes)
	195[1]	1.3. Clarinets	remove half note (had doubled 1.2. Oboes)
	195	1.3. Horns	change dynamic '*f*' to dynamic '*ff*'
	195	2.4. Horns	change dynamic '*f*' to dynamic '*ff*'
	196	Double bass	remove first five eighth notes of this bar (had doubled lower Cello part)
	196	Cello	add slur over sixteenth notes
	196	Double bass	add slur over sixteenth notes
26	203	Viola	remove crescendo marking
	203	Cello	remove crescendo marking
27	212	Timpani	add dynamic '*p*' at first beat
30	227	Double bass	add down-bow marking on half note A♭
31	234	1. Oboe	replace dynamic '*p*' with dynamic '*f*'
	234	2. Oboe	replace dynamic '*p*' with dynamic '*f*'
	234	1. Clarinet	replace dynamic '*p*' with dynamic '*f*'
	234	2. Clarinet	replace dynamic '*p*' with dynamic '*f*'
32	237	1.2. Bassoons	over last eighth note, add dynamic '*sf*' followed by decrescendo marking
	238	1.2. Bassoons	add dynamic '*ppp*' over first set of thirty-second notes
32	238	Double bass	replace whole rest with dotted half note C♮ tied to half note C♯ and eighth rest; add dynamic '*ppp*' at first beat and 'morendo' (at second half of the bar)
	240	1. Horn	replace dynamic '*pp*' with dynamic '*p*'
	240	2. Horn	replace dynamic '*pp*' with dynamic '*p*'

33	242	1. Horn	add 'cresc.' at sixteenth rest
	242	2. Horn	add 'cresc.' at sixteenth rest
	243	1. Horn	add dynamic '*f*' at first beat
	243	2. Horn	add dynamic '*p*' at first beat
	245	1. Horn	replace dynamic '*pp*' with dynamic '*p*'
	247	1.2. Horns	replace dynamic '*pp*' with dynamic '*p*'
36	246	2. Violin	add up-bow marking on last eighth note
	246	Viola	add up-bow marking on last eighth note
	246	2. Violin	add down-bow marking on first beat
	246	Viola	add down-bow marking on first beat
	263	All	add marking: 'Schwungvoll'
	265	1.2. Horns	replace dynamic '*p*' with dynamic '*f*'
	265	3.4. Horns	remove decrescendo marking at second half of the bar
37	266	1. Violin	remove down-bow marking (on eighth note D)
	266	2. Violin	remove down-bow marking (on eighth note D)
	267	All	remove marking: 'Schwungvoll'
39	284	1. Clarinet	replace second half of the bar with half rest (had doubled 1. Oboe)
	287	2. Bassoon	add sharp sign (♯) to third sixteenth
41	297	Double bass	add down-bow markings on first and third beats; add slurs over the first and third beats
	300	Cello	add '2 Pulte' at third beat
	300	Double bass	add '2 Pulte' at third beat
	301	Cello	add 'alle' at fourth beat
	301	Double bass	add 'alle' at fourth beat
42	311	1.3. Horns	replace dynamic '*p*' with dynamic '*f*' at first beat; replace dynamic '*f*' with dynamic '*sf*' at second beat

Second Movement

47	1	1.2.3. Clarinets	(in margin) remove '3.'
	4	1.2. Clarinets	replace '2.3.' with '2.'; remove 'zu 2'
	6	Solo Violin	add down-bow marking to sixteenth note A♮
	7	Solo Violin	add up-bow marking (V) to first beat
	10	Solo Violin	add down-bow marking to sixteenth note A♮
	11	Solo Violin	add up-bow marking (V) to first beat
48	19	Solo Violin	replace dynamic '*sf*' with dynamic '*sfp*'
	20	Solo Violin	replace dynamic '*sf*' with dynamic '*sfp*'
	27	Solo Violin	replace dynamic '*sf*' with dynamic '*f*'
	27	1. Clarinet	change last sixteenth note to a thirty-second note followed by a thirty-second rest
	28	1. Clarinet	change last sixteenth note to a thirty-second note followed by a thirty-second rest
	29	1. Clarinet	change last sixteenth note to a thirty-second note followed by a thirty-second rest

	35	1. Bassoon	replace eighth note C followed by two eighth rests with dotted quarter note C and tie to next bar
	36	1. Bassoon	added eighth note C (tied to previous bar) followed by two eighth rests
49	43	1. Violin	add down-bow marking on final eighth note
52	71	3. Horn	replace passage (had doubled Bassoon part) with rest
54	88	Contrabassoon	(in margin) replace Contrabassoon with 3. Clarinet; replace bass clef with treble and add key signature (top-line sharp)
	88–9	1. Flute	add slur to pitches D and C
	89	1. Flute	replace final eighth note with eighth rest
	90	1. Flute	replace passage (had doubled 1. Violin) with rest
	90	3. Clarinet	add part to double 1. Clarinet, including staccato dots and dynamic '*ff*'
	91–2	1. Oboe	replace passage with rests (had doubled 1. Violin)
	93	1. Flute	replace passage (had doubled 1. Violin) with rest
	93	3. Clarinet	add part to double 1. Clarinet
57	130	1. Horn	remove dynamic '*f*' followed by crescendo marking
	130	Viola	add slur (over entire bar)
	131	1. Horn	remove dynamic '*sf*' followed by crescendo marking
	131	Viola	add slur over first four sixteenth notes
	132	1. Horn	remove dynamic '*ff*' at first beat
59	142	1. Oboe	(in margin) change '1. Oboe' to '1.2. Oboe'
	142	1.2. Oboes	add 'a2' at first beat
	144	1.2. Oboes	add 'I.' (1.) at first beat
60	151	1.2. Flutes	change first eighth note F to a sixteenth note followed by a sixteenth rest; add dynamic '*sf*'
61	161	1.3. Horns	remove decrescendo marking under last three sixteenth notes
	163	1.3. Horns	remove crescendo marking under entire bar
	164	1.3. Horns	remove dynamic '*ff*' (at first beat) followed by decrescendo marking (under last two)
	166	1.3. Horns	remove crescendo marking under last two eighth notes
62	171	1. Violin	add decrescendo marking under last three sixteenth notes
	171	1. Violin	'+' sign, thus, add dynamic '*sf*' from above and decrescendo marking under last three sixteenth notes
	173	1. Violin	add decrescendo marking under last three sixteenth notes

	173	1. Violin	'+' sign, thus, add dynamic '*sf*' from above and decrescendo marking under last three sixteenth notes
	178	Cello	add 'Solo' at first beat
63	180	Cello	add 'alle'
	185	1.2. Trumpets	remove accent from first beat
	187	1.2. Trumpets	remove accent from first beat
64	206–7	Viola	add part to double 2. Violin, with dynamic '*p*' (but without the marking 'dolce' found in 2. Violin)
65	208	Cello (upper part)	add up-bow marking on first beat
	209	Cello (upper part)	add up-bow marking on first beat
	210	1.3. Flutes	add dynamic '*ff*' at first beat
	210	2.4. Flutes	add dynamic '*ff*' at first beat
	210	1.3. Oboes	add dynamic '*ff*' at first beat
	210	2. Oboe	add dynamic '*ff*' at first beat
	210	1.2. Bassoons	add dynamic '*ff*' at first beat
67	251	1.2. Cl. in B	(in margin) change to 2.3. Cl. in B.
	251	Bcl. in B	(in margin) remove marking (and entire part, from 251 to 261)
	254	2.3. Clarinets	replace 'zu 2' with 'a 3'
	254	Harp	replace dynamic '*pp*' with dynamic '*sf*' on first beat; add dynamic '*p*' on second beat
	255	1.2. Bassoons	remove ties to m. 256
	256	1.2. Bassoon	remove pitches tied from previous bar
	257–9	1.2. Bassoons	add part to double 2.3. Clarinets, with dynamic '*ff*'
	260	1.3. Flutes	add part to double 2.3. Clarinets
	260	Viola	remove slur to m. 261
	261	Viola	remove pitch 'A'
	261	1.2. Bassoons	add part to double 2.3. Clarinets
	261	Contrabassoon	add crescendo marking
	261	Double bass	add dotted quarter note D with dynamic '*pp*' (at first beat) and tie to next bar
68	262	1.2. Clarinets	(in margin) change '1.2.' to '1.2.3.'
	262 (from margin)–273	Bcl. in B.	remove entire part
	262–5	1.2. Oboes	add part to double Clarinets exactly, including dynamics and articulations
	262–5	1.2. Horns	add part (to double Contrabassoon)
	262–5	3.4. Horns	add part (to double Contrabassoon)
	262	Double bass	add part (tied from previous bar)
	263–4	1.2. Bassoons	add part (to double Clarinets), but without dynamic indication
	263	1. Violin	remove dynamic '*pp* subito'
	263	2. Violin	remove dynamic '*pp* subito'

	267	1.2. Bassoons	add dynamic '*pp*'
	267	Double bass	remove part (same as previous bar)
	269	Double bass	remove part (same as previous bar)
	271–3	Double bass	remove part (same bar 270)
	273	1.2. Flutes	remove dynamic (crescendo marking followed by decrescendo marking)
	273	3.4. Flutes	remove dynamic (crescendo marking followed by decrescendo marking)
70	297	1.2. Flutes	remove part (doubled in 3.4. Flutes)
	297	3.4. Flutes	replace dynamic '*f*' with dynamic '*p*' at first beat
72	330	Double bass	remove tie to bar 331
	331	Double bass	remove bar (tied dotted quarter note C)
73	339–40	Double bass	remove part (had doubled Cello, but an octave higher)
	341	Double bass	replace first two beats with rests; add dynamic '*pp*' to last beat
	341–2	Timpani	remove part (pitch C with same rhythm as found in the Double bass)
74	343–4	Timpani	remove part (pitch C with same rhythm as found in the Double bass)
	355–7	Timpani	remove part
	355	Bass clarinet	remove last two sixteenth notes (had doubled 1.2. Clarinets)
	356–7	Bass clarinet	remove part
	356	Cor anglais	remove part (had doubled Clarinets on first beat, followed by two eighth rests)
75	358	Cor anglais	remove part (had doubled Clarinets on first beat, followed by two eighth rests)
	358–60	Bass clarinet	remove part
	358–60	Timpani	remove part

Third Movement

	1	Cello	add marking 'D-Saite' (before first beat)
76			
	24	All	(above the system) add marking 'Nicht zurückhalten/streng im Tempo'
77	37	1. Violin	add 'espr.' after the first beat
80	90	1.2.3. Trumpets	move 'dim.' from first to fourth beat
	93	All	replace 'Wieder langsam' with 'Wieder a Tempo'
81	98	All	replace 'Immer noch zurückhaltender' with 'Zurückhaltend'
	107	3. Flute	remove part
	108	3. Flute	add dynamic '*pp*'
82	118–19	1.2. Clarinets	remove dynamic markings (crescendo marking followed by decrescendo marking)
	123	All	add marking 'Fliessender'
	128	2. Violin	add marking 'espr.'

83	141	3.4. Flutes	remove crescendo markings at first and third beats
	141	1. Oboe	remove crescendo markings at first and third beats
	141	2. Violin	remove crescendo markings at second and fourth beats; add up-bow markings at second and fourth beats
	141–2	Cello (upper part)	remove part (had doubled lower part)
	142	3.4. Flutes	remove crescendo markings at first and third beats
	142	1. Oboe	remove crescendo markings at first and third beats
	143	3.4. Flutes	remove part (had doubled Oboe)
	143	2. Violin	remove crescendo mark at first beat; replace dynamic '*pp*' (at third beat) with dynamic '*p*'
84	144–6	3.4. Flutes	remove part (had doubled Oboe)
	151	All	add marking 'Sehr fliessend'
	155	Cello (upper part)	remove marking 'molto espr.'
86	171	All	remove marking 'zurückhaltend'
	179	All	replace marking 'Langsam' with 'Wieder wie vorher'
	187	All	remove marking 'Etwas drängend'
87	192	All	add marking 'Fliessend'
	195	2. Trumpet	add part
88	196–7	Cor anglais	add part indicated (double Oboes, but with different dynamic markings)
	196		(in margin) replace '1. Trp.' with '1.2. Trp.'
	196	2. Trumpet	add part
	196–7	2. Violin	remove part
	197	1.2. Oboes	remove decrescendo marking; add marking 'cresc.' at fourth beat (above the staff) and crescendo marking at fourth beat (below the staff)
	197–8	1. Horn	add part (as written on page)
	197–200	Viola	remove sostenuto markings from all eighth notes
	197–200	Cello (both parts)	remove sostenuto markings from all eighth notes
	201	Trumpets	add marking 'I.' (1.) and 'offen'
89	204	Trumpets	(in margin) replace '1.2. Trp.' with '1. Trp.'
	210	All	add marking 'Wieder gehalten'
	210–11	1.2. Clarinets	replace part (had doubled Viola) with part to double Cor anglais
	210–11 (1st beat)	Bass Clarinet	add part to double Viola
	210–11 (1st beat)	1.2.3. Bassoons	add part to double Viola with dynamic '*ff*'
	210	Trumpet	replace 'zu 2' with 'I.' (1.)

	211	1.2. Oboes	replace marking 'dim.' with crescendo marking
	211	Viola	change whole note to half and double the Clarinet part in the last 2 beats
90	212	1. Oboe	add part
	212–13	Cor anglais	replace dynamic '*p*' with dynamic '*ff*' at first beat; add decrescendo from second beat to the end of the next bar
	214	All	replace 'Zurückhaltend' with 'Etwas zurückhaltend'
	219	All	add marking 'Sehr zurückhaltend'
91	237	1.2. Clarinets	add marking 'I.' (1. Clarinet)
92	260–2	1. Clarinet	remove part
	260	1. Violin	add 'a 2' at first beat
	260–2	2. Violin	add 'a 2' and 'tr' marking at first beat; rewrite part in octaves
	261	2. Violin	add octave pitches to the first and last beats
	260–2	Viola	revise part (found on pasteover)
	260–2	Cello (upper part)	remove part; replace with part marked (add eighth note D at the end of bar 261); double lower part in bar 262
	262	Double bass	remove part
	263	1.2. Flutes	replace dynamic '*pp*' with dynamic '*p*'
	263	1.2.3. Oboes	remove part
	263	1.2.3. Clarinets	replace dynamic '*pp*' with dynamic '*p*'
	263–6	1.2. Bassoons	remove part
	263	3. Bassoon	(in margin) replace '3. Fag.' with 'Contrafag.'
	263–6	2. Violin	add part (as originally found in Oboes); use dynamic '*pp*' at first beat of bar 263
	263–6	Cello	add part (to double 2. Violin at the octave)
	263–6	Double bass	add part (as originally found in the Bassoons); use dynamic '*pp*' at the first beat of bar 263
	264	1.2.3. Oboes	replace part with a doubling of the first beat of the Flutes
	266	1.2.3. Oboes	replace part with a doubling of the first beat of the Flutes, as revised above
	267	1.2. Flutes	make second note a thirty-second note followed by a thirty-second rest
	267	1.2.3. Oboes	make second note a thirty-second note followed by a thirty-second rest
	267	1.2.3. Clarinets	remove part
	267	1.2. Horns	add part
	267	3.4. Horns	add part
	267	1. Violin	replace second half bar with a rest
	268	1.2. Flutes	remove decrescendo marking
	268	1.2.3. Oboes	remove decrescendo marking
	268–9	1.2. Bassoons	remove part

	268	Contrabassoon	add notation 'nimmt 3. Fagott'
	268	2. Violin	remove trill marking and augmentation dot; replace dynamic '*p*' with dynamic '*sf*' and add 'pizz.'
	268	Viola	make second note a thirty-second note followed by a thirty-second rest
93	270	1.2. Bassoons	(in margin) remove '1. Fag.'
	270–5	1.2. Bassoons	remove part
	270	2.3. Bassoons	(in margin) replace '2.3.' with '1.3.'
	277	2.3. Clarinets	add part, 'a 2'
	277	1.3. Bassoons	add part, 'a 2'
	277	1.2. Horns	make eighth notes into quarter notes; remove rests
	277	3.4. Horns	make eighth notes into quarter notes; remove rests
	277	1. Violin	add part
	277	Cello	rewrite part in octaves (as notated in bottom margin)
94	278	1.2. Bassoons	add tie from previous bar
	278	3. Bassoon	add tie from previous bar
	278	Glockenspiel	replace dynamic '*p*' with dynamic '*f*'
	282	1.2. Flutes	add dynamic '*ff*' at the first beat
	282	1.2. Piccolos	add dynamic '*ff*' at the first beat
	282	1.2. Horns	replace part with the one in the lower margin
	282	3.4. Horns	replace part with the one in the lower margin
	283	1.2. Horns	add 'a 2' at first beat
	283	3.4. Horns	add 'a 2' at first beat
	282	1. Violin	add up-bow marking to second beat and down-bow to third beat
	282	2. Violin	add lower octave to existing part
95	288	1. Violin	(both staves) replace dynamic '*pp*' with dynamic '*p*'
	288	2. Violin	replace dynamic '*pp*' with dynamic '*p*'
	288	Viola	replace dynamic '*pp*' with dynamic '*p*'
	288	Cello	(both staves) replace dynamic '*pp*' with dynamic '*p*'
	290	1. Violin	(both staves) add marking 'Ton!'
	290	Viola	add marking 'Ton!'
	292	1. Violin	(lower part) add marking 'Ton!'
	296	1.2. Bassoons	replace dynamic '*pp*' with dynamic '*p*' at first beat; add 'espr.' at fourth beat
	296	1.2. Horns	replace dynamic '*pp*' with dynamic '*p*' at first beat; replace 'molto portamento' with 'espr.' at fourth beat
	299	1.2. Horns	replace dynamic '*pp*' with dynamic '*p*'
	299	Viola	replace dynamic '*pp*' with dynamic '*p*'

	303	All	add marking 'Fliessend'
	303	1. Violin	(lower part) change pitch A (had doubled upper part of 2. Violin) to double upper part of 1. Violin
96	315	Double bass	remove tremolo marking; tie whole notes to next bar
97	316	1.2. Flutes	remove dynamic '*p*'
	316	3.4. Flutes	remove dynamic '*p*'
	316	1.2.3. Oboes	remove dynamic '*p*'
	316	1.2.3. Clarinets	remove dynamic '*p*'
	316	1.2. Bassoons	remove dynamic '*p*'
	316–17	1.2. Horns	add part
	316–17	3.4. Horns	add part
	316	Double bass	remove tremolo marking; add ties from previous bar
	317	3.4. Flutes	add part (tie pitches from previous bar)
98	318	1.2. Flutes	(in margin) change '1.2. Fl.' to '1.2.3.4. Fl.'
	318	3.4. Flutes	(in margin) change '3.4. Fl.' to '1.2. Ob.'
	318	1.2.3.4. Flutes	replace dynamic '*p*' and 'cresc.—' with 'sempre ff'
	318	1. Violin	remove dynamic '*p*'
	320	1.2.3.4. Flutes	add 'a 4' and indicate 1.2. as 'sempre ff' and 3.4. with dynamic '*p*' followed by the crescendo marking to extend through the rest of the bar
	321	1.2. Oboes	replace dynamic '*ff*' with crescendo marking at the second half of the bar; remove accent marks
	322	1.2. Oboes	add dynamic '*ff*' at the first beat
	322	1.2.3.4. Flutes	remove decrescendo marking
	324	1.2.3. Bassoons	replace dynamic '*ff*' with dynamic crescendo *ff* decrescendo
	325	1.2.3. Bassoons	replace decrescendo with crescendo *ff* decrescendo
99	326–9	1.2. Flutes	add part
	333	2. Violin	add dynamic '*p*' and 'espr.' (at second beat)
	333	Viola	add dynamic '*p*' and 'espr.' (at second beat)
	339	Cello	(lower part) change half note to whole note (pitch 'D')
	344	3.4. Flutes	remove upper note 'G'
	345	3.4. Flutes	add dynamic '*pp*'
	346	3.4. Flutes	remove upper note 'G'
	347–50	Harp	(treble clef) remove part
	349–50	Harp	(bass clef) remove part
	351	Double bass	remove part (tied quarter note 'D')
	352	1.2.3. Clarinets	remove part (tied quarter note sonority)

Fourth Movement

100	1	1. Clarinet	change dynamic '*pp*' to dynamic '*ppp*'

	1	1. Horn	change dynamic '*pp*' to dynamic '*ppp*'
	1	Viola	change dynamic '*pp*' to dynamic '*ppp*'
	1	Cello	change dynamic '*pp*' to dynamic '*ppp*'
	5–6	Cor anglais	remove part
	5	Bass Clarinet	replace dynamic '*p*' with dynamic '*f*'
	5	1.2. Bassoons	replace dynamic '*p*' with dynamic '*f*'
	5–6	Timpani	add part
	5–6	2. Violin	remove part after first beat 'D'
	5–6	Double bass	remove part after first beat 'G'
	6	2. Bassoon	add dynamic '*ff*'
	6	Viola	remove part
	6	Cello	remove part
101	7–10	Cor anglais	remove part
	7	Viola	add dynamic '*pp*' (at second beat)
	7	Cello	add dynamic '*pp*' (at first beat)
	10	2. Violin	add open parenthesis '(' to indicate chord at third beat, and dynamic '*sf*'
	10	Viola	add open parenthesis '(' to indicate chord at third beat
	10	Cello	add open parenthesis '(' to indicate chord at third beat
102	12–16	Harp	remove treble part
	14	1.2. Flutes	remove dotted half note D (downstem) and quarter rest (replace with whole rest)
	16–17[1]	1. Violin	remove part
	17	Cor anglais	replace second half of the bar with rest
	17	1. Horn	add part in second half of the bar (to take over Cor anglais part) at dynamic '*pp*'
103	18–19	1.2. Bassoons	add half rest and upstem C at dynamic '*pp*' (in each bar)
	18–19	1. Horn	replace part (half rest followed by half note G) with tied whole notes B
	18–20	Cor anglais	remove part
	20	Harp	remove part
	21	Harp	add dynamic '*pp*' in both staves at first beat
	22	Harp	remove part
104	23–4	Harp	remove part
105	31–3	Harp	remove part
106	36–8	Becken	remove ties and tied whole notes after the first; add marking 'klingen lassen' after remaining whole note
110	58	1.2. Oboes	add marking 'sehr hervortretend'
111	60	1. Oboe	remove dynamic '*pp*' (at first beat)
	61	3. Bassoon	remove tie (to next bar)
	62	3. Bassoon	replace dynamic '*pp*' with dynamic '*ff*' followed by decrescendo marking

	63–5	1.2. Flutes	remove part
	66	Double bass	remove marking 'mit Dämpfer' after 'Ein Contrabass-Solo'
113	80–3	Harp	remove treble-clef part
	81–3	Cor anglais	remove part
114	84–6	Cor anglais	remove part
	84–5	Harp	remove treble-clef part
	85–6	Harp	remove bass-clef part
	87	Harp	add dynamic '*p*' at first beat
115	91	1. Violin	change first note to half note followed by half rest
	91	2. Violin	remove part
	93	1. Violin	change first note to half note followed by half rest
	93	2. Violin	remove part
	95	1. Violin	remove crescendo marking
	95	Viola	add lower pitch (E) (originally found in Cello)
	95	Cello	remove part
116	97	2. Flute	remove dynamic marking '*sf*' (at fourth beat)
	97	1. Violin	(upper part) remove crescendo marking
	97	1. Violin	(lower part) replace dynamic '*f*' at first beat with dynamic '*pp*'; remove decrescendo marking on second beat
	98	1. Violin	(lower part) remove dynamic '*sf*' at first beat
118	106–8	Becken	remove ties and tied whole notes after the first (in b. 106)
	111	1. Flute	replace whole note with dotted half note followed by quarter rest
	111	2. Flute	replace whole note with dotted half note followed by quarter rest
	111	1.2. Clarinets	replace whole note with dotted half note followed by quarter rest
	111	Double bass	replace whole note with dotted half note followed by quarter rest
119	112	1.3. Horns	replace whole note with dotted half note followed by quarter rest
	112	2.4. Horns	replace whole note with dotted half note followed by quarter rest
	113	1. Violin	replace whole note with dotted half note followed by quarter rest
	113	2. Violin	replace whole note with dotted half note followed by quarter rest
	113	Viola	replace whole note with dotted half note followed by quarter rest
	113	Cello	replace whole note with dotted half note followed by quarter rest

	113	Double bass	replace whole note with dotted half note followed by quarter rest
122	135	Viola	add part (to double 2. Violin) at dynamic '*pp*' at first beat
	136	1. Violin	replace dynamic '*pp*' with dynamic '*ppp*'
	136	2. Violin	replace dynamic '*pp*' with dynamic '*ppp*'
	136	Viola	replace dynamic '*pp*' with dynamic '*ppp*'
	143–6	Cor anglais	remove part
124	162	1. Violin	replace second quarter note with an eighth note followed by an eighth rest; remove rest of bar
	163	1. Violin	remove part
	162	Viola	remove part
	163	Viola	add dynamic '*ppp*' at first beat
	165–7¹	Viola	remove part
	167	Viola	(second half) add half note B at dynamic '*ppp*'
	168	Cor anglais	remove part
	168	Harp	remove part
125	169	Cor anglais	remove part
	169	Harp	remove part
	169	2. Violin	change first pitch from F♯ to D♯

Select Bibliography

The bibliography includes works consulted for this study dealing specifically with Mahler and his music, including various catalogues of manuscripts.

CATALOGUES AND BIBLIOGRAPHIES

ALBRECHT, OTTO E., *A Census of Autograph Musical Manuscripts of European Composers in American Libraries* (Philadelphia: University of Pennsylvania Press, 1953).

SEEBASS, TILMAN (ed.), *Musikhandschriften der Bodmeriana* (Cologny-Genève: Fondation Martin Bodmer, 1986).

STEPHAN, RUDOLF, *Gustav Mahler Werk und Interpretation: Autographe, Partituren, Dokumente* (Cologne: Arno Volk, 1979).

TURNER, J. RIGBIE, *Nineteenth-Century Autograph Music Manuscripts in the Pierpont Morgan Library: A Checklist* (New York: The Pierpont Morgan Library, 1982).

MANUSCRIPTS AND EDITIONS

Entries for manuscripts include cataloguing information found at the institution where they are currently stored. Since not all libraries and archives use call numbers for manuscripts, I have retained the original cataloguing and/or descriptive entries in lieu of self-determined alpha-numeric reference codes idiosyncratic to this study.

MAHLER, GUSTAV, [*Des Knaben Wunderhorn*]. '6 Wunderhornlieder'. Berlin, Staatsbibliothek der Stiftung Preußischer Kulturbesitz.

—— [*Des Knaben Wunderhorn*]. '5 Humoresken'. Vienna, Gesellschaft der Musikfreunde, VI.36886/A316.

—— [*Des Knaben Wunderhorn*]. *Fünfzehn Lieder, Humoresken und Balladen aus 'Des Knaben Wunderhorn' für Singstimme und Klavier*, ed. Renate Hilmar-Voit and Thomas Hampson (Gustav Mahler: Sämtliche Werke, Kritische Gesamtausgabe, 13; Vienna: Universal Edition, n.d. [1993]).

—— *Symphonie Nr. 3* (Sämtliche Werke: Kritische Gesamtausgabe, 3; Vienna: Universal Edition, 1974).

—— [*Symphony No. 3*]. 'III. Symphonie Partitur, 281 Seiten'. New York, Pierpont Morgan Library.

—— [*Symphony No. 3*]. 'III. Symphonie Autograph Partiturentwürfe von 3 Sätzen'. New York, Pierpont Morgan Library.

—— [*Symphony No. 3*]. 'Erste Skizze, drei Seiten (Mus. Hs. 22.794.)'. Vienna, Österreichische Nationalbibliothek, Musiksammlung.

—— [*Symphony No. 3*]. 'Sketches for the first movement (MLM, Box 8, 630)'. Stanford, [Calif.], Stanford University Library.

—— [*Symphony No. 3*]. 'Sketches for the first movement (MLM, Box 8, 631)'. Stanford, [Calif.], Stanford University Library.

—— ['Es sungen drei Engel']. 'III. Symphonie 5ᵉ Satz, 2 Seiten; Klavierskizze zum Frauenchor "Es sungen drei Engel"' (F21 Berg 31). Vienna, Österreichische Nationalbibliothek, Musiksammlung.

—— ['Es sungen drei Engel']. 'Was mir die Morgenglocken erzählen, 4 Seiten, autographe Partiturskizze'. New York, Pierpont Morgan Library.

—— ['Es sungen drei Engel']. 'III. Symphonie, 23 Seiten: Bearbeitung des 5. Satzes'. Vienna, Universal Edition Archive.

—— [*Symphony No. 4*], 'Gustav Mahler, IV. Symphonie G-Dur Partitur, XIII. 35824'. Vienna, Gesellschaft der Musikfreunde.

—— [*Symphony No. 4*], 'Gustav Mahler, IV. Symphonie G-Dur Partitur, Korrigierter Partitur mit früheren Korrekturen Mahlers'. Vienna, Internationale Gustav Mahler Gesellschaft Archive.

—— [*Symphony No. 4*], 'Gustav Mahler, IV. Symphonie. Abzüge mit Autographkorrekturen Mahlers'. London, Haas-Rosenthal.

—— [*Symphony No. 4*], 'Gustav Mahler, IV. Symphonie G-Dur Partitur, korrigierter Notenstich mit Korrekturen Mahlers, U.E. 2944'. Vienna, Universal Edition-Archive.

—— [*Symphony No. 4*], 'Gustav Mahler, IV. Symphonie G-Dur Grosse Partitur der Erstausgabe, Doblinger Platten Nr. 31'. Graz, Bibliothek der Grazer Musikhochschule.

—— [*Symphony No. 4*], 'Gustav Mahler, IV. 'Sketches for the 1st movement of the 4th Symphony (Case MS VM 1001 M21 s4)'. Chicago, The Newberry Library.

—— [Symphony No. 4]. 'Skizzen (Mus. Hs. 4366)'. Vienna, Österreichische Nationalbibliothek, Musiksammlung.

—— [Symphony No. 4]. 'Skizzen (Mus. Hs. 39.745)'. Vienna, Österreichische Nationalbibliothek, Musiksammlung.

—— [Symphony No. 4]. 'Skizzen (Mus. Hs. 30.898)'. Vienna, Österreichische Nationalbibliothek, Musiksammlung.

—— [*Symphony No. 4*]. 'Skizzenfragment zur 4. Sinfonie'. Cologny, Bibliotheca Bodmeriana.

—— [*Symphony No. 4*]. 'Skizze zur IV. Symphonie, 14 Seiten'. Vienna, Internationale Gustav Mahler Gesellschaft Archive (Photocopy Ph 60).

—— [*Symphony No. 4*]. 'Fragment II Mvt IV Symphony (Scherzo)'. London, Ontario, The University of Western Ontario. Music Library.

—— [*Symphony No. 4*]. 'Fourth Symphony Sketches'. Paris: Bibliothèque Musicale Gustav Mahler.

—— [*Symphony No. 4*]. 'Skizzen zur IVᵉ mit Klavierauszug letzten Satz'. New York, Pierpont Morgan Library. Lehman Deposit.

—— [*Symphony No. 4*]. 'Skizzenblatt aus der IV. Symphonie (MLM, Box 8, 633)'. Stanford, [Calif.], Stanford University Library.

—— [*Symphony No. 4*]. 'Symphonie Nro. IV (Humoreske)'. Cincinnati, Public Library of Cincinnati and Hamilton County [Ohio], Fine Arts Collection.

—— *Symphony No. 4* (Vienna: Ludwig Doblinger, [1902]).

—— *Symphony No. 4* (Vienna: Universal Edition, [1905]).

MAHLER, GUSTAV, *Symphony No. 4* (Vienna: Universal Edition, [1906]).

—— *Symphony No. 4* (Vienna: Universal Edition, [1910]).

—— *Symphony No. 4*, Introduction by Erwin Stein (Vienna: Universal–Edition, 1925).

—— *Symphony No. 4*, Introduction by Erwin Stein (Vienna: Universal–Edition, n.d. [1925?]).

—— *Symphony No. 4*, Introduction by Fritz Stiedry (London: Boosey & Hawkes, Ltd., 1943).

—— *Symphony No. 4*, Introduction by Erwin Ratz (Sämtliche Werke: Kritische Gesamtausgabe, 4; Vienna: Universal Edition, 1963).

—— *Symphony No. 4*, Introduction by B. Levik (Moscow: Musik, 1965).

—— *Symphony No. 4*, Introduction by Hans Ferdinand Redlich (London: Edition Eulenberg, 1966).

—— *Symphony No. 4*, Introduction by Erwin Stein (repr. of the 1963 Universal Edition score; Vienna: Universal Edition, 1966).

—— *Symphonie Nr. 7*, ed. Hans Redlich (London: Edition Eulenberg, [1965]).

—— [*Symphony No. 8*]. 'Veni creator spiritus'. New York: The New York Public Library, Lincoln Center.

—— ['Das himmlische Leben']. 'Wir geniessen die himmlischen Freuden'. (Universal Edition Nr. 2946; Vienna: Universal Edition, 1920; repr. New York: Edwin W. Kalmus, n.d.).

—— ['Das himmlische Leben']. 'Das himmlische Leben, Ein Humoreske, Nro. 4 (VII.36886)'. Vienna, Gesellschaft der Musikfreunde.

—— ['Das himmlische Leben']. '6 Wunderhornlieder (für) Singstimme und Klavier, Autograph auf verschiedenzeiligen Notenpapier'. Berlin, Bibliothek der Stiftung Preußischer Kulturbesitz.

—— ['Das himmlische Leben'] 'Kopistenabschrift mit Eintragungen Mahlers. Partitur mit Singstimme, G-Dur'. Vienna, Internationale Gustav Mahler Gesellschaft Archive. (Photocopy.)

—— 'Scherzo und Trio'. Vienna, Wiener Stadt- und Landesbibliothek, MH 654/c.

—— 'Unidentified Sketches'. New York, Pierpont Morgan Library.

—— *Symphonische Entwürfe. Faksimile nach den Skizzen aus der Wiener Stadt- und Landesbibliothek und der Pierpont Morgan Library, New York*, ed. Renate Hilmar-Voit (Tutzing: Hans Schneider, 1991). This is a facsimile of the 'Scherzo und Trio' (Vienna) and the 'Unidentified Sketches' (New York), both of which are listed above.

LETTERS AND REMINISCENCES

BAUER-LECHNER, NATALIE, *Erinnerungen an Gustav Mahler*, ed. H. J. Killian, introduction by Paul Stefan (Vienna: E. P. Tal & Co., 1923).

—— *Erinnerungen an Gustav Mahler*, ed. and annotated Knud Martner (Hamburg: Karl Dieter Wagner, 1984).

—— *Recollections of Gustav Mahler*, ed. and annotated Peter Franklin, trans. Dika Newlin (New York: Cambridge University Press, 1980).

—— 'Mahleriana'. Typescript ('dactylographie') of the original manuscript. Paris: Bibliothèque Musicale Gustav Mahler.

MAHLER, GUSTAV, *Briefe*, ed. Herta Blaukopf (Vienna: Zsolnay, 1982).

—— *Unbekannte Briefe*, ed. Herta Blaukopf (Vienna: Zsolnay, 1983).

—— *Selected Letters of Gustav Mahler*, ed. Knud Martner, trans. Eithne Wilkins, Ernst Kaiser, and Bill Hopkins (New York: Farrar, Straus & Giroux, 1979).

MARTNER, KNUD, *Mahler im Konzertsaal* (Copenhagen: Knud Martner, 1985).

MÜLLER, KARL-JOSEF, *Mahler: Leben, Werke, Dokumente* (Mainz: Schott, 1988).

REESER, EDUARD (ed.), *Gustav Mahler und Holland: Briefe* (Vienna: Universal Edition, 1980).

REILLY, EDWARD R., *Gustav Mahler und Guido Adler: Zur Geschichte einer Freundschaft* (Vienna: Universal Edition, 1978); English edn., trans. as *Gustav Mahler and Guido Adler: Records of a Friendship* (New York: Cambridge University Press, 1982).

WALTER, BRUNO, *Briefe 1894–1962* (Frankfurt am Main: S. Fischer, 1969).

WERFEL, ALMA SCHINDLER MAHLER, *Erinnerungen und Briefe* (Amsterdam: Propyläen, 1974); English edn., trans. as *Gustav Mahler: Memories and Letters*, ed. Donald Mitchell, trans. Basil Creighton (3rd edn., Seattle: University of Washington Press, 1975).

BIOGRAPHICAL STUDIES

BANKS, PAUL, AND MITCHELL, DONALD, 'Mahler, Gustav', *New Grove Dictionary of Music and Musicians*, ed. Stanley Sadie (London: Macmillan, 1980), xi. 505–31.

—— —— 'Gustav Mahler', in *The New Grove Turn of the Century Masters*, ed. Stanley Sadie (New York: W. W. Norton & Co., Inc., 1985), 79–181.

KENNEDY, MICHAEL, *Gustav Mahler* (London: J. M. Dent & Sons, Ltd., 1974; rev. edn., New York: Schirmer Books, 1991).

LA GRANGE, HENRY-LOUIS DE, *Mahler*, i (Garden City, NY: Doubleday and Co., 1973; repr. with corrections, London: Victor Gollancz, Ltd., 1974).

—— *Gustav Mahler: Chronique d'une vie*, i: *Vers la gloire 1860–1900* (rev. edn., Paris: Fayard, 1979).

—— *Gustav Mahler: Chronique d'une vie*, ii: *L'Âge d'or de Vienne 1900–1907* (Paris: Fayard, 1983).

—— *Gustav Mahler: Chronique d'une vie*, iii: *Le Génie foudroyé 1907–1911* (Paris: Fayard, 1984).

—— *Gustav Mahler*, ii: *Vienna: The Years of Challenge (1897–1904)* (Oxford: Oxford University Press, 1995).

—— 'Gustav Mahler Chronologie'. (Typescript).

MITCHELL, DONALD, *Gustav Mahler: The Early Years*, rev. and ed. Paul Banks and David Matthews (Berkeley, Calif.: The University of California Press, 1980).

—— *Gustav Mahler: The Wunderhorn Years—Chronicles and Commentaries* (Boulder, Colo.: Westview Press, 1980; repr. Berkeley, Calif.: University of California Press, 1980).

—— *Gustav Mahler: Songs and Symphonies of Life and Death* (Berkeley, Calif.: University of California Press, 1985).

REDLICH, H. F., *Bruckner and Mahler* (London: J. M. Dent & Sons, Ltd., 1955; rev. edn., London: Dent, 1963).

ANALYSES AND CRITICAL STUDIES: THE FOURTH SYMPHONY

ABRAHAM, LARS ULRICH, 'Zur Harmonik in Gustav Mahlers Vierter Symphonie', in *Neue Wege der musikalischen Analyse*, ed. Rudolf Stephan (Berlin: Merseburger, 1967), 43–4.

BONDS, MARK EVAN, 'Ambivalent Elysium: Mahler's Fourth Symphony', in *After Beethoven: Imperatives of Originality in the Symphony* (Cambridge, Mass.: Harvard University Press, 1996), 175–200.

HEFLING, STEPHEN C., ' "Variations *in nuce*": A Study of Mahler Sketches and a Comment on Sketch Studies', in *Gustav Mahler Kolloquium 1979*, ed. Rudolf Klein (Österreichische Gesellschaft für Musik, 7; Kassel: Bärenreiter, 1981), 102–26.

NEUWIRTH, GÖSTA, 'Sensationelle Entdeckung in Graz: Handschrift von Mahler', *Grazer Tagblatt*, 28 February 1979.

—— 'Zur Geschichte der 4. Symphonie', in *Mahler-Interpretation: Aspekte zum Werk und Wirken von Gustav Mahler*, ed. Rudolf Stephan (Mainz: Schott, 1985), 105–10.

STEIN, ERWIN, 'Eine unbekannte Ausgabe letzter Hand von Mahlers IV. Symphonie', *Pult und Taktstock*, 6 (1929), 31–2; English trans., 'The Unknown Last Version of Mahler's Fourth Symphony', in *Orpheus in New Guises* (New York: Rockliff, 1953), 31–3.

STEPHAN, RUDOLF, *Gustav Mahler: IV. Symphonie G-Dur* (Meisterwerke der Musik, 5; Munich: Wilhelm Fink, 1966).

—— 'Betrachtungen zur Form und Thematik in Mahlers Vierter Symphonie', in *Neue Wege der musikalischen Analyse* (Berlin: Merseburger, 1967), 23–42.

ZYCHOWICZ, JAMES L., 'Sketches and Drafts of Gustav Mahler 1892–1901: The Sources of the Fourth Symphony' (Ph.D. diss., University of Cincinnati, 1988).

—— 'Toward an *Ausgabe letzter Hand*: The Publication and Revision of Mahler's Fourth Symphony', *Journal of Musicology*, 12 (1995), 260–72.

ANALYSES AND CRITICAL STUDIES: OTHER WORKS

ADORNO, THEODOR W., *Gustav Mahler: Eine musikalische Physiognomie* (Frankfurt: Suhrkamp, 1960); English trans. by Edmund Jephcott, *Mahler: A Musical Physiognomy* (Chicago: The University of Chicago Press, 1992).

ANDRASCHKE, PETER, *Gustav Mahler IX. Symphonie: Kompositionsprozeß und Analyse* (Beihefte zum Archiv für Musikwissenschaft, 14; Wiesbaden: Steiner, 1976).

BEKKER, PAUL, *Gustav Mahlers Sinfonien* (Berlin: Schuster & Loeffler, 1921; repr. Tutzing: Hans Schneider, 1969).

CARDUS, NEVILLE, *Gustav Mahler: His Mind and his Music*, i (London: Gollancz, 1965).

FILLER, SUSAN M., 'Editorial Problems in Symphonies of Gustav Mahler: A Study of the Sources of the Third and Tenth' (Ph.D. diss., Northwestern University, 1976).

—— 'Mahler's Sketches for a Scherzo in C Minor and a Presto in F Major', *College Music Symposium*, 24 (1984), 69–80.

FINSON, JON W., 'The Reception of Gustav Mahler's *Wunderhorn* Lieder', *Journal of Musicology*, 5 (1987), 91–116.

FLOROS, CONSTANTIN, *Gustav Mahler*, i: *Die geistige Welt Gustav Mahlers in systematischer Darstellung* (Wiesbaden: Breitkopf & Härtel, 1977).

—— *Gustav Mahler*, ii: *Mahler und die Symphonik des 19. Jahrhunderts in neuer Deutung* (Wiesbaden: Breitkopf & Härtel, 1977).

—— *Gustav Mahler*, iii: *Die Symphonien* (Wiesbaden: Breitkopf & Härtel, 1985); English trans. by Vernon Wicker, *Gustav Mahler: The Symphonies* (Portland, Ore.: Amadeus Press, 1993).

FRANKLIN, PETER R., 'The Gestation of Mahler's Third Symphony', *Music and Letters*, 58 (1977), 439–46.

HEFLING, STEPHEN C., 'The Composition of "Ich bin der Welt abhanden gekommen"', in *Gustav Mahler*, ed. Hermann Danuser (Wege der Forschung, 653; Darmstadt: Wissenschaftliche Buchgesellschaft, 1992), 96–158 at 103–8.

—— 'The Making of Mahler's "Todtenfeier": A Documentary and Analytical Study' (Ph.D. diss., Yale University, 1985).

—— 'Mahler's "Todtenfeier" and the Problem of Program Music', *19th Century Music*, 13 (1988), 27–53.

—— 'Perspectives on Sketch Studies in Mahler Research', in *Das Gustav-Mahler-Fest: Hamburg 1989*. Bericht über den Internationelen Gustav-Mahler-Kongreß, ed. Matthias Theodor Vogt (Kassel: Bärenreiter, 1991), 445–58.

HILMAR-VOIT, RENATE, *Im Wunderhorn-Ton: Gustav Mahlers sprachliches Kompositionsmaterial bis 1900* (Tutzing: Hans Schneider, 1988).

HOPKINS, ROBERT G., *Closure and Mahler's Music: The Role of Secondary Parameters* (Studies in the Criticism and Theory of Music; Philadelphia: The University of Pennsylvania Press, 1990).

KLEIN, RUDOLF (ed.), *Beiträge '79–81: Gustav Mahler Kolloquium 1979* (Österreichische Gesellschaft für Musik, 7; Kassel: Bärenreiter, 1981).

MURPHY, EDWARD W., 'Sonata-Rondo Form in the Symphonies of Gustav Mahler', *Music Review*, 35 (1974), 54–62.

REDLICH, HANS FERDINAND, 'Gustav Mahler: Probleme einer kritischen Gesamtausgabe', *Musikforschung*, 14 (1966), 386–401.

REILLY, EDWARD R., 'An Inventory of Musical Sources', *News about Mahler Research*, 2 (1977), 2–6.

—— 'Mahler's Manuscripts and What They Can Tell Us', *Muziek & Wetenschap*, 5 (1995/96), 363–83.

—— 'A Re-examination of the Manuscripts of Mahler's Third Symphony', in *Colloque International Gustav Mahler* (Paris: Association Gustav Mahler, 1986), 62–72.

—— 'Die Skizze zu Mahlers zweiter Symphonie', *Österreichische Musikzeitschrift*, 34 (1979), 266–84.

ROMAN, ZOLTAN, 'Mahler's Songs and their Influence on his Symphonic Thought', 2 vols. (Ph.D. diss., University of Toronto, 1970).

ROSENZWEIG, ALFRED, 'Wie Gustav Mahler seine "Achte" plante: Die erste handschriftliche Skizze', *Der Wiener Tag*, 4 June 1933.

SCHMIERER, ELISABETH, *Die Orchesterlieder Gustav Mahlers* (Kieler Schriften zur Musikwissenschaft, 38; Kassel: Bärenreiter, 1991).

STEPHAN, RUDOLF (ed.), *Mahler-Interpretation: Aspekte zum Werk und Wirken von Gustav Mahler* (Mainz: Schott, 1985).

VILL, SUSANNE, *Vermittlungsformem verbalisierter und musikalischer Inhalt in der Musik Gustav Mahlers* (Frankfurter Beiträge zur Musikwissenschaft, 6; Tutzing: Hans Schneider, 1979).

WHAPLES, MIRIAM K., 'Mahler and Schubert's A Minor Sonata D. 784', *Music and Letters*, 65 (1984), 255–63.

WILLIAMSON, JOHN, 'Mahler's Compositional Process: Reflections on an Early Sketch for the Third Symphony's First Movement', *Music and Letters*, 61 (1980), 338–45.

—— 'Mahler's "Wunderhorn" Style and Zemlinsky's "Schneiderlein" ', in *Das Gustav-Mahler-Fest: Hamburg 1989*. Bericht über den Internationelen Gustav-Mahler-Kongreß, ed. Matthias Theodor Vogt; Kassel: Bärenreiter, 1991), 293–311.

ZYCHOWICZ, JAMES L., 'The Adagio of Mahler's Ninth Symphony: A Preliminary Report on the Partiturentwurf', *Revue Mahler Review*, 1 (1987), 77–113.

Index

References in **bold** indicate extended or primary discussions of an item.